Troubled Waters

Troubled Waters

Religion, Ethics, and the Global Water Crisis

Gary L. Chamberlain

ROWMAN & LITTLEFIELD PUBLISHERS, INC.
Lanham • Boulder • New York • Toronto • Plymouth, UK

All references from the Qur'an are from *The Qur'an*, translated by M. H. Shakir (Elmhurst, NY: Tahrike Tarsile Qur'an, Inc., 1997). All references from the Bible are from The Jerusalem Bible, © 1966 by Darton Longman & Todd Ltd. and Doubleday and Company, Ltd. A different version of chapter 6 was published as "Water Wars: Privatization and Public Goods," Summer 2006, *Journal for Peace and Justice Studies*, vol. 15, no. 2, 53–69. Used by permission.

ROWMAN & LITTLEFIELD PUBLISHERS, INC.

Published in the United States of America
by Rowman & Littlefield Publishers, Inc.
A wholly owned subsidary of The Rowman & Littlefield Publishing Group, Inc.
4501 Forbes Boulevard, Suite 200, Lanham, Maryland 20706
www.rowmanlittlefield.com

Estover Road
Plymouth PL6 7PY
United Kingdom

Copyright © 2008 by Rowman & Littlefield Publishers, Inc.

British Library Cataloguing in Publication Information Available

Library of Congress Cataloging-in-Publication Data

Chamberlain, Gary L.
 Troubled waters : religion, ethics, and the global water crisis / Gary L. Chamberlain.
  p. cm.
 Includes bibliographical references.
 ISBN-13: 978-0-7425-5244-9 (cloth : alk. paper)
 ISBN-10: 0-7425-5244-6 (cloth : alk. paper)
 ISBN-13: 978-0-7425-5245-6 (pbk. : alk. paper)
 ISBN-10: 0-7425-5245-4 (pbk. : alk. paper)
 1. Water—Religious aspects. 2. Human ecology. I. Title.
 BL450.C43 2008
 201'.77—dc22   2007023915

Printed in the United States of America

♾™ The paper used in this publication meets the minimum requirements of American National Standard for Information Sciences—Permanence of Paper for Printed Library Materials, ANSI/NISO Z39.48-1992.

Dedicated to my wife, Sharon, and my sons, Michael and Benjamin,
who support and encourage me in my work,
and to my students at Seattle University who have inspired and endured
me over these many years

"Son of man, take up a lamentation for Pharaoh the king of Egypt, and say to him: Thou art like the lion of the nations and the dragon that is in the sea; and thou didst push with the horn in thy rivers and didst *trouble the waters* with thy feet and didst trample upon their streams.
Ezekiel 32:2

~

Contents

	Acknowledgments	ix
	Introduction	1
Chapter 1	Water in Indigenous and Asian Traditions	11
Chapter 2	Water in Abrahamic Western Traditions	39
Chapter 3	Water: A Biography	63
Chapter 4	Water and the Human Cycle	79
Chapter 5	A Tenuous Relationship: Human Need and Water Resources	93
Chapter 6	Water Management: Privatization, Problems, and Resistance	115
Chapter 7	Rights to Water and a New Water Ethic	131
Chapter 8	"I Like Fountain Flow": Religion Revisited	155
Chapter 9	Where Do We Go from Here?	177
	Selected Bibliography	199
	Web Resources	211
	Index	215
	About the Author	227

Acknowledgments

I want to acknowledge the many people who have contributed to the research and development of this book. I simply could not have survived the effort involved without the essential work of my two research assistants, Erin Foran, senior English literature major, who wrote initial sections on Judaism, and Tobie Neely, senior history major. Their efforts, especially in the last days of writing, were unsurpassed. My colleagues at Seattle University helped a great deal with research as well, particularly Eddie Salazar who fed me more information constantly, Mike Bisesi who shared insights from public policy, June Johnson who shared her work on globalization, David McCloskey who inspired my interest in ecology, and Gareth Green who introduced me to important economic aspects of water management. I am indebted to former students, now Seattle University alums, Brooke (Hill) Rufo-Hill, who with her husband Jim, provided me with information about water conditions in the Dominican Republic (in chapter 4) and Danica Hendrickson, who delivered texts into my hands. Also I want to acknowledge the peoples of Belize and Japan whom I interviewed for parts of this work. I have included the knowledge and insights I gained from them and in my travels in those countries at appropriate places in the story. Finally, I want to acknowledge the help of my editors at Rowman & Littlefield: Brian Romer, who gave me the initial encouragement to examine this issue and subsequent support in writing this work; Sarah Stanton, editorial assistant; and Elaine McGarraugh, who had the difficult task of seeing the book through to completion as production editor.

~

Introduction

Water, water everywhere,
And all the boards did shrink;
Water, water everywhere;
Nor any drop to drink.

—Samuel Taylor Coleridge, "The Rime of the Ancient Mariner"

All day I face
The barren waste
Without the taste
Of water, cool water.

—Bobby Norton, "Cool Water"

These two images, one of the *abundant* but deadly seawater, the other of the *absence* of water in a barren desert, typify the quandary in which we find ourselves at the beginning of the twenty-first century. Certainly Coleridge did not foresee how prophetic his words would be for our world today. Nor was "Cool Water" composed with the millions in mind who lack fresh water. Yet, these refrains exemplify at least in part some of the struggles surrounding access to fresh water. Water is our most precious resource, essential for all living things and for the life of the planet itself. But reports about water today reveal a frightening scenario.

The Global Water Crises

According to the United Nations Development Report released November 9, 2006, 1.1 billion people have no access to clean water and some 2.6 billion lack good sanitation. The average U.S. citizen consumes 40 gallons of water per day while those 1.1 billion use 1.3 gallons per day. This imbalance caused the authors of the report to call for an end to "water apartheid." The results of declining access are deadly. In Pakistan, for example, 118,000 people die yearly because of diarrhea caused by contact with dirty water while the government spends forty-seven times more money on the military. In African cities such as Dar es Salaam, the commercial capital of Tanzania, people pay more for water than people in New York.

The impact on children is most dramatic. After respiratory infections, unclean water is the second leading cause of death, killing 1.8 million children younger than age 5 annually. In Peru, for example, where some families have toilets and clean water, children are 59 percent more likely to survive than those without. An important key in the report is the link between clean water and proper sanitation. Where those are developed together, child survival rates soar "almost overnight," in the words of the report's author, Kevin Watkins. The report calls for much greater attention to the central role of water in promoting health and breaking through poverty barriers.[1] The report argues that "The scarcity at the heart of the global water crisis is rooted in power, poverty, and equality, not in physical availability."[2]

I am neither hydrologist nor engineer, politician nor planner. I dwell on a Seattle ridge called Queen Anne, surrounded by the salt waters of Puget Sound to the west, visible from my home, and the fresh waters of Lake Washington to the east, a short drive away. To the north a channel cuts across my path connecting the two, bridged by high spans and drawbridges. I hear the horns cutting through the low early morning clouds of fog, and I walk around in the wet of what we call the "September to May Rain Festival." I hear of floods in my region along the "ish" river systems—the Skykomish, Stilligamish, and Snohomish rivers that flow into the low flood plains. I've stood in water in my basement from seepage due to saturated ground. On rare occasions of snow we sled down the hills on my street, or I travel 50 miles for cross-country skiing in the snows of the Cascade Mountains. I am circumscribed by water.

Yet at the beginning of the twenty-first century the waters around me and around the globe face unprecedented challenges—pollution from agriculture, industry, and human waste; oceans heating up and rising due to global warming; growing populations with increasing demands for clean water and more food grown through irrigation; expanding industries discharging waste into streams and rivers and ultimately the sea; increasing salinity of fresh water; blockage of the natural flow of rivers and dams or diversions for other needs, often preventing once-rushing rivers from reaching the seas.

This book involves the story of water, or rather several stories about water—religious stories, scientific stories, stories of people struggling to find safe sources of water and sanitation, stories about the Earth and its needs. I take seriously the note by ecofeminist Anna Peterson in her discourse on ethics that we can "construct a livable and lived ethic only in and through a process of listening to others and working through them."[3] If we are to aid in the efforts to provide clean water and sanitation, to restore the Earth's waters to wholeness, and to learn to live in balance with the world's waters to prevent pollution and even war, we must listen to the stories captured in people's religious traditions, their imaginative insights about water and water's struggle to liberate itself from pollution and mismanagement. The challenge before us is not just good management, but to effect deeper changes in understanding our relationships to water and changes in our motivations so we might act holistically on behalf of water. This will involve a new water ethic.

Peterson argues that most lived ethics have religious roots. In that case a large portion of this exploration will involve examinations of religious traditions in the hope that they can offer new ways of acting and new worldviews of relationships among humans, nonhuman users of water, and the Earth. Peterson's position derives from the reality, certainly in the West and particularly in the case of Christianity, that we live from earliest years in religious traditions that have been harmful to the Earth and water; consequently, "the urgent task for ethics is to uncover what might make people change their ways of understanding and living on the earth."[4]

So how do we define ethics and religion? How can we use them in relation to water and conservation?

Religion

Rarely in analyses and conversations about water are cultural, and in particular religious, dimensions brought to light. Yet for billions of the globe's peoples, their fundamental conceptions about the natural world and water are influenced to some degree by religious considerations, whether those are feelings of disdain, indifference, respect, or even love. Today as Buddhist David Loy asserts, a new "religion" has arrived on the scene to dominate many of the discussions about the natural world and water, namely, "the religion of the market."[5] This volume is dedicated to reviewing the sometimes buried and neglected significance of water in the great historical religions to provide meaning and motivation for an engagement in the preservation and enhancement of the globe's sacred waters.

Although there are a wide variety of definitions of *religion*, for my purposes I will utilize the words of cultural anthropologist Clifford Geertz in his now-classic definition of religion as ". . . a system of symbols that acts to establish powerful, persuasive, and long-lasting moods and motivations in men [*sic*] by formulating conceptions of a general order of existence and clothing these conceptions with such an aura of factuality that the moods and motivations seem uniquely realistic."[6] Certainly those symbolic representations may be reflected in a number of formal and informal ways, but for the purposes of this discussion I will utilize the religious traditions of indigenous peoples, Hinduism, Buddhism, Daoism and Confucianism, Judaism, Christianity, and Islam. At the same time, we must recognize the great variety of expression within each one of those traditions. Our coverage will recapture only general accounts and only some of the stories of water among the varieties of each tradition's expressions. These accounts and stories are those that I believe can provide new relationships with the natural world and water in particular.

Religious meanings must be considered in developing approaches to the global water crisis. Religions shape our understandings of who we are and how we relate to the natural world. We are in desperate need of new worldviews, new "cosmologies," or views of the universe, particularly a *new ethos* around water, to guide our decisions for the present as well as future uses of natural resources. I utilize the work of Charles Kammer III to define worldview. A worldview is a ". . . general presumption about the final principles and powers that underlie the existence of both natural and human history."[7] As Kammer notes, our worldviews are composed not only of cognitive conceptions, but just as importantly of symbolic, largely unconscious perceptions, sensibilities, and personal and group experiences found in our stories and the stories of our cultures. Religious perspectives provide the bases for those worldviews, and although religious cosmologies alone will not solve water issues, they can contribute greatly to people's understandings, involvement, and motivations in making the necessary, even revolutionary changes called for in a new water ethic. At the same time, the world water crisis challenges religious traditions to engage in the reshaping of our basic responses to this profoundly real as well as symbolic place of water.

In their recent work *Reflections on Water*, political scientists Joachim Blatter and Helen Ingram argue convincingly that the primary meanings ascribed to water in the twentieth century were circumscribed by those interested in controlling water through engineering, law, and economics to the neglect of other meaning systems. To the authors these "narrow, bounded meanings" reflected an "individualistic, rational, and utilitarian perception of water" that must in the twenty-first century be balanced by other understandings from both science and the humanities. These other understandings will challenge the dominant models of human rationality and human control. The result is not the absence of rationality and control, but the inclusion of other perspectives and visions.[8] The cultural and religious dimensions of people and places are essential in developing the water management practices and policies necessary for the years ahead.

Religious voices for far too long have been silent not just about water but about our human relationships to the environment. In 1990 Russell Train, chair of the World Wide Fund for Nature, expressed his puzzlement that the continuing lack of response of religion to the ecological crisis ". . . has been nothing less than extraordinary. Here we have issues that go to the heart of the human condition, even to humanity's ultimate survival. Here we have problems that can be said to threaten the very integrity of Creation. And yet the churches and other institutions of organized religion have largely ignored the whole subject."[9] Fortunately in recent years philosophers, theologians, and ethicists in all the world's religious traditions have been reexamining those traditions for new insights, discoveries, and reinterpretations that support a more holistic relationship among all created beings. Yet Train's words remain as a major challenge to those who nurture and develop these new understandings and formulations and perhaps more fundamentally to those responsible for translating beliefs and values into practice. The challenge involves not only a reconfiguration of fundamental scriptural texts, teachings, themes, and ritual practices to allow ecological insights to emerge, but, more than that, it requires a transformation to an entire new cosmology.

Religions provide symbolic meanings and ethical perspectives necessary to support a new water ethos and ethic critical for the twenty-first century. Precisely because religious symbols around the natural world, in this case water, are so much a part of the human consciousness, and our unconscious structures of meaning, they can aid greatly in this struggle to secure water for all peoples, creatures, and the Earth itself.

Ethics

A second major theme in these discussions lies in developing the guiding ethical reflections that are necessary and useful in shaping the debate over water access, management, allocation, and use. These reflections will appear throughout the book and will be treated specifically in chapter 7, where I examine several ethical traditions and their contributions to the development of key principles for management and use of water. It is precisely management policies and practices that the United Nations 2006 Report, *Water: A Shared Responsibility: United Nations World Water Development Report 2*, views as the key to *resolving* the world water crisis and *restoring* the globe's water supplies to health.[10]

Although there are a variety of understandings of the very meaning of ethics, one approach helpful for our discussion views ethics as a "systematic reflection upon human actions, institutions, and character."[11] Theologian Daniel Maguire adds the understanding that ethics is ". . . the art/science that seeks to bring sensitivity and method to the discernment of moral values." He notes that such reflection includes not only principles and reason, but personal and group experiences, affective dimensions, imagination in symbols and stories, creativity in looking at alternatives.[12] Reflecting insights of feminist ethics, Mick Smith states the following in a metaphor appropriate to our study of water ethics: "Like the river's flowing, the ethical stream shapes the landscapes of our lives, it springs forth from hard rock, cuts deep canyons, carries and deposits the alluvium of our hopes and dreams. Its ripples echo through the soul."[13] In these times of water struggles, it is hoped that new springs of water will indeed ripple through our collective soul as communal peoples, as well as our personal souls, and merge into a new water ethos.

I argue that a new water ethos, i.e., a master viewpoint, and a consequent new water ethic must be built characterized by the lived experiences of local communities and through organized, participatory, democratic policies based on solidarity with those in marginalized and poor situations of water deprivation. Such a water ethos and ethic will be rooted in the stories of peoples around the globe who are struggling to meet their own water needs, who are called to consume less, and who sense themselves as an integral part of the natural world. Such an approach is essential to the discussion of *resolution and restoration* mentioned above. On the one hand policies must be rooted in broad ethical guidelines that support long-term sustainability, yet at the same time ethical reflections need to utilize the contexts of particular people and places.

Such approaches in outlooks, principles, and practices challenge the dominant paradigm of the twentieth century—large-scale development, centralization, corporate management, nonrepresentation of local stakeholders—which has guided development in general and water issues in particular. Here new worldviews, shaped by new insights from the world's religions, will require a sharp break with the tenacious hold of a mechanistic, utilitarian, materialistic view of the natural world. Consequently, we must shift from technological, large-scale, *hard* approaches to water issues to more communitarian, democratic, local, small-scale, and technologically *soft* movements based on valuing, respecting, and reverencing water, not just for our immediate or future benefit but also for the future of the globe.

Throughout the text I have included stories, an integral element in ethical reflection—my own encounters with water marvels, those of friends, and importantly the encounters of communities around the world with water issues, such as farmers, dam opponents, city people and rural people. These stories reveal the interrelationships among us all around the globe, people from Porto Alegre, Brazil; Stockton, California; India; China; Africa; Europe; Asia. One story in particular, that of Cochabamba, Bolivia, reveals the problems and the promise around water—a story of privatization and resistance, of people's practices and principles of justice in action. The Cochabamba story illustrates ethical actions that both express guiding insights and principles and foster new guiding principles. The very relationships among us and with the watery Earth are key to any attempt to bring about the needed ontological and epistemological shifts in our viewpoints on water, its reality, and its intrinsic knowledge of sustainability. For I firmly believe that water, particularly as expressed partly in the symbols of our religious traditions and partly in our bodies and psyches, reflects images of knowing *from which* we must learn and *which* we must learn. Water teaches.

In this discussion a basic premise is that access to water is a fundamental right and not a result of market supply. At the same time, such a *right* imposes *obligations* upon users that include various forms of payments and reimbursements. I will also discuss several directions that support the development of sustainable water programs of use, delivery, and cost. Such programs must include the water needs of others than humans and of the Earth itself.

Hopefully this discussion will assist religious groups and others deeply concerned about the global water issues, water poverty, and issues of development to find meaning in their traditions and the motivation to take steps in their personal lives and join with others in supporting solutions. In addition, this book may fill an important role in the broader discussions of religious studies and ecological/environmental studies. I hope that it will advance both of these fields and provide important interdisciplinary links for interested readers.

Method

In the opening chapters I examine several religious traditions for their import in understanding the various meanings of water and their contributions to a new water ethic, beginning in chapter 1 with indigenous traditions, Hinduism, Buddhism, Taoism, and Confucianism. Chapter 2 continues the discussion with a look at the religions rooted in the Abrahamic traditions: Judaism, Christianity, and Islam. The chapter concludes with insights from psychiatry into the hidden, unconscious meanings of water carried in human cultural memory.

Moving from the place of water in religious traditions, chapter 3 provides a look at the story of water as told from the perspective of contemporary sciences. Here the wonders of water, its character, and behaviors provide a different sense of awe and wonder than that found in religion. Then in chapters 4 and 5, I explore the current water crises, their causes, human and otherwise, and the difficulties in which we now find ourselves. Since as the United Nations recent report argues, the key dimension of water provision is now water management, I explore issues of water management, privatization, public policies, and resistance to those policies in chapter 6. Out of these stories from around the world emerge the guiding insights, reflections, and principles needed for proper water management and policies to direct the access to and the distribution of water for the world's needs.

Then in chapter 7, before examining the ethical insights needed for a new water ethic, I undertake an exploration of international legal statements on water that only gradually over the course of the past thirty years have seen the United Nations and international agreements support the premise that, first, water is a basic right for humans and the planet and that, second, the management of water must be based on principles of ecological sustainability and local, democratic policies. The major section of the chapter focuses on the ethical principles essential to the new water ethos. Some of these principles derive from the religious traditions studied while others reflect more recent insights emerging from the experiences of persons and communities redefining human relations with the natural world, and thus with water. Although operative earlier in several parts of the book, these reflections emerge from examinations of several key ethical theories in both Eastern and Western traditions.

No one approach will suffice, but rather principles from several theories are needed to promote the new water ethos in ways that complement one another. The water ethos now needed must incorporate not only some forms of payment for water use and allocations, but must promote management policies around water that reflect an equitable, sustainable, local, democratic approach. At the same time as the requisite water ethos will incorporate such principles in management policies at local, national, and even international levels, there must be a set of principles that challenge consumerist attitudes and behaviors around water use and that support personal responsibility and a humble approach to water. These discussions necessarily involve a host of issues around water rights, human rights to water, and biotic, nonhuman rights around water. In this sense I argue that the Earth too has a correlative right to water necessary for its flourishing and intentions. This exploration is essential in providing concrete specifications to the religious worldviews surrounding water developed in the early chapters. While those chapters explore potential resources for motivating action and imbuing those actions with significant meaning, such visionary understandings of the religious dimension of water must be grounded in ethical principles that can be applied practically to concrete policies.

In chapter 8 we return to the religious traditions to examine their contributions to the new water ethos. The interpenetration of ethical principles and religious meanings and motivations is essential in moving the new water ethic into practice. Neither ethical principles alone nor religious traditions in themselves are sufficient for the tasks of developing a new water ethos or worldview, and a new water ethic. Principles without guiding motivations remain abstract, unable to provide guides for active engagement, and religious traditions without principles cannot guide policies for practical action.

Finally, in the last chapter, I highlight some of the many ways in which small, participatory and democratic, local, sustainable solutions to water issues are emerging through recovery of old technologies as well as in the application of new technologies. These provide a hopeful antidote to what seem to be the grim reminders of the water crises seen and heard daily in the news.

Notes

1. Robyn Dixon, "Targeting 'Water Apartheid,'" *The Los Angeles Times* as reported in *Seattle Times*, Nov. 6, 2006, Sec. A; United Nations, *Water: A Shared Responsibility. The United Nations World Water Development Report 2* (New York: Berghahn, 2006), 46 (cf. ch. 6).

2. Quoted in Peter Bosshard, "A Drop-Sized Way to Bring Clean Water to a Thirsty World," *Christian Science Monitor*, 10 November 2006.

3. Anna Peterson, *Being Human: Ethics, Environment, and Our Place in the World* (Berkeley: University of California Press, 2001), 238.

4. Peterson, *Being Human*, 238.

5. David Loy, "The Religion of the Market," in *Visions of a New Earth*, eds. Harold Coward and Daniel C. Maguire (Albany: State University of New York Press, 2000), 15–28.

6. Clifford Geertz, "Religion as a Cultural System," in *The Religious Situation*, ed. Donald R. Cutler (Boston: Beacon, 1969), 643.

7. Charles Kammer III, *Ethics and Liberation* (Maryknoll, NY: Orbis, 1988), 20–21.

8. Joachim Blatter and Helen Ingram, eds., *Reflections on Water: New Approaches to Transboundary Conflicts and Cooperation* (Cambridge, Mass.: MIT Press, 2001), 5, 16, 32.

9. Quoted in John F. Haught, *The Promise of Nature* (New York: Paulist Press, 1993), 2–3.

10. United Nations, *Water: A Shared Responsibility*.

11. Arthur J. Dyck, quoted in Kammer, *Ethics and Liberation*, 11–12.

12. Daniel Maguire, *On Moral Grounds* (New York: Crossroad, 1991), 34; see chaps. 8–13 for further development of these categories.

13. Mick Smith, *An Ethics of Place: Radical Ecology, Postmodernity, and Social Theory* (Albany: State University of New York Press, 2001), 189.

CHAPTER ONE

∼

Water in Indigenous and Asian Traditions

The Kogi peoples of northeast Colombia trace their ancestry back to a time before the arrival of the Spanish conquistadores when they fled into the high Sierra Nevada to pursue their life and livelihood. Today they continue that livelihood with few incursions of modern civilization. In Alan Ereira's marvelous description of their struggles, *The Elder Brothers*, the Kogi send a message to the rest of the world's peoples, whom they call the Younger Brothers. They admonish the Younger Brothers for harming the Earth. Besides ripping out the Earth's entrails, we have changed the waters, beginning with the glacial snows of the Paramo, the most sacred part of the Sierra. "We could see immediately [from the helicopter] the first signs that worried the Kogi. Glacier mountains were empty of ice. Large lakes of dark waters showed clearly that they had shrunk dramatically,"[1] writes Alan Ereira of his trip to the snow-covered peaks of the Sierra.

For the Kogi, water is the origin of all reality. Water is *Aluna*, the primordial "stuff" of the universe. For the Kogi people, the very structure of the world is maintained by water from all sources—from the highest of the Sierras to the runoff at the sea. In water is the metaphysics of the many "worlds" of reality, from dreams to structures of daily life, to visions into the meaning beyond the everyday. "Why do we say 'water'? In the beginning we were formed in the water. The Mother formed us there. And all the trees, all of them had water. . . . We all need water. We cannot live without it."[2]

The next two chapters follow the stream of water as it flows through various religions traditions—indigenous religions and the Asian traditions of

11

Buddhism, Hinduism, Taoism, and Confucianism. The second chapter will take up the Abrahamic monotheisms of Judaism, Christianity, and Islam.

We begin with a definition of religion taken from anthropologist Clifford Geertz. Geertz defines religion as ". . . a system of symbols which acts to establish powerful, persuasive, and long-lasting moods and motivations in men [sic] by formulating conceptions of a general order of existence and clothing these conceptions with such an aura of factuality that the moods and motivations seem uniquely realistic."[3] Religion provides a set of symbols that serve as models of reality and for reality, breaking in upon the limits of physical endurance, moral insight, and analytic capacity in order to prove meaning. The religious dimension moves beyond the everyday "taken-for-granted" world, asks a total commitment, and induces a set of motivations through beliefs and ritual practices.

Religion is a group phenomenon. The members of the group share common values, beliefs, and organization nurtured by myths and rituals, resting upon symbols. A symbol can be a term, name, picture, or image familiar in daily life and possessing specific meanings in addition to its everyday meaning. The symbol in myth and ritual, such as "crucifix," "Star of David," or "lotus," breaks through the everyday meaning to a world in which one "knows" by participating, and such participation produces a sense of rightness and happiness. Thus the symbols of Sun, Moon, water, Earth, father, mother refer to a larger, religious viewpoint beyond what we immediately see, and they integrate humans into it. So water, as we will see, not only cleanses the physical body but also cleanses the spirit.

One of the most important scholars of religious symbolism, Mircea Eliade, tells us that water, given its ability to dissolve substances, is universally both the origin and the dissolver of realities. In every culture, water symbolizes the potentialities of existence, potentialities brought into existence in peoples and cultures through immersion and reemergence.[4] Eliade writes, "Principle of what is formless and potential, basis of every cosmic manifestation, container of all seeds, water symbolizes the primal substance from which all forms come and to which they will return. It will always exist."[5]

Immersion into the waters nurtures, fertilizes, and multiplies potentialities in a preformed or unformed state, while emergence brings reentry into a formed reality—new life, new livings. From time immemorial, through deluges to birth and death, water has taken on characteristics found in every religious tradition. Using Eliade's basic analysis, we will examine the symbolism of water in each tradition in such categories as (1) origin and birth; (2) initiation, immersion; (3) healing/restoration and life/eternal life; and (4) epiphanies and divinities.[6]

Indigenous Traditions

Creation: Origins and Birth

Whether we are talking about the Hopi of the U.S. Southwest, the Salish of the Northwest, the Cree of Eastern Canada, the Australian aboriginals, the Ashanti of Africa, the Karaja of Brazil, or the Kogi of Colombia—water, along with Earth and sky, dominates the religious symbol system. Water is the birthplace or the creation of all things, of peoples and of the Earth itself. The Karaja of Brazil "still lived in the water,"[7] and the Kogi are "formed in the water."[8] For the Dagara of Burkina Faso and Ghana, life itself emerged from water; the Earth began as a union of fire and water. According to Dagara elders, "this primal water originally came from the 'Other world' and spilled into Earth at the moment when the veil between the two worlds was thinned."[9] Among the Dogon of Mali, water is "a divine green seed" impregnating the Earth and so "(bringing) forth twin green beings, half man, half serpent"; the male seed, oil, combines in the womb "with the moisture of the vaginas in a helix symbolizing the creative vibrations."[10] Water can be both the creation of life and life itself.

In the United States, Madonna Thunderhawk of the Lakota speaks of water as "the life blood, the key to the whole thing."[11] For the Western Shoshone, "All the water that comes from the Mother Earth, that's her blood. It's the Mother Earth's blood."[12] The Taos of the U.S. Southwest believe that the Blue Lake in the Sangre de Christo Mountains is where "the Great Spirit created humans,"[13] and for the Omaha Nation in the Great Plains area, ". . . all creatures once floated disconsolately on a wholly submerged Earth until a great boulder rose from the deep."[14] Among indigenous people of southern Alaska and the Pacific Northwest, the ocean is seen as Mother. Various totem poles include "drowned man" because ocean fishermen were often "taken home" by their Ocean Mother, the stormy North Pacific, who gets lonely for her human children.[15] Water as source, as origin of all, ushers human and animal into life through the birth waters and takes back living things into itself.

Initiation

A second theme coalesces around water in initiating new life, purifying and giving social "birth" into the group. In the rituals after childbirth among many sub-Saharan peoples, a midwife sprays a mouthful of water over the newborn, and the water's touch makes the infant cry out and so "officially" receive speech.[16] Immersion, as Mircea Eliade notes, is another form of purification. In whatever form, "in water everything is 'dissolved,' every 'form' is broken up, everything that has happened ceases to exist. . . . Breaking up all forms, doing away with all the past, water possesses this power of purifying, of giving new birth."[17]

Healing, Restoration, and Divinities

Water too has tremendous powers of healing, both physically and spiritually, restoring body tissue and torn social relationships. In indigenous traditions, behind the healing powers of waters are the spirits and divinities that use and in some cases inhabit them. In whatever form water takes—from seawater to rivers, streams, waterfalls, storms, even water in tubs—those who practice Haitian Vodou feel the presence of the spirits; all the major female divinities associate with water in some way. Water animals, such as whales, snakes, and fish, and even water vessels symbolize water power.[18] By using the magical powers of water, Haitians, descendants of slaves from Africa, are attempting to connect to the mythical Africa of their ancestors by means of subterranean waters that "constitute a world of their own and teem with human activities of every kind." By pouring water out in front of the altar at ceremonies, Haitians are summoning up spirits from the underworld.[19]

Similar beliefs are held by peoples around the world, including the African peoples of Benin, Togo, and Nigeria. According to the Fon people, water spirits reside in Benin's Oueme River and its surrounding lakes. The Yoruba and Bini people of Nigeria say that the river spirit Oshun and the saltwater god Yemoja bring them wealth and fruitfulness. The powers of water spirits also extend to Caribbean and South American descendants of West African peoples, bringing them love, fertility, and prosperity across the Atlantic Ocean.[20]

Water Rituals

Water rites are essential in accessing the sacred powers of water. Given the important place of water in the parched deserts of Australia, for example, aboriginals for centuries have relied upon ceremonies and rainmakers to retain contact with the rain ancestors. Rainmakers must learn the rain songs and the rain sites and their sacred meanings, and they must be able to read the clouds. The sites are critically important and are often places that attract lightning and, if elevated in the paths of rain clouds, bring rain.[21]

Rainmakers continue to perform important sacred rituals in many African villages and communities. Using "rain stones" that have "fallen from the sky," burning "rain leaves" so that the smoke "catches" the rain, the rainmakers are highly esteemed leaders. Other rituals involve symbolic actions that call rain from the sky, for example, "drawing water from wells, sprinkling water on groups of people, and collecting perspiration and spraying it into the air." Historian John Mbibi writes of these ritual beliefs: "As it comes from above, so rain links man [sic] with the divine. Rain is a deeply religious rhythm, and those who deal in it transact business of the highest religious caliber."[22] Young Zulu girls are secluded for some weeks, then purified by taking "a ritual bath in the river" and washing off "the red clay with which they have daubed themselves"[23]; they then rejoin the group.

Every spring, Pueblo spiritual leaders in the Southwest United States pray at a ceremony marking the "cleaning" of the *acequia* ditches, which divert water from rivers to serve the needs of the people living there. In a combination of ancient practices with their Catholicism, the people march in procession along the banks of the ditches with the image of San Isidro, the Catholic patron saint of agriculture. The water is considered the people's lifeblood, the *acequias*, the veins.[24]

Probably the best-known water ritual in the Americas is the sweat lodge, where water in the form of steam provides the basis for the cleansing ritual. The lodge, symbol of birth and regeneration, is built in the shape of an oval or womb, symbolizing Mother Earth. Participants enter the lodge naked through a small entrance, marking their humility. Sitting in the pitch-black darkness (the womb), each person purifies mind and spirit as the body is purified. Cold water is thrown on the hot stones, and the steam pours into the participants' pores. Sacred songs are chanted, prayers are recited, and at times a pipe is passed from one participant to another. Some experience visions, hear voices, or have transforming experiences.[25] Whatever the responses, the ritual is an important part of the rhythms of indigenous peoples.

Conclusion

In all of these examples from peoples around the world, we see the powerful, often hidden, meanings of water in creation stories, myths of initiation and purification, tales of healing, abodes of divinities, and rituals. Water is often the very "stuff" from which the universe, all creatures, and particularly humans, sprang. Whether brought to Earth by gods and invested with power or the abode of divinities themselves, water's potency for bringing new life is transferred symbolically into new, literal births and ritually into purification from wrongdoing, into protection against harmful spirits. "In initiation rituals water confers a 'new birth,' in magic rituals it heals, and in funeral rites it assures rebirth after death."[26] The very fluidity of water and its absolute necessity for life renders water a potent and actual symbol for life's basic rhythms, whether the life of the planet or all living things. In the sections to follow, we will investigate how these basic elements transfer into the historical religious traditions of East and West.

Traditions of Asia

Hinduism

When Westerners view the Ganges River, the Ganga, at the holy city Varnasi, they are often overwhelmed and puzzled by the huge numbers of pilgrims bathing in what seem at that point terribly polluted waters. In addition, every year thousands of bodies are burned at the *ghats*, areas along the river bank where bodies are incinerated atop funeral pyres and the remains then thrown into the river. How, one asks, can such an "unclean" river provide the basis for rituals of burial, cleansing, purification, and salvation?

This is only one of the many questions that surround the meaning and place of water in Hindu religious teachings, rituals, and customs. In this section of the chapter, we will explore how those teachings, rituals, and customs can become sources and resources for directing religious beliefs and actions into civic actions for cleaning up India's polluted and often putrid rivers, countering more dam building, and providing alternatives to Western-style, large water development projects. In the course of the discussion, three rivers among the most sacred rivers of India will be our focus: the Ganga, the Narmada, and the Yamuna. All three are truly in great danger.[27]

Origins: Creation

Although India is not the only place where Hindu beliefs are practiced, India is the home of the great religion of Hinduism. In our short course on the complexity of Hinduism, we will start with the assertion from the sacred texts that everything, all cosmic matter (*prakrti*), is sacred. Thus water itself is a sacred reality, one of the five elements of the created world: Earth, air, fire, water, and space, all interconnected and interdependent.[28] One of the earliest texts, the *Rig Veda*, written about 3700 B.C.E., reads: "Darkness was there, all wrapped around by darkness, and all was Water indiscriminate."[29] Another Vedic hymn emphasizes the nurturing, maternal elements of water: "The waters, which are our mothers and which desire to take part in the sacrifices, come to us following their paths and distribute their milk to us."[30]

Rivers themselves are linked to gods and goddesses, mainly female, since water is seen as generative and nurturing. Vandana Shiva, Indian ecological thinker, recounts the story surrounding the arrival of the goddess Ganga to Earth:

King Sagar [the ocean king] had slain the demons on Earth and was staging a horse sacrifice to declare his supremacy. Indra, the rain god, feared losing his power of the sacrifice and stole Sagar's horse and tied it to the ashram of the great sage Kapil. . . .

King Sagar's grandson Anshuman, eventually successful in recovering the horse, reported to his grandfather that the sage had burned Sagar's 60,000 sons [sent to recover the horse] out of anger; the only way for the sons to reach their heavenly abode was if the Ganges could descend from Heaven so its water could cleanse the sons' ashes. . . .

Finally, Anshuman's grandson Bhagirath went to the Himalayas and started meditating at Gangatori. After a long meditation, the Ganges appeared to him in bodily form and agreed to descend to Earth if someone would break her mighty fall, which would otherwise destroy the Earth. King Bhagirath appealed to Shiva, who eventually agreed to use his hair to soften the descent of the Ganges [hence the forests of the Himalayas]. The river followed Bhagirath to where the ashes of King Sagar's sons were piled, purified their souls, and paved the way to the heavens.[31]

This simple yet powerful tale encapsulates not only the understanding of the river's sacred status, but also its key place in purifying souls on their way to salvation and ritually purifying those who bathe in its waters. The tale also reflects the more general belief that every river and stream and the sea itself share in this sacredness. "Bathing in the sea, river, stream, or pond near the temple is said to grant salvation."[32] The origin of this belief lies in a variety of sacred texts about the nature of the universe and creation. For example, in the Bhagavad Gita, ". . . the universe, composed of sentient matter and non-sentient matter, forms the body of the Vishnu. . . . Vishnu is the personal name given to the Supreme Being, or Brahman. . . . All of creation has the Supreme Being as its soul."[33] Water, one of the five fundamental elements, is especially prized.

Several sacred texts go on to support the importance of keeping the waters clean and pure. In the Ayurvedic texts, polluted waters are seen as dangerous to people's health. Referring to the "Mother Ganga," the Gautama Dharmasutra issues these injunctions: "One must not splash water with his [sic] feet nor enter water when one is full of dirt; one must not discharge into water blood, excreta, urine, spit, and semen."[34]

Along with the Ganga, the Narmada, the largest westward river in India, is one of India's most sacred rivers. Yet the Narmada is one of the most polluted rivers in India from industrial discharge, agricultural runoff, and human use for bathing and other activities. The vision of the Narmada as goddess is one of the oldest in India. There are thousands of temples to Ganga and Shiva along its banks, and annually hundreds of thousands of pilgrims make the sacred journey up the Narmada valley and back. For the inhabitants of the long valley, their physical and spiritual roots are tied to the land and the river, the goddess Narmada. Their gods are rooted to the place, and they cannot move without their gods.[35]

The Yamuna flows into the Ganga, and it too is sacred but polluted. In the Bhagavata Purana, the Yamuna is one of the sights that particularly delights Krishna, the very body of god. Yamuna's story, appearing in the Regveda scriptures, concerns her "excessive love" for her twin, Yama, the god of death, who rejects her and tells her to find another man. The beautiful sixteenth-century Sanskrit hymn "Yamunastakam" describes Yamuna's descent to Earth to meet with her beloved Krishna to "purify the world." The hymn distinguishes the powers of Yamuna from those of Ganga, also a lover of Krishna:

> By herself, Ganga can grant only liberation, not love; in contrast with Yamuna, who is filled with love and compassion, Ganga is associated more with knowledge and asceticism. . . . Ganga prepares one for liberation through bathing in her waters, whereas Yamuna prepares one for devotional love through sipping her waters. . . . [B]y sipping her water, comparable to a mother's milk, one is spared the agony of death, since Yama, Lord of Death, is her older brother.[36]

Like the Ganga and the Narmada, the physical form of the Yamuna allows devotees to reach beyond to the river's spiritual level and then to the goddess herself. Each form encompasses the other in a hierarchical pattern.[37]

Rituals, Purification, and Salvation

We have examined several rituals in telling the stories of the three rivers as examples of the sacredness of all water that falls from the sky. Here an interesting pattern develops. Each of these rivers is now tremendously polluted, "unclean" in our Western understanding, yet the spiritual power of the river remains to "purify." "[T]he rivers—embodied as women—absorb the moral dirt and then come to the Ganga, the grand purifier, to purify themselves."[38] Here there is a connection between physical dirt in the rivers themselves, moral dirt of sin, and ritual purity.

In the Ganga and other bodies of water one achieves salvation through the purifying waters. Anyone bathing in the waters has sins removed and can achieve salvation. Not only are residents along rivers granted such gifts, but the millions of pilgrims who journey every year to various parts of India to worship at sacred sites along the rivers are likewise gifted. While the temples of Varnasi are best known to Westerners, there are hundreds of smaller tem-

ples along the Ganga, Narmada, and Yamuna, as well as other bodies of water. Traditionally, pilgrims along the Yamuna come to the river, place water
on their fingertips, and then shake the water into their mouths, purifying
themselves with just a few drops. At the temple sites along the Yamuna, "the
temple deities are bathed in Yamuna water, and this water is then traditionally drunk as consecrated water. It is still a fairly common sight to see residents and pilgrims . . . worshiping the Yamuna River, offering milk, sweets,
and incense to the aquatic form of the goddess."[39]

From late July to early August, the million pilgrims who come to the
Ganga at Hardwar collect Ganga water and transport it to a temple dedicated
to Shiva, over 60 miles downstream. Others walk and climb over 180 miles
and as far away as Delhi to offer the Ganga water to Shiva, recapturing the
myth of Ganga's descent to Earth in Shiva's matted hair.[40] Perhaps the best-
known rituals are performed at the junction of the Ganga and the Yamuna
during the Great Kumba Fair, the six-week religious festival Maha Kumba
Mela. The festival gathers over thirty million people who come to bathe in
the sacred waters, visit the hundreds of holy people, and scatter the ashes of
their loved ones into the waters to mingle with the purity and divine wisdom
symbolized in the rivers. The experience of bathing in the waters brings a
spiritual awakening and heightened reality for millions.[41]

Conclusion

Hundreds of texts attest to the sacred nature of water, its reality as goddess
nurturing all creation, its purifying qualities, and its importance as a way to
salvation. Millions of Indian pilgrims traverse the routes to the sacred rivers,
carry water to shrines, and drink or immerse themselves in waters of sea,
rivers, ponds, and pools. Yet there is little outcry, at least based on these religious writings, traditions, and ritual practices, from religious leaders and the
millions of religious pilgrims to clean up India's polluted waters, to save wells
and other ancient water storage systems from development, to regulate agricultural waste, and even to influence humans in decreasing their output of
waste into these waters. A grand disjunction exists between personal piety
and civic and responsible action. Hinduism provides us with a particularly
telling example. However, this disjunction exists to some extent in all of the
subsequent traditions as well—a separation of personal piety from the fate of
the natural world as impacted by the devotee's own behavior.

Vasudha Narayanan points to several reasons for these discrepancies. First,
in the hierarchy of the gods, the goddess of wealth, Sri-Lakshmi, holds more
importance than the Earth goddess, Bhu-Devi/Prithvi, "and the quest for
wealth seems to be more intense than reverence for the Earth"[42] and by

implication the waters of the Earth. Second, there seems to be a belief that the rivers cannot be polluted because they are inherently pure. Finally Narayanan points to the emphasis on individuality in some Hindu traditions and refers to Anil Agarwal for support.

According to Agarwal, Hinduism

> . . . looks into the self, emphasizing the *atman* [self] as the key to spiritual ascent. *Dharma*, or social responsibility, focuses first on oneself, emphasizing one's own behavior. The consequences of one's behavior on others plays a secondary role. . . . Hinduism believes in pollution, but only to the extent that it affects one's self directly. . . . [T]he concern focuses on keeping the pollution away from one's own being, not on making certain that the pollution does not hurt someone else.[43]

Kelly Alley makes a similar argument in her analysis of the distinction between "cleanness" and "purity" made by religious practitioners, pilgrims, priests, and others. While the Ganga could become unclean, she cannot be impure because as a goddess she has the power to absorb worldly impurities.[44] For these religious leaders and pilgrims, the industrial pollutants and other wastes into the river are the responsibilities of government, not their duties.[45] Alley's conclusion is sobering indeed: "I suggest that if environmental activism continues to develop in India, it will likely expand out of coalitions between nongovernmental activists and public interest lawyers long before it does so at the crossroads of religious and political movements."[46]

While these analyses give pause to any simplistic claim that sacred texts and ritual practices lead directly to programs and calls to keep water clean, potable, and available, they remain powerful forces for the many efforts under way in India, which will be detailed later, and expanding consciousness among Hindus. Narayanan is a bit more optimistic when he calls for a shift to sacred texts and practices that more directly relate to everyday behavior and notes that devotion to a river goddess has led some to work for safe drinking water and river cleanup.[47] Agarwal calls for Hindus "to reexamine, ruthlessly, their religion. . . . There is a vast reservoir of tenets, practices, and beliefs that can help Hindus to reform Indian society."[48] We end this discussion, then, on notes of hope, given the rich traditions we have explored in this section.

Buddhism

Seeking the supreme state of sublime peace, I wandered by stages through the Madadhan country until eventually I arrived at the Senanigama near Uruvela. There I saw a delightful stretch of land and a lovely woodland grove, and a *clear flowing river* with a delightful forest so I sat there thinking, 'Indeed this is an appropriate place to strive for the ultimate realization of that unborn supreme security from bondage, Nirvana.'[49]

This quotation attributed to Prince Siddhartha, the future Buddha, illustrates the importance that natural settings held for Buddha in his quest for nirvana. Woodlands and forests appear prominently throughout his entire life, from the time he was born to his enlightenment under the Bodhi tree to his death "between the twin *sala* trees blooming with flowers out of season."[50]

Origins

While at first glance Buddhism seems to move the practitioner through various forms of meditation and rituals away from engagement in the world, Buddhism has deep roots in the world of nature. In Buddhism, there is no creator god; the cycle of life has no beginning and no end. There is no permanence in things; nothing exists in itself, but only as a context of relations. All is dynamic, changing; there is no static structure to things. Rain is not a noun, "which appears to name a *thing*"; rather "rain is nothing but the *process* of drops of water falling from the sky."[51] But human ignorance in the form of ego projects its desires and needs onto this relationality and sees individual realities. Such a perception brings unhappiness and suffering. The goal of one's life, then, is to strive for the transcendence of passion and desire through enlightenment or nirvana, the realization of emptiness that releases humans (and in the Mahayana tradition, animals also) from attachment. This path is achieved only through a succession of rebirths in which one works out one's karma.

Since suffering is an inevitable part of existence, caused not only by ignorance of reality as it is but also by the violence of one creature against another, then the Buddhist is governed in the struggle for enlightenment to seek a nonviolent way, *ahimsa*. The story of the Buddha's distress in watching a farmer plow a field is illustrative of this theme: "Thinking of all the suffering the plowing was causing the small organisms in the ground, the Buddha was distressed and wept for them." David Kinsley notes two themes in this story: First, Buddhists must cultivate empathy toward others' suffering and in all their actions practice *ahimsa* so they will not increase suffering; and second, this empathy is meant to extend to all creation.[52]

In addition, because of the doctrine of reincarnation, humans have intimate connections with nonhuman reality. All life is intricately joined. This reality is expressed by Vietnamese Buddhist Thich Nhat Hanh: "We should deal with nature the way we should deal with ourselves! We should not harm ourselves; we should not harm nature. Harming nature is harming ourselves, and vice versa."[53] The Thai Buddhist Ajahn Pongsak adds that "The true nature of Buddhism is wisdom—the knowledge and understanding of the true worth of nature according to the Natural Law which is Truth. . . . When we destroy nature we destroy the truth and the teachings. When we protect nature, we protect the truth and the teachings."[54]

Instead of an interpretation of the doctrine of *sunyata* or universal non-substantiality to mean that phenomenal existence is somehow denigrated, another understanding yields the conviction that the doctrine denies the permanent and independent status of phenomena. *Sunyata* "is the very mode by which their essential nature as a mutually interdependent, cooriginating whole becomes manifest." In this cosmology the universe is understood as a coherent whole in which ". . . human consciousness is an intrinsic self-expression of that larger reality." If humans understand themselves as a part of and dependent upon the whole cosmos, then they will be guided in their concern for the Earth community.[55]

In addition, the five basic elements we saw in Hinduism—space, Earth, air, fire, and water—become in Buddhism an important factor in achieving nirvana. In some Buddhist traditions the five elements have their counterpart in the human psyche as related to forms of consciousness that must be purified of "the five poisons" and transformed into "the five pristine cognitions." In our context, then, the example would be water:

> The globally embedded arrogance, which makes possible the overt delusion, inflation of ego operations, that man [sic] is independent of nature, is represented by the water element, internally constituted as feelings, and, externally, watery cohesion, which allows multinational and personal greed to become the modus operandi without noticing the consequences.[56]

We see that the very transformation of oneself in Buddhism is linked to the state of the natural world. Thai Buddhist monk Buddhadasa Bhikkhu writes:

> The entire cosmos is a cooperative. . . . When we realize that the world is a mutual, interdependent, cooperative enterprise, that human beings are all mutual friends in the process of birth, old age, suffering, and death, then we can build a noble, even heavenly environment. If our lives are not based on this truth, then we'll all perish.[57]

In the view of Thich Nhat Hanh, water itself is "a good friend, a bodhisattva [Buddha-like person who steps aside from entering nirvana in order to help others], which nourishes the many thousands of species on Earth."[58]

In addition to the ontological perspective of nonduality between nature and humans that provides an integral connection with the natural world, Buddhism illustrates the intimate interconnection through the aesthetic sensibility of the arts, such as painting and poetry. For example, the connection with the river Ajakarani is expressed in the Poems of the Elders:

> Whene'er I see the crane, her clear bright wings
> Outstretched in fear to flee the black storm cloud,
> A shelter seeking, to sage shelter borne,
> Then doth the river Ajakarani give joy to me. . . .
> Safe is the Ajakarani. She brings us luck.
> Here it is good to be.[59]

Water in its various forms serves as a powerful symbol in Buddhism. The lotus, which grows in water rather than soil, is a central image in many Buddhist traditions and art. Here water serves as the material of possibilities, "the image of the primordial substance of the world" and serves as "the image of the soul." "The lotus-stream of the Buddha rises up from the waters of the soul, just as the spirit, illumined by knowledge, frees itself from passive existence."[60] These viewpoints form important meanings for a deep reverence for the Earth and Earth's waters.

Rituals and Practices

Water rituals and practices such as those found in Hinduism are not a strong feature of contemporary Buddhism, yet water is an important feature in birthing ceremonies and in Buddhist funerals. For example, as water is poured into a bowl placed before the dead body and overflows, the monks say the words: "As the rains fill the rivers and overflow into the ocean, so likewise may what is given here reach the departed."[61] In the Mahayana tradition, friends and relatives gather around the deceased for a bathing ceremony in which water is poured over one hand of the dead.[62]

Other rituals involve a variety of points on the body. Foot cleansings utilize clean water mixed with sandalwood as one of eight typical offerings. By such a cleansing of an enlightened person, one's own karma is cleansed.[63] In Tibetan Buddhism, the Kalachakra ceremony employs water throughout a twelve-day series of rituals of initiation, cleansing, and blessing meant to "clear away the defilement of evil deeds" in life. The focus is on a giant sand mandala, six feet in diameter with a circular design representing chambers and the world where the deities reside; the design symbolizes dimensions of the enlightened mind. Some seven hundred gods and goddesses, all manifestations of Kalachakra, appear in the mandala in plant, animal, and human form. Prior to viewing the mandala the practitioners pass through the Water Initiation, seven rites involving sanctified water. The water, resting in a sacred vase in the shape of a conch shell, has special purifying qualities and symbolizes the virtues of the various deities involved. At some point in each rite, a holy one touches the disciple with a conch shell filled with water at five spots, the crown of the head, shoulders, upper arms, thighs, and hips. Water is then sprinkled on those five spots to cover the disciple with the spirit of the deities and eliminate any obstacle to enlightenment. The disciple then drinks the water and so is provided with wisdom and compassion for everyday life.[64]

In addition, there are important prohibitions on water. Monks may not pollute grass and water with bodily fluids, such as saliva, feces, or urine. Not only is grass an object of contemplation, it is also food for animals. Water, in its various forms in rivers, ponds, or wells, is a public good; it must be kept clean for the next user.[65] These ethical and aesthetic practices rest upon the inherent human-nature link in Buddhism and can be used for prohibitions against the more dramatic forms of pollution today. Here then, water functions as a symbol rather than as an aspect of the divinity or any transcendent reality. In Buddhism in general, as in all traditions, water has a cleansing and purifying function; however, for the most part, water remains something functional rather than actually being an aspect of a reality beyond itself.

In Buddhism, meditation is the tool by which one achieves enlightenment, and for many traditional Buddhists their environmental concerns are served by meditation alone. Thus, through meditation the reducing of egoism, fostering of empathy, deepening an appreciation for one's surroundings, the curbing of violence, clarifying of purpose, and increasing the sense of oneness with the universe serve the good of the environment. Such an ascetic and disciplined mindfulness is an important component of a frugal and reverent approach to water and the entire environment.

Conclusion

Ruben Habito has noted that Buddhism, particularly in its Zen form, can turn practitioners inward, toward a path of self-discovery, and the impact of the Zen practice of "living in the present" can develop "an attitude of indifference toward the future"—the future of both the practitioners and other Earth beings. Therefore the rivers used so often in Zen can refer only to "merely idealized images" "with no connection at all . . . to the rivers reeking with chemical pollutants."[66] However, Habito then goes on to explore the ways in which Zen practices, and by extension other Buddhist practices and rituals, deepen one's awareness not only of oneself, but because of the interconnectedness of all and the dissolution of the subject-object dichotomy, one's awareness of all being. Here Habito quotes the thirteenth-century Japanese Zen master Dogen: "I came to realize clearly, that mind is no other than mountains and rivers and the great Earth."[67]

In this way, the various particular aspects of nature—rivers, mountains, and the great Earth itself—are manifestations of the true self. "One is enabled to feel as one's very own the pain of the whole Earth being destroyed by human selfishness and greed and shortsightedness: the mountains being denuded, the rivers being polluted. . . . In all this, one feels one's own body racked in pain."[68] As a result this awareness should bring about rituals and practices that protect, revere, and celebrate rivers and other waters.

In this Buddhist perspective, the symbols of rivers and other aspects of nature do not, as in the Judeo-Christian heritage, point to some transcendent reality beyond nature, but instead refer to the very realities they symbolize. This is certainly the case in the religious and aesthetic traditions of Japanese Buddhism, and in the broad Mahayana schools of Buddhism we can trace important religious/aesthetic elements and applications for outlooks and actions on water issues. In spite of what seems to be a tradition turned *away* from the Earth, then, Buddhism provides unique insights and practices that integrate the human and the natural worlds.

Taoism and Confucianism

Heaven is my father and Earth my mother, and even such a small creature as I finds an intimate place in their midst. Therefore that which extends throughout the universe I regard as my body and that which directs the universe I consider as my nature. All people are my brothers and sisters, and all things are my companions.[69]

The great Tao flows everywhere, both to the left and to the right. It loves and nourishes all things, but does not lord it over them, and when good things are accomplished, it lays no claim to them. The Tao having done everything, always escapes and is not around to receive any thanks or acknowledgment. *Like water,* the Tao always seeks the lowest level, which man [sic] abhors. It does not show greatness and is therefore truly great.[70]

These quotations by a neo-Confucian philosopher and from the Tao Te Ching, allegedly written by Lao-tzu, founder of Taoism, point to great similarities between these two ancient Chinese religions. Unlike Hinduism and Western religions, in these religions there are no gods who created the world; the world simply is, and humans are among the inhabitants of a world/

universe shot through with vital force or *ch'i*, perhaps best translated as energy. The universe is alive.

In both of these ancient traditions, "reality" involves a seamless interconnectedness among the divine, human, and natural world—"an anthropocosmic worldview," in one author's words.[71] A continuity pervades the dynamic movements of nature through seasons and agricultural cycles. We will begin our discussion by examining terms central to them both. By the beginning of the Han dynasty, 220–206 B.C.E., the ideas of *Tao, ch'i, yang* and *yin* had become common in all various philosophical schools of Taoism and Confucianism.[72]

Ch'i

Tao itself is seen as primal chaos, as water is seen in other traditions—"When Heaven and Earth were not yet shaped, It [Tao] was amorphous, vague . . . a blur." It seethed and churned until in its center was formed a "drop" of primordial breath (ch'i). We are rooted in ch'i (material force), and the goal of personal cultivation in Confucianism and Taoism is to be in harmony with the natural and human while attentive to the Tao (Way).[73]

The two traditions share several common characteristics, namely, "continuity, wholeness, and dynamism." All things are interrelated and so interdependent. The universe is complete, whole, not created, not fallen nor subject to ignorance. Changes of all kinds are merely reflections of the organic whole. Pervaded by ch'i, the universe is dynamic, changing, but always leaning toward harmony.[74]

Yang and Yin

The principles of yang and yin are the complementary, interacting manifestations of ch'i. Yang signifies Heaven, the male, Sun and heat, mountains, while yin signifies Earth, the female, water, and nourishing rivers. The light yang ch'i moves up to the heavens while the heavy yin ch'i sinks down to form Earth.[75] They are two poles but always complementing one another. Here there is no dualism of opposing forces, but constant interplay, bringing changes in harmony.

Feng Shui

In Chinese thought, *feng shui* is the search for ch'i "as it is interpreted in the geophysical environment."[76] We have already seen that "Water is the root of all things and the source of all life. . . . Water is the blood and breath of the Earth, functioning in a similar fashion to the circulation of blood and breath."[77] This association of water with ch'i in the human body, chi's physiological base, finds its counterpart in its geophysical base, the Earth itself. In one noted text, for example, a prince is trying to persuade his father, the king, from damming rivers against the danger of floods:

> I have heard that those who ruled in ancient times did not . . . raise the marshes, obstruct the rivers, nor drain the swamps. . . . Rivers are channels for qi [ch'i], and swamps are concentrations of water. When Heaven and Earth became complete, they had . . . gathered creatures in the low (marshes). They had cut through rivers and valleys, to channel their qi, and had dammed and diked stagnant and low-lying water, to concentrate their fertility.[78]

The relationship among topography, qi [ch'i], and water derives from the principle that "Qi [ch'i] is the mother of water—where there is qi there is water."[79] In other words, ch'i birthed water. This explains the natural relationship between them. We have the bases for the flow of ch'i in the human body (arteries) and in the land (streams, pools, and rivers).

Perhaps nowhere is this as well observed as in the directions for choosing the proper burial site, which should be at the point where water transverses the axis of advancing mountains. The water must not be too swift (swift waters mean grief), nor divergent (lack of prosperity), nor stagnant (decline). The flowing water in its meandering around the burial site energizes the bones of the deceased with ch'i and enhances the chances of good fortune for the living.[80]

Chinese gardens all contain a pool or a lake that serves as the spiritual center of the garden. Quiet waters, also found in wells, symbolize wisdom, clarity, and good judgment. Sitting with the waters calms strong emotions and quiets the spirit. The waters also represent the positive force of ch'i, especially when fish are present. In whatever form, water in feng shui represents the flow of communication, fostering the interchange of ideas in the arts, music, and literature.[81] Feng shui provides a key element in understanding the place of ch'i in these Chinese traditions.

Taoism

The Tao is the origin of all things, silent and unchanging. A major Taoist thinker, Chuang Tzu (399–295 B.C.E.) writes: "Before heaven and Earth came into being, Tao existed by itself from all time. . . . It created heaven and Earth. . . . It is prior to heaven and Earth."[82] The phenomenal world is changing; there is constant gain and loss "in the form of yin and yang superseding each other. All that exists uses these processes." The human environments of moral ways and social interactions are based upon the interchanging relations of yin and yang. When the Tao is not respected, division and disharmony inevitably follow.[83]

In Taoism one achieves harmony through *wu-wei*, described as "actionless action." Taoism itself is often viewed as water, which does not resist but flows gracefully, eventually bringing changes through its effortless flow, and so humans accomplish harmony through the "flow" of their actions in harmony with the rest of nature. The image of water resembles strongly the action of the Tao, as recorded in these words of Lao-tzu (sixth century B.C.E.) in the Tao Ti Jing: ". . . the highest good is like water. Water benefits the myriad things but never strives against them. It rests at the lowest place that everyone dislikes. Hence it is similar to the Dao." Earlier in the text, a sage ruling a country is seen as "like the sea: he is willing to stay downstream and endure all manner of filth."[84] The questions that arise from this quotation are how much filth must the waters, and by extension the sage, endure—and can humans restore the harmony of the heavens, Earth, and humans, given the ills of water in our world?

E. N. Anderson notes that the world described in Taoism represents a coming together of various themes from early Chinese folk religion surrounding a belief that the cosmos is held together by breath (or ch'i, as we have seen), which "circulates along channels similar to veins."[85] However, these views represent an idealized rural life of isolated villages. At the time the texts were taking final shape in the early Han dynasty of the third century B.C.E., they could not reflect the reality of the rich agricultural life of later Chinese civilization. Anderson goes on to note that the Taoists are not real ecologists; that role fell to Confucians. Rather, Taoism was meant more for rulers as advice for running their societies.[86] For our investigation we note that water in Taoism remains largely a *symbol* of adapting to the changing nature of reality rather than either a divine force or a central dimension and reflection of a creative force.

Yet, we find that Taoism can serve as a basis for conservation and sustainable management of water resources. For example, along the Dujiang Yan irrigation system lies a Taoist temple, making the Taoist masters major engineers of water management. Acting as guardians of waters flowing from mountains, Taoists become managers of ch'i, the life-giving breath of nature. In this manner, taking care of the mountain and its waters becomes a ritual of purification of self.[87]

Confucianism
Confucian thought focuses on kinship with all beings, reserving a special place for humans. Humans are engaged in active participation in managing

creation, working toward harmony of all things. Confucius in the *Analects* was concerned mainly with proper *human* conduct, "questions of ethical conduct, ritual, good government, education, and self-cultivation" rather than with more philosophical questions reflecting on ch'i or yin/yang. The heart of Confucianism in general lies in "the referent of worth or excellence that can be commended to anyone seeking a moral, intellectual, or spiritual orientation to life."[88]

However, this can be accomplished only through the cultivation of virtues in engagement with others and nature itself. The Confucian virtues include benevolence, responsibility, faithfulness, wisdom, and propriety; these are especially important in five areas of relationships: ruler and subject, older and younger friend, father and son, husband and wife, and older brother and younger brother.[89] In relation to the natural world and its proper care and refinement (as distinguished from the Taoist orientation to let things be), only certain virtuous people can carry out this role: "To become a guardian, steward, or elder sibling to the rest of creation requires special preparation. It requires that one become a person who is cultivated in the mysteries and rites of human behavior and culture and fully comprehends the nature of reality and the way of the world."[90]

Mencius

The Confucian scholar Mencius (371–288 B.C.E.), along with a later philosopher Hsun Tzu, developed the more reflective dimensions of ch'i in relation to the natural world, and in particular to the forces of nature. Confucianism, as distinct from Taoism, is very concerned with and embedded in history, which means in the natural world. Ch'i is not just a spiritual force but is material energy as well. Much more than for the Taoist, history is material for philosophical thought because the world is real, not just symbol; it is careful attention to "the realities of the world" that encourages human flourishing.[91]

For Mencius the concept of the human place in the natural world helped underscore a "conservationist view of human interaction with nature."[92] Although water as a separate reality does not appear strongly in Confucian thought, Mencius interestingly cultivated his own defenses of Confucianism through the use of important water images. Based on an ancient account of a great inundation of water that Mencius noted had inundated the Middle Kingdom [China],[93] he used the water symbol to describe a world not yet "perfectly reduced to order." Because of the meaning this great inundation had for people, Mencius connected the law of water with the law of morality: a good ruler would bring order to the world *and* to the water. Here are a few thoughts from Mencius on the relationship between good rule and flowing water: "The people turn to a benevolent ruler as water flows downward. . . . The tendency of man's nature to good is like the tendency of water to flow downwards. . . . Benevolence subdues its opposite just as water subdues fire."[94] Thus the moral ruler's progress was ". . . like the falling of opportune rain, and the people were delighted."[95]

Mencius used water as a metaphor replete with perceptions of the chaos of a mythical great deluge to relate his Confucian tenets of the moral bearing of the great ruler.

> By using the figurative language [of water] the ethical standards that he was advocating were raised in the auditor's [listener's] mind to a level as significant as water. . . . To Mencius, though water is powerful, benevolence and righteousness are even more encompassing. One with these virtues was able to solve any problem including a disaster caused by water.[96]

Although Confucianism is mainly concerned with order and relationships among humans, many Confucian scholars took seriously the connection with nature. In Japan, Confucian scholars built a conservationist theory of nature, based upon the writings of Mencius, which resulted in the sound forestry policies of the Tokugawa government of the seventeeth to nineteenth centuries. Although usually anthropocentric, Mencius's writings would furnish today's environmentalist with notions of the obligation to respect the natural world. After all, it was Mencius who noted that the ruler would not remain untouched by the suffering of sacrificial animals and who lamented the ruinous deforestation of Ox Mountain in North China.[97]

Neo-Confucians

The medieval neo-Confucians and today's new Confucians advance even more fully the idea of human involvement with nature. Writing in the eleventh century, Chou Tun-I refrained from cutting the grass in front of his window through his recognition that "the feelings of the grass and his own feelings are the same."[98] The world is one; this requires a care for all things. In the fifteenth century, Confucian scholar Wang Yang-ming noted: "Everything from ruler, minister, husband, wife and friends to mountains, *rivers*, spiritual beings, birds, animals, and plants should be truly loved in order to realize my humanity that forms one body with them, and then my clear character will be completely manifested, and I will really form one body with Heaven, Earth, and the myriad things."[99] Writing with some concern for today's new Confucians in relation to the ecological crisis, John Berthrong argues that contemporary Confucian scholars must make use of other sources, such as Taoism that is more sensitive to nature, in order to bring an environmental aspect to Confucianism.[100]

While water or even nature as such does not appear directly in Confucian thought, human obligations to develop harmony among Heaven, Earth, and the human—the holy triad—can include helpful tools for aspects related to the global water crisis, from water conservation to access to drinkable water and water reclamation. Confucius was said to have wanted "to swim in a stream during the spring with his friends,"[101] and Mencius saw water as a primal and basic metaphor for ethical guides upon rulers and ruled. If the waters are blocked, polluted, hindered, then there will be no more bathing in streams and the ruler's benevolence will not flow freely.

Conclusion

Although there are many different schools of thought in both Taoism and Confucianism, these two Chinese traditions provide a dynamic view of the universe that integrates Heaven, Earth, and the human. As one author notes, "The East Asian traditions of Confucianism and Taoism remain, in certain ways, some of the most life-affirming in the spectrum of world religions."[102] With their cosmological view of the place of the human in the natural world and their emphasis upon the dynamics of change through the interactions of yang ch'i and yin ch'i, Taoism and Confucianism offer profound insights into natural realities such as water.

Heaven, Earth, and the human are part of a triadic ordering through which ch'i as "material energy" flows in the universe. Yang and yin are not opposing forces, but rather their dynamic interaction accounts for all change, in both physical realities as well as spiritual.

There are certainly clear differences between these two traditions. For example, the seventeenth-century Japanese Confucian scholar Kaibara Ekken clearly distinguished Confucianism from Taoist and Buddhist ideas of emptiness and passivity for fear of neglecting the human's ethical obligations to intervene in this world.[103] Yet, together they both show a reverence, if that is not too strong a word, for the natural world. Perhaps the difference between them is best summed up by E. N. Anderson:

> Daoist mystical ecology grows within a wider universe of mystical geography and cosmology. . . . [T]he desire is to transcend visible reality and put oneself in harmony with subtle flows and Ways—the inferred processes behind perceived facts. . . . Natural things, such as rhinos and tigers [and rivers], are mere exemplars.

> By contrast, the Confucian tradition . . . reveals a genuine knowledge of, understanding of, and desire to work with nature. . . . Conservation was ritually represented and ritually sanctioned. . . . Mencius, perhaps more than any environmentalist before or since, understood both the practical and the spiritual reasons why conservation is necessary to individuals and states.[104]

Even though in this text the Confucians are the real ecologists, Anderson shows that in time the Taoists followed the Confucian lead and began to set rules for nature preservation and conservation. By focusing on a mystical Way that directed human energy outward toward the rest of nature, Taoists "provided an environment-oriented counterbalance to the Confucian focus on human life." Anderson continues with the assertion that the "vast and devastating onslaught on China's fragile environment" went along with the decline of Taoism in the twentieth century.[105]

More particularly, however, in neither tradition does water have the central place that it occupies in indigenous, Hindu, or even Buddhist traditions. Water appears in Taoism primarily as a *symbol* of the reality of the Tao rather than as a reality itself. In Confucianism water is one of the elements, a foundational one at that, which requires good management by the wise ruler. Again, water, although significant for life of all the Earth, appears to be valued for its usefulness, to be at best conserved and preserved for human utility and the use of those life forms associated with human society.

Summary

One theme has flowed throughout this exploration of the significance of water in religious traditions: water is not only sacred, but to some degree the sacred resides in water or is manifested in the water itself. These traditions echo the theme that water is either a divinity in itself, possesses divine characteristics, or manifests divine powers. While that theme is not as strong in all traditions, particularly in Taoism where water seems more symbolic of divinity, the central place of water's connection to the divine or cosmic powers is confirmed. These beliefs concerning the nature and origins of water form a "water" consciousness that can enhance awareness and lead to significant practices in the current water crises. With their calls for inner purification, renewal, cleansing, rebirthing, these traditions also have developed rituals and ceremonies that respect the waters and at least form important bases for policies and programs. Such policies and programs can help to conserve waters, clean polluted waters, share waters more equitably, and through meditation and rituals renew attitudes and practices that respect and grasp the importance of water and even establish new attitudes and practices.

Our next exploration of Western religious traditions provides strong initial contrasts. For in the desert-origin, Abrahamic religions of Judaism, Christianity, and Islam, with their strongly monotheistic belief system, water is definitely *not* divine, and to attribute a "sacred" dimension to water seems like a threat to the absolute divinity of the God of Abraham. However, as we will see, each tradition has a special reverence for water and rituals and practices similar to those we have already seen.

Notes

1. Alan Ereira, *The Elder Brothers* (New York: Vintage, 1993), 223.

2. Ereira, *Elder Brothers*, 176.

3. Clifford Geertz, "Religion as a Cultural System," in *The Religious Situation*, ed. Donald R. Cutler (Boston: Beacon, 1969), 643.

4. Mircea Eliade, *Images and Symbols* (New York: Sheed & Ward, 1969).

5. Mircea Eliade, *Patterns in Comparative Religion* (New York: Sheed & Ward, 1958), 188.

6. Eliade, *Comparative Religion*, 193–212.

7. Eliade, *Comparative Religion*, 191.

8. Ereira, *Elder Brothers*, 176.

9. Nathaniel Altman, *Sacred Water: The Spiritual Source of Life* (Mahwah, N.J.: Hidden Spring, 2002), 17.

10. Camille Talkeu Tounounga, "The Liquid of the Gods," *Unesco Courier* 5 (May 1993): 38.

11. Corbin Harney, *The Way It Is: One Water, One Air, One Mother Earth* (Nevada City, Calif.: Blue Dolphin, 1995), 218.

12. Harney, *The Way It Is*, 8.

13. Louis Sahagun, "Holy Waters, Slot Machines and a Gamble in Taos, New Mexico: A Ruling May Close Tribal Casinos," *Los Angeles Times*, 11 January 1996.

14. Phillip Ball, *Life's Matrix: A Biography of Water* (New York: Farrar, Straus, & Giroux, 1999), 4.

15. Leslie Marmon Silko, *Sacred Water: Narratives and Pictures* (Tucson, Ariz.: Flood Plain Press, 1993), 58.

16. Tounounga, "Liquid of the Gods," 38.

17. Eliade, *Comparative Religion*, 194.

18. Marilyn Houlberg, "Sirens and Snakes: Water Spirits in the Art of the Haitian Vodou," *African Arts* 29, no. 2 (Spring 1996): 32.

19. Tounounga, "Liquid of the Gods," 39.

20. Houlberg, "Sirens and Snakes," 33.

21. Richard G. Kimber, "Australian Aboriginals' Perceptions of their Desert Homelands: Part One," *Arid Lands Newsletter* 50 (Novermber/December 2001), http://ag.arizona.edu/OALS/ALN/aln50/kimberpart1.html (14 April 2006)

22. Altman, *Sacred Water*, 49.

23. Tounounga, "Liquid of the Gods," 38.

24. Electronics Industry Good Neighbor Campaign, *Sacred Waters: The Life-Blood of Mother Earth* (Tucson, Ariz.: Southwest Network for Environmental and Economic Justice, and Campaign for Responsible Technology, 1997), 80.

25. Altman, *Sacred Water*, 141–143.

26. Eliade, *Comparative Religion*, 189.

27. David L. Haberman, "River of Love in an Age of Pollution," in *Hinduism and Ecology: The Intersection of Earth, Sky, and Water*, eds. Christopher Key Chapple and Mary Evelyn Tucker (New Delhi: Oxford University Press, 2001), 348.

28. K. L. Seshagiri Rao, "The Five Great Elements (Pañcamahābhūta): An Ecological Perspective," in *Hinduism and Ecology: The Intersection of Earth, Sky, and Water*, eds. Christopher Key Chapple and Mary Evelyn Tucker (New Delhi: Oxford University Press, 2001), 24–25.

29. Quoted in Maggie Black, *The No-Nonsense Guide to Water* (Oxford: New International, 2004), 8.

30. Quoted in Gaston Bachelard, *Water and Dreams* (Dallas: Pegasus Foundation, 1983), 118. Originally published as *L'Eau et les Reves* (Paris: Librairie Jose Corti, 1942).

31. Vandana Shiva, *Water Wars: Privatization, Pollution, and Profit* (Cambridge, Mass.: South End Press, 2002), 132–133.

32. Vasudha Narayanan, "Water, Wood, and Wisdom: Ecological Perspectives from the Hindu Traditions," *Daedalus* 130, no. 4 (Fall 2001): 185.

33. Narayanan, "Water, Wood, and Wisdom," 185–186.

34. Quoted in Rao, "The Five Great Elements," 33.

35. William H. Fisher, "Sacred Rivers, Sacred Dams: Competing Visions of Social Justice and Sustainable Development along the Narmada," in *Hinduism and Ecology: The Intersection of Earth, Sky, and Water*, eds. Christopher Key Chapple and Mary Evelyn Tucker (New Delhi: Oxford University Press, 2001), 413.

36. Haberman, "River of Love," 345.

37. Haberman, "River of Love," 350.

38. Narayanan, "Water, Wood, and Wisdom," 192.

39. Haberman, "River of Love," 349.

40. Stephen Alter, *Sacred Waters: A Pilgrimage up the Ganges River to the Source of Hindu Culture* (New York: Harcourt, 2001), 4–5.

41. Altman, *Sacred Water*, 197–198.

42. Narayanan, "Water, Wood, and Wisdom," 198.

43. Anil Agarwal, "Can Hindu Beliefs and Values Help India Meet Its Ecological Crisis?" in *Hinduism and Ecology: The Intersection of Earth, Sky, and Water*, eds. Christopher Key Chapple and Mary Evelyn Tucker (New Delhi: Oxford University Press, 2001), 172–173.

44. Kelly D. Alley, "Separate Domains: Hinduism, Politics, and Environmental Pollution," in *Hinduism and Ecology: The Intersection of Earth, Sky, and Water*, eds.

Christopher Key Chapple and Mary Evelyn Tucker (New Delhi: Oxford University Press, 2001), 357.

45. Alley, "Separate Domains," 371–372.

46. Alley, "Separate Domains," 381.

47. Narayanan, "Water, Wood, and Wisdom," 202.

48. Agarwal, "Hindu Beliefs and Values," 178.

49. Donald K. Swearer, "The Hermeneutics of Buddhist Ecology in Contemporary Thailand: Buddhadāsa and Dhammapitaka," in *Buddhism and Ecology: The Interconnection of Dharma and Deeds*, eds. Mary Evelyn Tucker and Duncan Ryūken Williams (Cambridge, Mass.: Harvard University Press, 1997), 8 (emphasis mine).

50. Dipak Kumar Barua, "Ecological Ethics and Conservation of Forests and Wildlife," in *Buddhism and Ecology*, ed. S. K. Pathak (New Delhi: Om Publications, 2004), 59–60.

51. Lily de Silva, "The Hills Wherein the Soul Delights," in *Buddhism and Ecology*, eds. Martine Batchelor and Kerry Brown (London: Cassell, 1992), 18.

52. David Kinsley, *Ecology and Religion: Ecological Spirituality in Cross-Cultural Perspective* (Englewood Cliffs, N.J.: Prentice-Hall, 1995), 85.

53. Quoted in Kinsley, *Ecology and Religion*, 88.

54. Kerry Brown, edited talks with Ajahn Pongsak, "In the Water There Were Fish and the Fields Were Full of Rice," in *Buddhism and Ecology*, eds. Martine Batchelor and Kerry Brown (London: Cassell, 1992), 98–99.

55. Brown, "In the Water There Were Fish," 132.

56. K. Sankarnarayan, "Buddhist Ecology and Scriptures of Mahayana," in *Buddhism and Ecology*, ed. S. K. Pathak (New Delhi: Om Publications, 2004), 25.

57. Swearer, "Hermeneutics of Buddhist Ecology," 7.

58. Thich Nhat Hanh, "Look Deep and Smile: Thoughts and Writings of Thich Nhat Hanh," in *Buddhism and Ecology*, eds. Martine Batchelor and Kerry Brown (London: Cassell, 1992), 105–106.

59. Padmasiri de Silva, *Buddhism, Ethics and Society: The Conflicts and Dilemmas of Our Times* (Clayton, Australia: Monash University Press, 2002), 155.

60. Titus Burckhardt, "The Symbolism of Water," in *Seeing God Everywhere: Essays on Nature and the Sacred*, ed. Barry McDonald (Bloomington, Ind.: World Wisdom, 2003), 210.

61. Bodhidharma, quoted in Julie Abrams, "Buddhism," at www.thewaterpage.com/religion (accessed 12 June 2006).

62. Buddah Dharma Education Association Inc., "Rituals in Buddhism: Buddhist Funeral Rites," at www.buddahnet.net (accessed 2 May 2006).

63. "Bathing in Hospitality," *Daily Om*, 4 November 2005, at http://www.dailyom.com.

64. Altman, *Sacred Water*, 178–180.

65. de Silva, "Hills," 25.

66. Ruben L. F. Habito, "Mountains and Rivers and the Great Earth: Zen and Ecology," in *Buddhism and Ecology: The Interconnection of Dharma and Deeds*, eds.

Mary Evelyn Tucker and Duncan Ryūken Williams (Cambridge, Mass.: Harvard University Press, 1997), 165–67.

67. Quoted in Habito, "Mountains and Rivers," 168.

68. Habito, "Mountains and Rivers," 172.

69. Kinsley, *Ecology and Religion*, 77.

70. Quoted in "Taoism/Daoism," *Meditations and Reflections in Zen, Buddhism, Taoism, Mystical Religions, and Early Christianity*, at www.yakrider.com (accessed 3 May 2006) (emphasis mine). The term *Daoism* is found in some texts rather than *Taoism*; I will use *Daoism* only where a quotation contains that form. Likewise I will use *ch'i* except where a quoted author employs *qi*.

71. Mary Evelyn Tucker and John Berthrong, eds., *Confucianism and Ecology: The Interrelation of Heaven, Earth, and Humans* (Cambridge, Mass.: Harvard University Press, 1998), xxxviii.

72. John Berthrong, "Motifs for a New Confucian Ecological Vision," in *Confucianism and Ecology: The Interrelation of Heaven, Earth, and Humans*, eds. Mary Evelyn Tucker and John Berthrong (Cambridge, Mass.: Harvard University Press, 1998), 249.

73. Tucker and Berthrong, *Confucianism and Ecology*, xxvii.

74. Kinsley, *Ecology and Religion*, 69–70.

75. Zhang Jiyu and Li Yuanguo, "The Concept of 'Mutual Stealing among the Three Numinous Powers' in the *Scripture on Unconscious Unification* (Yinfu jing)," in *Daoism and Ecology: Ways within a Cosmic Landscape*, eds. N. J. Girardot, James Miller, and Liu Xiaogan (Cambridge, Mass.: Harvard University Press, 2001), 114–115.

76. Stephen L. Field, "In Search of Dragons: The Folk Ecology of Fengshui," in *Daoism and Ecology: Ways within a Cosmic Landscape*, eds. N. J. Girardot, James Miller, and Liu Xiaogan (Cambridge, Mass.: Harvard University Press, 2001), 187.

77. From the *Guanzi*, quoted in Field, "In Search of Dragons," 188.

78. From the *Zhouyu*, compiled in 431 B.C.E., quoted in Field, "In Search of Dragons," 189.

79. From the *Zangshu*, quoted in Field, "In Search of Dragons," 190.

80. Field, "In Search of Dragons," 194–195.

81. Altman, *Sacred Water*, 107–109.

82. Quoted in Michael Glenhorn, "Taoism and Christianity," at http://www.probe.org/content/view/892/65 (accessed 3 May 2006).

83. Tao Ti Jing, chap. 20, quoted in Michael Glenhorn, "Taoism and Christianity," at http://www.probe.org/content/view/892/65 (accessed 3 May 2006).

84. Quoted in Jiyu and Yuanguo, "'Mutual Stealing,'" 118–119.

85. E. N. Anderson. "The Flowering Apricot: Environmental Practice, Folk Religion, and Daoism," in *Daoism and Ecology: Ways within a Cosmic Landscape*, eds. N. J. Girardot, James Miller, and Liu Xiaogan (Cambridge, Mass.: Harvard University Press, 2001), 174.

86. Anderson, "Flowering Apricot," 174–177.

87. Thomas Hahn, "An Introductory Study on Daoist Notions of Wilderness," in *Daoism and Ecology: Ways within a Cosmic Landscape*, eds. N. J. Girardot, James Miller, and Liu Xiaogan (Cambridge, Mass.: Harvard University Press, 2001), 204–211.

88. Berthrong, "New Confucian Ecological Vision," 248, 241.

89. Ingrid H. Shafer, "Confucianism," revised 6 January 2002, at www.usao .edu/~usao-ids3313/ids/html/confucianism (accessed 25 July 2006).

90. Kinsley, *Ecology and Religion*, 78.

91. Berthrong, "New Confucian Ecological Vision," 252.

92. Berthrong, "New Confucian Ecological Vision," 242.

93. Quoted in R. Ma, "Water-Related Figurative Language in the Rhetoric of Mencius," *Rhetoric in Intercultural Contexts*, eds. A. Gonzalez and D. V. Tanno, *International and Intercultural Communication Annual* 22: 123.

94. Quoted in Ma, "Water-Related Figurative Language," 123, 125.

95. Ma, "Water-Related Figurative Language," 125.

96. Ma, "Water-Related Figurative Language," 125.

97. Berthrong, "New Confucian Ecological Vision," 255, 238, 257.

98. Rodney L. Taylor, "Companionship with the World: Roots and Branches of a Confucian Ecology," in *Confucianism and Ecology: the Interrelation of Heaven, Earth, and Humans*, eds. Mary Evelyn Tucker and John Berthrong (Cambridge, Mass.: Harvard University Press, 1998), 53.

99. Quoted in Taylor, "Companionship," 54.

100. Berthrong, "New Confucian Ecological Vision," 250.

101. Berthrong, "New Confucian Ecological Vision," 258.

102. Mary Evelyn Tucker and John Grim, "Series Foreword," in *Confucianism and Ecology: the Interrelation of Heaven, Earth, and Humans*, eds. Mary Evelyn Tucker and John Berthrong (Cambridge, Mass.: Harvard University Press, 1998), xxvii.

103. Mary Evelyn Tucker, "The Philosophy of Ch'i as an Ecological Cosmology," in *Confucianism and Ecology: the Interrelation of Heaven, Earth, and Humans*, eds. Mary Evelyn Tucker and John Berthrong (Cambridge, Mass.: Harvard University Press, 1998), 201.

104. Anderson, "Flowering Apricot," 167.

105. Anderson, "Flowering Apricot," 171.

~

CHAPTER TWO

Water in Abrahamic Western Traditions

When we turn to the Western religious traditions, we encounter striking differences from indigenous and Asian traditions in the relationships among gods, humans, and nature, Heaven, Earth, and humans: one divinity, one God, emerges as the creator of, but separate from, all of creation. In contrast to the interrelatedness of all creation emphasized in indigenous and Asian traditions, the Abrahamic traditions separate the human and natural worlds in a hierarchical ordering of human, animal, plant, and inorganic matter. Although humans have a distinct role, that of caretaker (Judaism), steward or manager (Christianity), or vicegerent (Islam), the Western traditions emphasize the transcendence of the divine in relation to the created world. Nonetheless, in these traditions nature does have an intimate relationship with humans and the divine, and water has a central place both as a symbol and as a reality in itself.

Judaism

In her essay "Waiting for a Miracle: A Jew Goes Fishing," Marjorie Sandor reflects on a time when she stood waist-deep in the Colorado River and felt judged by the dozen Hasidic Jews gazing down on her from a bridge:

> What kind of chutzpah was this, a Jew trying to walk in harmony with nature?
> Is there a posture in the world that smacks more of the desire for premature transcendence than this business of standing midstream, trying to raise fishes from the deep?[1]

Sandor's experience led her to explore the symbolism of fish and water in Judaism, proving to herself that her religion and her desire to commune with nature were not incompatible. She discovered that water in Judaism is "a metaphor for the environment of the Torah itself." Water and charity are one: "Your charity is like the waves of the sea" (Isaiah). Sandor writes, "In the beautiful logic of this commentary, it follows that the *tzaddik* or holy man who dwells in it is—metaphorically speaking—a fish."[2] Sandor's story moves us into a brief discussion of Judaism.

Origins

The arid desert areas of the Middle East, the birthplace of Judaism, Christianity, and Islam, are a rich source for religious beliefs surrounding water. Egypt's male god Hapi was depicted with two breasts, from which flowed the waters of the upper and lower Nile. Aspu, the Sumerian god, governed the Sweet Waters. Mesopotamian Ea, god of water, set his palace at the confluence of the Tigris and Euphrates, and Gilgamesh placed the Tree of Life in the same location. Nun, god of Babylonia, provided the view that water was the origin of all life from which the Earth sprang as did all creation.[3]

The Jewish account of the origin of water reveals strong similarities:

> In the beginning God created the heavens and the earth. Now the earth was a formless void, there was darkness over the deep, and God's spirit hovered over the water. . . . God said, "Let there be a vault in the waters to divide the waters in two." And so it was. God made the vault, and it divided the waters above the vault from the waters under the vault. God called the vault "heaven." . . . God said, "Let the waters under heaven come together into a single mass, and let dry land appear." And so it was. God called the dry land "earth" and the mass of waters "seas," and God saw that it was good.[4]

The world was created from water, and water "symbolizes the primordial ocean from which all fertility is derived and in which the formless takes shape."[5] These rich statements underline the dramatic nature of water in Judaism, and consequently in Christianity and Islam.

Creation: The Primordial Ocean

Irving Friedman writes that the ancient Hebrews viewed the sea as the mother of all the elements that emerged in the guise of gods. After dividing the waters, God subdued the monsters of the deep and ". . . impelled the winds to drive the waters that brought the great flood. He [sic] parted the waters of the Red Sea for Israel's escape from Egypt, and He opened a path through the Jordan River for Israel to enter the promised land."[6] Judah ben Pazi, quoting the wise Rabbi Ismael, reports: "In the beginning the world consisted of water within water; the water was then changed into ice and again transformed by God into earth. The earth however rests upon the waters, and the waters on the clouds."[7] This summary statement captures what we now call the hydrologic cycle and amplifies in poetic manner the centrality of water.

In the Hebrew Bible, the prophet Isaiah asserts that God created the chaotic darkness out of which the rest of creation came, while in Genesis the darkness and deep waters existed in the beginning and God created the rest of the world out of them. For Isaiah the very power of God pours forth from the depths of the Earth: "For in the wilderness shall waters gush out, and streams in the desert. And the parched ground will become marsh and the thirsty land spring of water. . . . And through it will run a path for them which will be called the sacred Way" (Isaiah 35:4, 6–8). In both accounts, however, it is clear that water existed before the other elements and the rest of creation, proving its significance to the Abrahamic people.[8]

In the words of the prophet Jeremiah, the Lord Yahweh, one of many Hebrew terms referring to God, is called "the fountain of living waters." Isaiah had called people to hear God's word by the exclamation, "Everyone who thirsts, come to the waters."[9] Yahweh God is the source of spiritual drink, nourishment, a conviction echoed in the Christian scriptures; at the same time, Yahweh God is the origin of the physical waters that nurture God's people.

Evan Eisenberg calls Eden "the worldpole of wilderness," from which energy and life flow to the world in the form of water: "The two rivers that run from El's mountain have been doubled [in the Genesis account] . . . so that they may reach and refresh the very corners of the world, dividing it neatly in four quarters."[10] In this way all the Earth is nourished by the waters that flow from Eden.

However, although water is powerful and is the very substance of creation, it is secondary to the power of and is contained by the Hebrew god, Yahweh. Jewish scholar Eric Katz reminds us, "Humanity does not own the natural world. *In Judaism, the world belongs to God.*"[11] Water is not sacred in itself, but is sacred because it reflects God's creation and God's mastery.[12]

Water's power, or rather the power of God as expressed in water, became a key element in the story of Hebrew deliverance, the exodus, from the oppression of the Egyptian pharaoh. The exodus story relates the many times Moses used water for deliverance. He took water from the Nile and turned it into blood. He parted the waters of the Red or Reed Sea, allowing the Hebrew people to escape from Egypt and the Pharaoh's pursuing army. By striking a rock with his rod, Moses brought water to the people in their journey across the Sinai desert.[13]

Ritual and Restoration

Water's irrigation of the Earth symbolizes the quenching of spiritual as well as physical thirst and the cleansing and purification of the soul as well as the soil. The priests of the temple washed with water from a bronze vessel before entering the temple, and the tradition of ritual washing continues to the present day. Jews wash and sprinkle areas with water in order to separate the living from the dead and the sacred from the profane.[14]

Washing of the hands and feet has the purpose of restoring the believer to his or her original state of purity. Ritual washing of hands is a common practice before and after meals. For the Sabbath meal, hands are washed before the meal begins. After the rabbi recites the blessing on the meal, the *Kiddush* (Sanctification), hands are washed again. The sacred *seder* meal on the first night of Passover, commemorating exodus and deliverance from bondage in Egypt, includes a series of blessings over food that is followed by washing of hands.[15] In addition, especially in Orthodox Judaism, observance of religious law also includes washing hands after sleep, after elimination of bodily fluids, before daily prayers, and after being in the presence of the dead.[16] Water cleanses humanity, bringing humans closer to God.

Aside from these everyday uses of water, special ablutions traditionally are practiced by priests, converts to Judaism during their initiation ceremony, and women. For example, the water of the *mikveh*[17] bath is used for both initiation and purification. An observant Jewish woman is obliged by tradition to immerse in the mikveh at the end of her menstrual or "impure" period, called "*niddah*."[18] She must first count seven "clean" days after the end of her period before immersing and cannot resume sexual activity until after immersion. The mikveh must contain a certain amount of *mayim chayim*, "living water," in order for it to retain all of its purifying powers. Living water is water from a natural source, such as rain or a stream.[19]

The mikveh is important to women particularly because it is connected to the belief that water symbolizes fruitfulness and fertility.[20] When a woman immerses in the bath, the body must be prepared, with all barriers between the water and the naked self eliminated. Also, vessels for eating can be purified by immersion in the mikveh waters, and the cleansed vessel will then purify the food served in it.[21] Although the mikveh is often interpreted as sexist, Rabbi Elyse Goldstein hopes to counter the idea that women and their menses are unclean by promoting the mikveh as a symbol of "conscious feminist rebirth."[22] Mikveh then involves not just purification but also an awareness of one's power as a woman.

The mikveh is also used in the ceremony for new initiates into Judaism, whether male or female. According to Friedman, water's downward flow represents the downward transmission of wisdom. This transmission was another rite of initiation in the Middle Ages, when immersion in water by a master and his pupil was required before transmission of the name of God. Standing in the water the master would proclaim, "The voice of God is over the waters!"[23]

We see another example of water's purifying power in the ceremony called *Tashlich*, which hinges on water as a dissolver and container of sins. Tashlich, meaning "to cast away" in Hebrew, is a Jewish ceremony that takes place during *Rosh ha-Shanah*, the opening of the year in the Jewish calendar. Jews recall the prophet Micah's words: "He will cover up our iniquities; You will hurl all of our sins into the depths of the sea."[24] People empty their pockets and symbolically cast their sins into natural bodies of water.

One final concept reveals the ecological importance of certain features of the Jewish tradition, namely, the principle of *bal tashchit*, "do not destroy." The text in Deuteronomy 20:19–20 reads: "When in your war against a city you have to besiege it a long time, you must not destroy the trees wielding the axe against them." While initially a prohibition against wanton destruction, such as the cutting of trees during war and vandalism, later rabbis extended the prohibition to peacetime issues, such as air and water pollution, and even to human artifacts: "Whoever breaks vessels, or tears garments or clogs up a fountain violates the prohibition of *bal tashhit*."[25] Such a prohibition would directly relate to issues of pollution today.

Conclusion

Each of the elements—fire, air, Earth, and water—have symbolic weight in Judaism, but water is the mother of the elements because in Judaic tradition the original unity of the elements is symbolized by the river of Eden, which parted into four rivers to flow over the Earth.[26] This river draws its strength from the Holy One, and if the human conforms to the will of the Holy One, he or she will assume the form of the river and master the elements in order to sustain the world.[27]

The water story in Judaism continues its flow in the Christian story.

Christianity

Christianity shares the Judaic creation story: God's spirit hovered over chaos, and out of the waters came the created world. Yet the two Abrahamic traditions develop very different meanings of the significance and role of nature and of water. In the Christian tradition, the reconfiguration of nature, including water, expresses the power and majesty of a transcendent God, often removed from the context of the natural world. Historically, water and nature are not seen as places of God's revelation; rather, the history of humans becomes the locus of God's manifestation and relation to humans, as seen in this quote from the 1966 statement of the World Council of Churches:

> The biblical story . . . places creation—the physical world—in the context of covenant relation and does not try to understand it apart from that relation. The movement of history, not the structure of the setting, is central to reality. Physical creation even participates in this history; its timeless and cyclical character, as far as it exists, is unimportant. The physical world . . . does not have its meaning in itself.[28]

This statement reflects a view of the natural world deriving from an emphasis on the transcendent, on the next life, on sanctification of the soul separate from the body. Thanks to the neo-Platonic teaching of several early Christian writers, the "world" was viewed as a place of trial, of temptation in relation to the afterlife. Historian Lynn White calls this development the "desacralization" of the Earth, and in his famous 1967 article, "The Historical Roots of Our Ecologic Crisis," published in *Science* magazine, argued that Christian "desacralization" paved the way for the contemporary ecological crisis by reinforcing a policy of domination and subordination of nature. White writes, "To a Christian a tree can be no more than a physical fact. The whole concept of the sacred grove is alien to Christianity and to the ethos of the West."[29] Such is the nature of water: part of the world, a natural world subordinate to the historical world of humans. With dualities between humans and nature, the spiritual and the bodily, the afterlife and this life, grace and sin, the Christian tradition—with notable exceptions—has reinforced a view of the natural world that sees it at best in the service of humans. Humans may be called to be "stewards" perhaps, but the natural world is at the service of humans for their purposes.

New studies are emerging in an effort to place Christian thought in the service of ecological reform and to develop new visions of human relationships to the natural world. Theologians Dieter Hessel and Rosemary Radford Ruether, for example, join a growing trend among Christian theologians and philosophers who reexamine the tradition and mine the gems of biblical, theological, and philosophical literature for a more holistic relationship with the natural world. Their hope and that of others is to achieve "a sustainable human-earth relationship by utilizing the relationality paradigm of contemporary physics and ecology and connecting it effectively with the eco-justice sensibility of biblical thought."[30] Here I will examine the tradition for its role in establishing a new water ethic.

There are many accounts of water in the tradition that build upon its inherent sacred nature. The second- and third-century theologian Tertullian wrote that water is the first

> seat of the divine Spirit, who gave it preference over all the other elements. . . . Water was the first to produce what has life, . . . Therefore all natural water, because of the ancient privilege with which it was honored from the first, gains the power of sanctifying in the sacrament. What used of old to heal the body now heals the soul.[31]

Many of the ancient pre-Christian practices and beliefs about the sacred powers of waters persisted in Christianity. The Celts in particular venerated well waters and local springs, placing them under the protection of the mother goddess. Many of the great rivers of Europe such as the Rhine, the Seine, the Marne, the Clyde, and others still retain Celtic names. Christian leaders quickly recognized the powers associated with these waters, and the waters themselves were "Christianized," often named after a Christian saint or the Virgin Mary. For example, the well waters at Chartres, St. Winifred's and St. Beuno's wells in Wales, Chalice Well of Glastonbury, or the "miraculous" spring at Lourdes are regarded as sacred precisely because they produce miracles of healing.[32] R. C. Hope, writing his account *The Legendary Lore of the Holy Wells of England* in 1893, found that one hundred twenty-nine wells in England had been transferred to Christian saints, the most common the Virgin Mary. The Grimm brothers, authors of fairy tales used for generations, in their text *Teutonic Legends*, named many examples of Christianized wells in the Rhine basin. They also noted that "The heathen practice of sprinkling a new born babe with water closely resembled Christian baptism."[33]

Even in the twenty-first century, sick children are dipped three times in St. Mandron's well in Cornwall, England, in hopes of a cure.[34] There are estimated to be some three thousand holy wells in Ireland alone. From the thirteenth century even into the early twentieth century, dipping a crucifix or a statue of Mary into water was seen as a way to end drought and produce rain. Pilgrimages to these holy waters involved a ritual called "the pattern," recitation of prayers and performance of rites for healing. Such beliefs have persisted in spite of the persecution of all such water cults by the Christian churches.[35] Cistercian monks in particular shared an affinity for the sacredness of water with the Celts and chose lands near water temples. The architecture centered around fountains, and fonts of water were built for ritual purposes of purification and initiation, and even for the mundane task of cleansing hands before eating.[36]

Initiation

Jesus, as a devout Jew, was baptized in the holy waters of the Jordan. For Christians, baptism has become the basic sacrament of Christian living, a place where God's love is present in the ritual. Although baptism has become associated with infants, adolescents and adults are still baptized. Baptism initiates an individual into new life in the Christian community, provides spiritual birth, and purifies the initiate from past sins. Not only a symbolic link to Jesus' own immersion and rebirth as God's beloved servant, baptism replaces circumcision in the Jewish tradition in becoming an adult in the faith.[37] The waters dissolve past misdeeds, and the initiate emerges from the waters reborn. A new garment of a new life is put on—a powerful symbol at a time when baptism was primarily a ritual for adults. Baptism was not just a cleansing from sin but an experience of spiritual birth.

John Chrysostom, a fifth-century theologian of the early Eastern church, saw that baptism "represents death and burial, life and resurrection. When we plunge our head into water as into a tomb, the old man [sic] is immersed, wholly buried; when we come out of the water, the new man [sic] appears at that moment."[38] Jesus' "going under" the waters becomes a first sign of his own death, working through the chaos of the waters,[39] while his emergence from the waters is symbolic of new awareness.

Purification and Salvation

Other segments of Jesus' life reveal the power of water as a central symbol for purification, healing, and sanctification. In one instance, he spits upon the ground, makes a paste, and rubs the paste on the eyes of a blind man, telling him to go and "wash in the pool of Siloam," a holy pool (John 9:6). On another occasion, Jesus comes upon a sick man near the pool of Bethesda in Jerusalem. The people believed that an angel would sometimes stir the waters, curing the first person to enter the waters. Jesus healed him in body and spirit that day (John 5:1–18). After asking a Samaritan woman for water from a local well, Joseph's well, Jesus transforms the physical waters of the well into spiritually life-giving waters: "Whoever drinks of the water that I shall give shall never thirst, but the water that I shall give shall be a well of water springing up into everlasting life" (John 4:13–14). Here the bodily need for water serves as a metaphor for spiritual thirst for the divine of all people. St. Paul also alludes to water as a need similar to the need for right relationships with God, writing that we "thirst after righteousness."

Jesus' crucifixion also illustrates the importance of water in salvation, when the Roman centurion pierces his side and water flows along with blood from the wound. Then, as a Jew, Jesus' body would have been washed in water to purify the body for burial. Finally, meeting his disciples after his resurrection, he commands them to baptize with water as a way of cleansing from past sins and entering a new way of life. In these incidents Jesus used the physical characteristics of water to form new rites of spiritual healing, purification, and belonging.

Jesus' ministry also incorporated the sea in his works, particularly the Sea of Galilee. Jesus sailed the sea several times, often as a prelude to a restful retreat, calmed its riotous waters, and even is imaged as walking on the sea. Although a carpenter, he recruited seamen to carry out his mission; at least seven of the twelve disciples were fishermen, implying that the waters were an important resource for Jewish subsistence. Likewise, the Mediterranean Sea was essential for the apostle Paul's travels to Cyprus, Grecian cities, and Rome in his three missionary journeys between 47 and 58 C.E. Furthermore, the symbol of identity among Christians even to this day is a fish, symbol of Christ since the Greek letters in the word for fish mean "Jesus Christ, son of the living God." Nathaniel Altman notes that for Christians, "fishing has not only been a symbol of looking into the soul, but also searching for souls,"[40] that is, reaching out to those who are thirsty for spiritual nourishment.

Rituals and Practices
Catholicism is replete with water rituals and practices. Upon entering a church or other sacred place, the entrant dips fingers into special "holy" water to purify himself or herself, to set aside the impurities of the world outside, and to prepare for the sacred rituals to come. Since the ninth century, at the Mass in preparation for reception of the communion host signifying the body of Christ, the priest will often sprinkle the congregation. During the Mass water is mixed with wine, recalling the mixing of water and blood at Jesus' crucifixion; the water symbolizes his humanity while the wine/blood symbolizes his divinity. During the Easter rituals a large candle, incised with symbolic emblems, is lit and then plunged into the waters of the font three times. This "immersion" represents the baptism of Jesus whereby the waters

became sanctified, possessed of sacred powers of regeneration.[41] In the ritual, the priest plunges the candle, symbolically fire, the masculine, into water, the feminine, recapturing archetypal symbols of human intercourse. These waters then become the "holy water" used throughout the rest of the year at rituals and ceremonies, such as baptism.

Boats, houses, animals, and other possessions are sprinkled with water as part of their dedication for God's purposes. For example, during the annual Blessing of the Fleet festival in many U.S. and European ports, Saints Peter and Anthony are called upon both to protect sailors and to ask for abundant fishing, because Peter was a fisherman and Anthony preached to the fishes, who listened with their tails in the air. The ceremony calls for divine protection of both the fishermen and their boats and also remembers those who lost their lives at sea.[42]

Hands are washed before prayer; as a third-century theologian of the Eastern church writes: "Although the hands are already pure, unless we have washed them thoroughly, we do not raise them in prayer."[43] In addition, holy water is used as a powerful instrument to ward off the attacks of the devil, especially in the exorcism of evil spirits from people and places.

Finally, as in other traditions, at a funeral water is sprinkled on the casket or cremation urn, symbolizing both a return to the Earth as the water flows away and as a final purification as the spirit moves into new life. The coffin itself has the shape of an ancient baptismal font, an immersion in the depths again to be reborn to new life in the Resurrection. All of these rituals remind us of the importance of water in our bodily and spiritual lives and serve as symbols of the divine presence among us.

Water as Sacrament

While the tradition recognizes baptism as a sacrament, namely, a sign of God's indwelling presence in the world, Eastern Orthodox Christian theologian John Chryssavgis notes that the Earth itself has moral and sacramental value: the Earth "is a bearer of God, a place of encounter with Christ, the very center of our salvation." Chryssavgis carries that insight ever further: "Were God not present . . . in the beauty of a forest, or in the sand of a desert [and we could add "in a drop of water"], then God would not be present in heaven either. So if, indeed, there exists today a vision that is able to transcend . . . tensions, it may well be that of our environment understood as sacrament of the Spirit."[44] This theme of God's Spirit at work in the world recaptures the theological insight that the Spirit has always been present in the works of the created world, of nature, and is an important element in developing a renewed intimacy with water on the part of Christians.

Water and the Book of Revelation

One of the richest texts for discussion in the Christian Bible is the Book of Revelation, a text seldom read by most Christians. Although often cited as referring to the "end times," "the last things," "the *eschaton*," contemporary scholars see the Book of Revelation as a scathing attack on the despotic Roman Empire of the first century C.E. in its depiction of the cities of Babylon, the Empire, and Jerusalem, God's kingdom. For our purposes, we want to look at this book for what it says about rivers and seas.

Barbara Rossing, a Christian scripture scholar, begins her discussion of the Book of Revelation with an assessment of the Roman Empire's economic reliance on seafaring trading in the Mediterranean Sea. Revelation challenges Rome's claim to supremacy and economic prosperity for the elite by questioning the role of the sea itself; in the new Jerusalem "the sea is no more," along with death, mourning, weeping, or pain (Rev. 21:1, 4). The writer John does not declare the sea to be a beast, evil, but rather the sea is the basis for a pattern of world domination: *the sea will no longer be used for enriching Rome* (Rev. 18:19). In the new Jerusalem, by contrast, God will provide the essential goods of life, including water, "without payment" (Rev. 21:6; 22:17)—an extraordinary vision indeed.

A central image in the new Jerusalem is the river or fountain of living water. Rossing writes: "Water, freely given by God, flows through this paradisiacal landscape. When God's own voice speaks from the throne for the first time in the book, it is to offer water to those who thirst. Twice God extends the invitation to come and receive the water of life 'without cost.'" Rossing notes that the invitation to drink from the living waters possesses a healing imagery, in contrast to the bloody, undrinkable springs described earlier and in relation to the exploitative mercantilism of Rome so dependent on the sea.[45] Rossing's important commentary on this key Christian text can well support a renewed Christian vision for waters—a new water ethos—for the waters of the new Jerusalem are not spiritual waters, but refer to the waters of a great urban center. This vision instills motivation to clean polluted waters, share water resources more equitably, and envision God's spirit flowing throughout the rivers of the Earth.

Conclusion

Although not sacred in itself, water in the Christian tradition is powerfully symbolic as an instrument of God's powers for healing, purifying, and cleansing. This is particularly true in the initiation ritual of baptism, but also finds its place in the symbolic mixing of water and wine in the Eucharist/communion rituals, blessings, and burial rites. Interesting questions emerge about "holy" water, or really, holy waters: what makes the water holy and imbues it with power? Is the water "holy" only symbolically or is the water "holy" and powerful in itself as in exorcism rituals, the healing powers of wells, or the waters of Lourdes, which can even be bought over the Internet as a "medicine" for healing?[46]

Christianity has instilled a set of religious values in water whereby baptism as descent into the abyss of the waters counters the destructive powers of the Deluge. Christ is the new Noah rising from the waters to lead the newborn peoples. Christ appears as the new Adam because through baptism (in the words of Tertullian) we regain our resemblance to God, as Adam was created in God's image. Eliade argues that in Christianity water itself is not so much valorized, but water symbolism forms a typology of a biblical valorization. That is, in baptism, the initiate renounces the darkness of the abyss, now known as Satan, and the sacrament itself, the baptism ritual rather than the waters, becomes the only representative that mediates salvation. The waters themselves no longer purify spiritually or bring salvation; the rituals do. In this way Christianity uses the natural symbol of water, but adds to it new value.[47]

While this new valorization of the spiritual meaning of water forms a central tenet in Christianity's understanding of rebirth in Christ Jesus, this understanding cannot diminish the importance of physical water. If the waters are to wash away the old and initiate the new, the waters cannot be polluted, and they must be in sufficient supply so that they still provide bodily nourishment to people seeking to slake their spiritual thirst. No water, no baptism, no rebirth in Christ.

Islam

Among the Abrahamic traditions, Islam's beliefs, rituals, and practices form a singularly cohesive core in relation to the faith itself. There is always a strain between belief and practice in most traditions; yet a study of Islam reveals an integral relationship between beliefs about water and actual use.

In Islamic thinking, the laws of nature reflect the interpenetration of the divine, nature, and the human. According to the Qur'anic view of the world, Allah has created a natural world and the human as signs, *ayat*, of the divine. In this sense Allah communicates with humans through the natural world. Humans do not possess any superior powers or authority but rather serve as Allah's regents in the world, taking care of the gift of nature, which in turn shows forth the mercy and wonder of Allah. Allah holds humans accountable for care of the natural world. This interrelationship among Allah, humans, and the natural world means that any harm to the natural world also harms humans. Furthermore, any injury to the natural world is an injury to Allah.

Allah creates natural laws, revealing that nature, like humans, submits to divine commands: "the inanimate elements of nature perform the act of worshipping Allah without verbal communication by functioning in conformity with the divine ordinances known as the laws of nature." The only superiority that humans possess lies in human spiritual volition, bestowing upon humans "a greater measure of balance between their conscious and unconscious minds, thus enabling them to make the best use of their freedom."[48] Thus when humans misuse nature and interfere with Allah's natural laws, humans prevent nature and themselves from true submission, which is at the heart of the very word *muslim*, i e , submission.[49]

Submission to Islamic natural laws ensures justice, providing an ethical framework for treatment of the natural world. Islam alone among the Abrahamic traditions receives no command to "subdue" the Earth or to have "dominion." "Certainly the creation of the heavens and the earth is greater than the creation of the men [sic], but most people do not know."[50] The human serves Allah through care for the Earth, and Allah strictly prohibits any harm or injury to nature.

Origins

Allah's merciful rule over creation provides the foundation for Islamic beliefs. As "vicegerents," humans practice humility and worshipful praise. Even further, nonhuman nature too joins in praise of Allah. Thus there are significant reasons why humans must show responsible treatment toward the environment: (1) "abusing the earth violates Allah's will"; (2) "creation provides humans with 'signs' of the sovereignty and grace of Allah"; and (3) "nonhuman creation is ordained to praise Allah along with humans."[51]

The Islamic creation story views Allah's creation as one harmonious organism. This places humans in biological connection to natural elements, including water.[52] Allah demands that in return for giving life humans not waste any element of creation on "pointless ventures," nor should humans hurt or harm creation. Although the language of the Qur'an could refer only to those creatures that serve human utility, Qur'an scholars are quick to point out that the prohibitions involved refer to at least all "moving creatures." While references to the use of inanimate matter are not as clear,[53] Islam promotes a use of land and the inanimate world that produces harmony.

In an incisive revival of Islamic thought, Islamic scholar Seyyed Hossein Nasr develops the notion that the world of nature is a mirror reflecting the

Divine God as immanent and transcendent. "By refusing to separate man [*sic*] and nature completely, Islam has preserved an integral view of the Universe and sees in the arteries of the cosmic and natural world order the flow of divine grace."[54] There are not then two orders, sacred and profane, but a cosmic Unity. Nature is a reflection of the Paradise that we still remember, and creation moves not in linear, evolutionary fashion but in cycles.[55] Furthermore, Allah's creative power continues in the ongoing creation of the cosmos; in one sense the world is recreated in every moment.[56] These insights of Unity, a sacred creation, human care and responsibility, and the worshipful response of all creation are central contributions from Islam to a renewed ecological care for the Earth.

Water, then, as part of the "flow of divine grace," participates in praise of Allah and is a sign of Allah's immanent presence in the world. Everything was created out of water: "And Allah has created from water every living creature: so of them is that which walks upon its belly, and of them is that which walks upon two feet, and of them is that which walks upon four [*Qur'an* 24:45]. . . . And Allah it is who has created humans from the water [*Qur'an* 25:54]."[57]

The meaning of water permeates every aspect of Islam. Water symbolizes Paradise, a reminder of Allah's gift in a harsh, desert climate. All fresh waters originate from underneath the Dome of the Rock in Jerusalem. Throughout the Islamic world, great gardens with pools, fountains, and canals serve as places of rest and communion with Allah. Wells, too, find their place in the Muslim world and are especially venerated because of water's scarcity in the desert regions where most of the Muslim world lives.

The well at Zamzam near Mecca is the most revered well in Islam. According to legend, God sent the angel Jibreel (Gabriel) to Hazrat Hajira (Hagar, Abraham's second wife) and Hazrat Ismail (Ishmael, Abraham's son) at a very difficult time. They had been forced to settle in an arid part of the country; their food was gone, and Hajira dashed back and forth between cities to find nourishment. On her seventh trip, the angel appeared, and a spring, Zamzam, had emerged by his heel. The water became food for the mother, who could then give milk to the son. One belief is that Mohammad drank from the well and carried its water to pour on the heads of the sick and to provide them drink; miraculous healings resulted.[58] The well today is a place on the sacred pilgrimage route to Mecca. When scientifically tested, the Zamzam waters contained high concentrations of calcium and magnesium salts and fluorides, which may explain why the waters have such rejuvenating powers and bring relief to those suffering from illness in the stomach, liver, and kidneys.[59]

Purification

Similar to Jewish and Christian traditions, purification from physical as well as spiritual defilement is an important characteristic of Islamic belief and ritual practices. In common with all of the traditions addressed so far, ritual cleansing centers around times of transition, such as initiation, and contact with defiling elements such as blood, bodily fluids, and even certain foods.

The importance of water's purity emerges in the *muhtasib* practice, the development of good and removal of evil: "Caring for the environment falls within the jurisdiction of the *muhtasib*. . . . Water should not be wasted; remember *wudu* (ablution or ritual cleansing with water) is the ultimate symbolic action that the Muslim performs every time he prepares himself for prayer. Water therefore should not be wasted even when it is used to prepare for prayer."[60] These strict prohibitions ensure that water remains pure.

Rituals

Similar to Catholics upon entering a church, Muslims wash themselves at mosques, but the ritual is much more elaborate than the sublimated dipping of fingers in a font of holy water. The Qur'an describes ritual cleansing: "When you come to fulfill the prayers, wash your faces and your hands as far as the elbows, and rub your heads and your feet up to the ankles" (*Qur'an* 5:6). This ritual, *faraid al-wudu*, must be undertaken before the five daily prayers in a humble spirit of obedience to Allah. Depending upon the particular branch of Islam, the ritual is performed in various manners. Whether starting from the elbows first and washing the right before the left hand according to the Jafari believers, or rinsing the mouth and drawing water into the nose in addition to hands, face, and feet as among the Hanbalis, Muslim practitioners view water as a purifying agent, preparing one to address Allah. Mosques may have courtyards with pools for washing inside, but most have water sources for ablutions outside.[61] In the absence of a mosque, buckets or containers of water are used. In small villages in northern Ghana, for example, Muslims pour water from plastic teapots to wash their hands, faces, and feet before prayer.[62]

Nathaniel Altman describes in great detail another central ritual, total immersion or *ghusl*, used with certain kinds of impurities and recommended after intercourse, menstruation, childbirth, and nocturnal emissions, all associated with defilement from bodily functions, and after washing a corpse. Altman writes: "As in the Jewish mikveh, Islamic law requires that the water used in ghusl must touch all parts of the body, including every hair; yet in contrast to the mikveh, which is used only for ritual bathing, ghusls often take place in an ordinary plunge pool located in the local *hamman*" or sweat bath,[63] which serves several purposes in Islam. The *hamman* is a community gathering place, once reserved for men only and now open to women. Those *hammans* associated with mosques are used for rituals of purification, especially after illnesses, long journeys, or difficult times. Once again, external purification symbolizes internal purity. Many sweat baths are built using natural or artificial hot springs. This creates moving waters, because Muslims view bathing in still waters as bathing in one's own filth.[64]

An ancient Islamic ritual involves washing the bodies of the dead. The body must be buried on the day of death itself; so the washhouse becomes an important center for ritual prayer and final cleansing. The body is first thoroughly washed with soap, every piece of skin. Then the preparers rinse the body with water mixed with berry leaves, while chanting from the Qur'an. Next, water with camphor is used for a rinse, followed by a final rinse. Last, the body is sprinkled with dust to remind believers of their return to the Earth.[65]

Practices and Prohibitions

The prophet Mohammed issued several sayings, *ahadith*, about respecting the natural world and its treatment. The *hadith*, Islamic law, is replete with emphasis on avoiding waste and unnecessary destruction of nature just to serve human greed, and the *ahadith* place strong emphasis on cleanliness and on avoiding pollution of waters.[66] Furthermore, the Muslim law codes on water, developed over decades in the arid lands under Muslim control, describe water as primarily a communal resource. The codes forbid private ownership of water, at least in its natural state. There is a hierarchy among uses of this scarce good according to need and amount per consumer: first is the right of thirst, i.e., no one can be denied the water necessary to drink since life may be involved; then all are allowed water for their daily needs of bathing, cleaning, cooking, and so forth; next comes the right to provide water to livestock; and last comes the irrigation of crops, which consumes the most water. Only when water has been placed in a vessel, a cistern, or some other object that separates the water from its source in a river, stream, well or fountain is water considered a private good. At that point, the water can be stored, sold, or disposed of in nonwasteful ways.[67] In these and other codes the relationship between the divine lawgiver and the reality of the natural world finds its moral base: Allah created the world, not humans.[68] The texts provide a thorough basis for the conservation and protection of water, seen as a creation of Allah for the full use of the Earth.

Conclusion

Water is sacred, the source of all living things created by Allah. Just like humans and other parts of nature, water too praises Allah: "everything which Allah has created praises Him [sic] in some way or other. . . . Everything in creation is obedient to Allah in this way, no matter whether it is non-living like the air, the earth or the oceans, or living like the animals, the plants, the bacteria and the fungi." In its faithful obedience water finds its purpose.

In addition to these strong beliefs about the relationships among Allah, the creator, and Allah's creation, the natural world, Islam also provides teachings and sayings for a way of life. In the case of water, the rituals surrounding cleanliness remind Muslims of the sacredness of water in purifying body and spirit. The practices and prohibitions around water laws and rights help settle disputes among desert peoples as well as provide measures for sustainability of a scarce resource. In short, Islam offers important traditions for meeting the challenges of the water crisis, particularly in arid areas of the world. While the rituals and practices emerge from understanding the interrelationships between humans and the world of nature, Islam as a religion provides the necessary motivations to carry out those rituals and practices not just for human betterment but for the welfare of the world itself.

Water as Psychic Symbol: The Deep Waters Within

Another view of the deep symbolism surrounding water found in the religious traditions we have examined lies in the place of water in the human psyche, namely, in dreams and imaginative expressions such as poetry, novels, and so forth. These "sources" ascribe values to water beyond the simply rational analyses found in the purity of water's physical and chemical properties. While the *purity* of water remains a *natural* fact, its value precisely as *pure* is lodged deeply in our unconscious, both social and personal.

For example, French psychotherapist Gaston Bachelard examines a text by the Greek thinker Hesiod: "Never urinate at the mouth of rivers which flow into the sea, nor at their source: be very careful about this. Do not satisfy your other needs there either; it is no less dangerous."[69] On the one hand, these prohibitions seem simple enough: they are matters of hygiene and make a great deal of sense rationally. Yet on another, unconscious level Bachelard argues that the clue to what the prohibitions mean is found in a part of the text which reads, "Do not urinate while standing facing the sun." This prohibition certainly has no directly hygienic, utilitarian value. Bachelard notes that the "purity" of water derives from a "permanent, unconscious drive" against pollution. The message is more than utilitarian; urination in water resources is a deep offense against other humans and "an outrage against nature, the mother."

Impure water then is a "receptacle for evil." It can be cursed, laden with evil spells; just a slight impurity means a loss of value. "We can see that the moral axiom of absolute purity, destroyed forever by one pernicious thought, is perfectly symbolized by water that has lost a little of its limpidity and its freshness."[70] This implies that while the waters are physically polluted, on a deep, unconscious, symbolic level the waters are still purifying, helping explain the curious feature we encountered in chapter 1 with the polluted waters of India's great rivers. Furthermore, while the pure waters purify the "soiled" soul, it is not necessary to be immersed in the water; much more often just a sprinkling will suffice. Even a small amount of water can purify a large mass. "Aspersion," not immersion, "is the maximum psychological reality." Quoting Psalm 50 from the Hebrew scriptures, "Purge me with hyssop, and I shall be clean," Bachelard notes that hyssop was a small flower, probably used for sprinkling: aspersion precedes washing. One does not need to wash before "purifying" oneself with drops of water; such is the great power of water in the imagination and in the symbolic rituals of religion.[71]

Through further examinations of legends, ancient and contemporary poets, and writers, Bachelard makes his case that water has been perceived by humans as essentially feminine, maternal in its nurturing, life-giving character. He reminds us of the connection of nurturing water with nurturing milk and selects citations from Hindu texts to illustrate his point: "The waters, which are our mothers and which desire to take part in the sacrifices, come to us following their paths and distribute their milk to us."[72] Again, utilizing a psychoanalytic framework, Bachelard provides a fascinating insight into the deeper significance of water as the primal nurturer: all water is a kind of milk.[73] From the first memories of being nurtured, the adult human recalls the first liquid that passes into the mouth in infancy. From this moment on water assumes the deep symbolic significance of maternal milk, reinforcing the feminine, maternal aspect of water.

Bachelard's analysis of water in human imagination presents insights into water symbolism in the world's religions and in psychic life, as in Hamlet's attempt to "wash away" the stain of guilt surrounding his father's murder, and the importance of washing the body for burial to be transported in purity to a new reality (and a host of other water rituals). Highlighting the value of "pure" water in the human psyche, especially in its association with nurturing milk, Bachelard emphasizes the importance given to water in the largely unconscious symbols of water, water spirits, sprites, of its healing powers, even of its vengeful powers in storms and floods. "The human mind has claimed for water one of its highest values—the value of purity. Water draws to itself all images of purity. . . . Here we have an example of the kind of *natural morality* learned through meditation on a fundamental substance."[74] In these comments Bachelard uncovers an understanding that pure waters run deep in the psyche.

Although he generally omits sacred texts or rituals and instead utilizes poetry and narrative, Bachelard notes the correspondence between the distresses of the soul and those of the water, whether in the violent storm, the raging sea, or the roiling river. The psyche projects its torments onto the waters and is affected by the waters as well. Is it, then, only a coincidence that in the Pacific Northwest sea areas, with rain, floods, dark clouds, and often no sun for days, the suicide rate is so high? Bachelard writes: "to the distress of a soul corresponds the misery of an ocean. . . . Violent water is one of the first settings for universal anger. Therefore there can be no epic without a storm scene."[75] While speculative in nature, such ruminations break upon our consciousness like waves upon the cliffs of reason; such is the nature of the imaginative place of water among humans. More than a material compound, a chemical reality, water influences our personal and general unconscious. In one fundamental sense, the care of water corresponds to the care of our inner life in addition to our physical life. Religious rituals use water to transform, "purify," that rich inner life.

Bachelard further explores another fundamental aspect of water for religion and any symbolic expression such as poetry or narrative, namely, the *sounds* of water. The "babbling brook," the "cascading falls," the "crashing waves," "the gurgling waters," "the stammering stream"—these and other water sounds form in the words of Wordsworth "a music of humanity."[76] Equally important are the *sights* of water: the "winking droplet" after a rain, "the quivering waters" in reflected light. Water sights and sounds resonate with the human spirit beyond just the onomatopoetic nature of the sound or the fleeting reflection of the sight. The imagination connects what is heard and seen which *expresses* and *reflects* the moods and motivations so central to the religious symbols surrounding water of nurturing, sustaining, purifying while also challenging, changing, immersing.

Conclusion

This insight into water's profound significance not just for material sustenance but also for spiritual insight, reflection,[77] purification, and nourishment provides us with yet further motivation to care for water. In fighting pollution and degradation of water, in struggling so that all peoples have pure, clean water and enough of it, in ensuring that the sea waters are not too salinated for living creatures, in keeping fresh waters flowing from snowmelt to deltas for the lives of myriad animals, insects, and plants, we are also making sure that we maintain our own selves as filled with life, with fresh, liquid life, not dried up or too brittle to form bonds with one another. We are water people, composed mainly of water, surrounded by water; water is "in our bones," but more importantly water is "in our selves," in our dreams, our fundamental rituals of religion and of daily life. Inasmuch as religion provides *meaning* and *motivation* through *symbols* in the words of Clifford Geertz cited at the beginning of this discussion, water begins our lives in the "uterine waters" and "mother's milk" and ends our lives as we literally run out of fresh waters in our bodies. It is no wonder then that water is at the heart of our spiritual traditions.

These religious revelations and psychoanalytic ruminations provide us with important perspectives to challenge the dominant paradigms of late twentieth-century water management, use, and distribution. In the next chapters we will examine water in its scientific wrappings, helpful in analyzing the marvel of water itself, but limited as a holistic view of the meaning of water in our human–nature interrelated world today. It was significant and key for understanding the place of water in human consciousness and in the world of living creatures and the Earth itself to begin with water's symbolic and unconscious, even preconscious meanings. While water shapes us and the Earth physically in many ways, we shape our responses to water psychically, on a personal and collective level. As we pursue the investigation into the nature of water from a contemporary, scientific approach, we need to keep in mind the significant meaning of water in our lives as whole persons, body and spirit. That will become especially important when we explore the ways in which humans have used and abused water over the centuries, particularly in our present times.

Perhaps this reality is expressed well in the words of Julia Whitty, nature film documentarian, writing about "The Fate of the Ocean" in the March/April 2006 issue of *Mother Jones* magazine: "I'm alarmed by what I'm seeing. Although we carry the ocean within ourselves, in our blood and in our eyes, so that we essentially see through seawater, we appear blind to its fate."[78] What *are* we seeing?

Notes

1. Marjorie Sandor, "Waiting for a Miracle: A Jew Goes Fishing," *Georgia Review* 53, no. 2 (Summer 1999): 265.

2. Sandor, "Waiting for a Miracle," 270.

3. Marc de Villiers, *Water: The Fate of Our Most Precious Resource* (New York: Houghton Mifflin, 2000): 51.

4. Genesis 1:1–10; all Bible quotations are taken from *The New Jerusalem Bible* (Garden City, N.Y.: Doubleday, 1966).

5. Irving Friedman, "A River Went out of Eden," *Parabola* 20, no. 1 (Spring 1995): 70.

6. Friedman, "River," 66.

7. Quoted in de Villiers, *Water,* 51.

8. Neil Gillman, "Creation in the Bible and in the Liturgy," in *Judaism and Ecology: Created World and Revealed Word,* ed. Hava Tirosh-Samuelson (Cambridge, Mass.: Harvard University Press, 2001), 140–142.

9. Jeremiah 2:13 and Isaiah 55:1; quoted in Nathaniel Altman, *Sacred Water: The Spiritual Source of Life* (Mahwah, N.J.: Hidden Spring, 2000), 185.

10. Evan Eisenberg, "The Ecology of Eden," in *Judaism and Ecology: Created World and Revealed Word,* ed. Hava Tirosh-Samuelson (Cambridge, Mass.: Harvard University Press, 2001), 43.

11. Eric Katz, "Judaism and the Ecological Crisis," in *Worldviews and Ecology,* eds. Mary Evelyn Tucker and John A. Grim (Maryknoll, N.Y.: Orbis, 1994), 59.

12. Katz, "Judaism," 67.

13. Exodus 4:9, 14:21; Numbers 20:11; cf. Altman, *Sacred Water,* 190–191.

14. Friedman, "River," 66–72.

15. Mark Erik Hecht, "A Pure Perspective on Water," *Human Rights Tribune* 9, no. 3 (30 April 2003): 2.

16. Altman, *Sacred Water,* 128.

17. Alternately spelled miqveh, mikva, or mikvah.

18. Lisa Anteby, "'There's Blood in the House': Negotiating Female Rituals of Purity among Ethiopian Jews in Israel," in *Women and Water: Menstruation in Jewish Life and Law,* ed. Rahel R. Wasserfall (Hanover, Mass.: Brandeis University Press, 1999), 74.

19. E. J. Kessler, "Taking the Waters," *Forward* 31 (13 September 1996): 22.

20. Friedman, "River," 66–72.

21. "Discovering the Dead Sea Scrolls," Inscription, Seattle Center House exhibit, 31 October 2006; Altman, *Sacred Water,* 130.

22. Elyse Goldstein, "Taking Back the Water," letter to ed. *Canadian Forum,* December 1998, 6.

23. Friedman, "River," 70.

24. Charles Austin, "Symbolic Sins Cast on Water for Rosh Ha-Shanah," *New York Times,* 9 September 1983, late edition, sec. B.

25. Quoted in Hayim Perelmuter, "'Do Not Destroy'—Ecology in the Fabric of Judaism," in *Ecological Challenge,* eds. Richard Fragomeni and John Palowski (Collegeville, Minn.: Liturgical Press, 1994), 132–133.

26. Genesis 2:10.

27. Friedman, "River," 72.

28. Quoted in Wesley Granberg-Michaelson, "Creation in Ecumenical Theology," in *Ecotheology: Voices from South and North*, ed. David G. Hallman (Maryknoll, N.Y.: Orbis, 1994), 96.

29. Lynn White Jr., "The Historical Roots of Our Ecologic Crisis," in *Readings in Ecology and Feminist Theology*, eds. Mary Heather MacKinnon and Moni McIntyre (Kansas City, MO.: Sheed & Ward, 1995), 33.

30. Dieter Hessel and Rosemary Radford Ruether, *Christianity and Ecology* (Cambridge, Mass.: Harvard University Press, 2000), xxxix. Other writers who have contributed to this effort include in particular "geo-logian" Thomas Berry with Brian Swimme, *The Universe Story* (San Francisco: HarperCollins, 1992); John Haught, *The Promise of Nature* (New York: Paulist Press, 1993); Michael Himes and Kenneth Himes, "The Sacrament of Creation," in MacKinnon and McIntyre, *Readings in Ecology and Feminist Theology*; and many others.

31. Quoted in Mircea Eliade, *Patterns in Comparative Religion* (New York: Sheed & Ward, 1958), 196–197.

32. "By the year 2000 more than 5,000 'miraculous' cures had been documented [at Lourdes] for which there was no simple scientific or natural explanation." Altman, *Sacred Water*, 163.

33. Quoted in de Villiers, *Water*, 53.

34. Eliade, *Comparative Religion*, 193, 196.

35. Sean McDonagh, *Dying for Water* (Dublin: Veritas, 2003), 99.

36. Altman, *Sacred Water*, 90, 114.

37. Altman, *Sacred Water*, 170.

38. Quoted in Eliade, *Comparative Religion*, 197.

39. Quoted in Eliade, *Comparative Religion*, 197.

40. Altman, *Sacred Water*, 79.

41. Tim Unsworth, "Holy Waters Run Deep," *U.S. Catholic*, February 1996, 50.

42. Altman, *Sacred Water*, 31.

43. Unsworth, "Holy Waters," 50.

44. John Chryssavgis, "World of the Icon and Creation: An Orthodox Perspective on Ecology and Pneumatology," in Hessel and Ruether, *Christianity and Ecology*, 90–91.

45. Barbara Rossing, "River of Life in God's New Jerusalem: An Eschatological Vision for Earth's Future," in Hessel and Ruether, *Christianity and Ecology*, 215–216.

46. See Discount Catholic Products at http://www.dcp3.com (accessed 12 August 2006).

47. Mircea Eliade, *Images and Symbols* (New York: Sheed & Ward, 1969), 154–155.

48. Al-Hafiz Masri, "Animal Experimentation: The Muslim Viewpoint," in *Animal Sacrifices: Religious Perspectives on the Use of Animals in Science*, ed. Tom Regan (Philadelphia, Penn.: Temple University Press, 1987), 176.

49. S. Nomanul Haq, "Islam and Ecology: Toward Retrieval and Reconstruction," in *Islam and Ecology*, eds. Richard C. Foltz, Frederick M. Denny, and Azizan Baharuddin (Cambridge, Mass.: Harvard University Press, 2003), 125–132, 136.

50. Qur'an 40:57, trans. M. H. Shakir (Elmhurst, N.Y.: Tahrike Tarsile Qur'an, 1997).

51. Roger E. Timm, "The Ecological Fallout of Islamic Creation Theology," in Tucker and Grim, *Worldviews and Ecology*, 88–89.

52. Masri, "Animal Experimentation," 181.

53. Masri, "Animal Experimentation," 183, 189.

54. Seyyed Hossein Nasr, quoted in Marjorie Hope and James Young, "Islam and Ecology," *Cross Currents* 44, no. 2 (Summer 1994): 187.

55. Hope and Young, "Islam and Ecology," 187–189.

56. Timm, "Ecological Fallout," 85.

57. The Qur'an.

58. Altman, *Sacred Water*, 166–167.

59. Recounted in Altman, *Sacred Water*, 167.

60. Mawil Y Izzi Dien, "Islamic Ethics and the Environment," in *Islam and Ecology*, eds. Fazlun Khalid and Joanne O'Brien (London: Cassell, 1992), 33.

61. Altman, *Sacred Water*, 134.

62. Erin Foran, Seattle University student and research assistant, personal observations during study abroad in Ghana, October 2005.

63. Altman, *Sacred Water*, 134–135.

64. Altman, *Sacred Water*, 135–136. A similar, but not religious, custom exists in Japan, where one first bathes before entering the *ofuro* or hot tub to soak and heal soreness.

65. Jamie Tarabay, "Shiite Burial Services in High Demand," *Morning Edition*, National Public Radio, 24 April 2006.

66. Seyyed Hossein Nasr, "Islam, the Contemporary Islamic World, and the Environmental Crisis," in eds. Richard C. Foltz, Frederick M. Denny, and Azizan, *Islam and Ecology: A Bestowed Trust*, (Cambridge, Mass.: Harvard Univesity Press, 2003), 98.

67. Othman Abd-ar-Rahman Llewellyn, "The Basis for a Discipline of Islamic Environmental Law," in eds. Richard C. Foltz, Frederick M. Denny, and Azizan, *Islam and Ecology: A Bestowed Trust*, (Cambridge, Mass.: Harvard Univesity Press, 2003), 203–205.

68. S. Nomanul Haq, "Islam and Ecology: Toward Retrieval and Reconstruction," 146.

69. Quoted in Gaston Bachelard, *Water and Dreams: An Essay on the Imagination of Matter* (Dallas, Tex.: Pegasus Foundation, 1983), 137; first published as *L'Eau et les Reves* (Paris: Librairie Jose Corti, 1942).

70. Bachelard, *Water and Dreams*, 139.

71. Bachelard, *Water and Dreams*, 141–142.

72. Quoted in Bachelard, *Water and Dreams*, 118.

73. Bachelard, *Water and Dreams*, 118–119.

74. Bachelard, *Water and Dreams*, 14 (Bachelard's italics).

75. Bachelard, *Water and Dreams*, 173, 177.

76. Quoted in Bachelard, *Water and Dreams*, 194, from *Lyrical Ballads*.

77. "Reflection is a water term." Joanne H. Stroud, "Foreword," in Bachelard, *Water and Dreams*, ix.

78. Julia Whitty, "The Fate of the Ocean," *Mother Jones* 31, no. 2 (March–April 2006): 34.

CHAPTER THREE

~

Water: A Biography

Driving along Highway 2 in central Washington State, you cannot miss the sign for the turnoff to Dry Falls—just the name is enticing. About a mile south on state route 17, there it is—a giant drop-off into the plain below where only small pools remain to tell the tale of a waterfall three to four times greater in volume than Niagara Falls. Scientists have long been puzzled by the shapes of the "coulees" of eastern Washington, giant Earth "islands" that seem to have been carved out of the surrounding terrain. Now satellite photos reveal that in the glacial period, a giant ice dam in western Montana broke and released flood walls that gouged and scalloped out huge portions of the rugged plains, eventually sending billions of gallons of water over the giant falls.[1]

A few miles north, at Coulee Dam, the story of the mighty Columbia River plays in laser lighting along the face of the huge dam holding back the waters that form Roosevelt Lake. As the lights play across the dam's cement walls, the river speaks and tells its story, a wonderful story of a once rugged, wild river, carving out its home from the northern borders of Montana through Idaho and north and central Washington until it found its way to the sea between what is now Oregon and Washington. The river once was a sacred place for the tribal people along its path, providing abundant supplies of fish, especially salmon, fresh water for animals, vegetation and crops, and a place for spirits to roam. Then, the scene of the wild river is replaced by the taming of the river by the gigantic building projects of the Depression years, and the power in the story moves from the river to the engineers and builders. The shift is dramatic and reminds the listener of voices long since silenced. Today the once wild Columbia is tamed by the giant Grand Coulee Dam and a series of dams all the way to the ocean, its waters diverted for the rich agriculture of eastern and central Washington, for electricity, barge shipments up and down the river, and fishing on the massive waters behind the dams. The competing interests involved often provide pitched battles among indigenous tribes, commercial interests, farmers, and sports fishermen.

These two glimpses into the water story from my perch in Washington State, a Northwest "island" on an island of a continent, reveal the power and beauty of waters that command a near reverence today and a literal reverence for many still. The waters also play important practical roles as sources of energy, shipping routes, commercial interests, farming needs, and so on. So how did these waters come to be, or in the case of Dry Falls, to be gone? What is water's story?

Water's Story

Long before picking up Phillip Ball's *Life's Matrix: A Biography of Water*, I had already felt that water does have a "story," has a certain character and characteristics, exhibits behaviors that vary greatly, and leaves its mark daily through its activities. Ball provides an important understanding of water's "biography" that helps describe such a reality: "like a person, water has immediate, evident, and familiar characteristics that can be understood only, if at all, by a consideration of its deeper makeup, of the hidden factors that shape its behavior."[2]

In many ways water is a person with a story, possessing three basic expressions, definite characteristics, known and unknown behaviors, and an inner life for billions of humans who animate it with divine, mystical, healing, and destructive powers. Beyond water's religious, historical, and symbolic meanings in various cultures, we will meet the character, "characteristics" and "hidden factors," and origins and behaviors that describe the chemical and physical reality of water. Beyond our usual expectations that water freezes at 32 degrees F and turns to vapor at 212 degrees F, it also can be liquid at −46 degrees F, is found in the intense heat of the Sun, and in its ice expression takes up to twelve forms!

What is or are the origins of water/waters on planet Earth? Why does water behave in such ways? What paths have the waters taken throughout Earth's history and continue to take today? Answers to these questions provide us with important information to understand further the religious and ethical claims water makes upon humans in the twenty-first century and, in turn, the demands humans make upon water.

Birth Origins

The chemical formula for water, H_2O, seems such a simple recipe—two parts hydrogen and one part oxygen. Yet how complex a reality—how did the two combine in the first place? Where did each atom come from? How can water take on different forms of solid, liquid, air? Even the ancient Greeks and other religious traditions that view water as a basic element, indivisible, didn't exactly get it right: water is a *molecule*, a *compound* made up of two elements.

Most scientists today agree that hydrogen originated in the cooling period after the initial Big Bang explosion. At first, "protons—the nuclei of hydrogen atoms—condensed out of the [Big Bang] fireball about a millionth of a second after time and space were born."[3] With temperatures at that instant about a trillion degrees, the protons were too hot to hold onto electrons, necessary to form atoms. When the temperature cooled to about 7200 degrees F, protons grabbed the necessary electrons, and hydrogen atoms birthed. Almost three-fourths of the mass of the Universe is composed of this simple atom.[4] The dramatic story continues with the next actor, gravity: "As the pull of gravity made matter collapse in on itself, the stuff heated up. Stars ignited and began blazing . . . , and out of their fiery hearts come the elements needed to make worlds."[5]

> The secret to the mix lies in the interior of stars, where hydrogen nuclei, the "heart" so to speak, fuse together to make heavier elements, such as helium. With a little dash of carbon recycled from its heady mix with hydrogen, new elements arise: three kinds of nitrogen and one of oxygen. But this form of oxygen, isotope 15, is too light for the oxygen isotopes 16, 17, 18 needed for water. Those isotopes only emerge as stars age, heat up, utilize their nuclear energy sources, and collapse in upon themselves under gravitational forces. Although small in amount, after hydrogen and helium oxygen is the third most abundant element in the Universe; air on planet Earth today is 21 percent oxygen.[6]

The next stage of the "birthing" process of water on Earth lies in the collisions over much time of rocky bodies of gases and dust. Some 4.5 billion years ago the planet Earth appears to have smashed into another large planet-sized object and "sheared off enough material to form the moon, boiled away any atmosphere that the Earth then possessed, and left the planet a ball of molten rock (magma) for millions of years, its surface awash with the fiery ocean from pole to pole."[7]

In the midst of this fiery furnace was enough water in various compounds that as the planet cooled and formed the inner core and the outer crust, the lighter, more volatile compounds such as hydrogen, nitrogen, carbon oxides, and most importantly water vapors were released into the atmosphere. Hydrogen, too light for Earth's gravity, was soon gone, while the others surrounded the cooling planet. Finally, some 4 billion years ago, when the temperature was low enough for water to condense, clouds formed and the rains came. Whether they came in a huge deluge or more gradually is still a subject of inquiry, but rains did come and water covered the Earth.[8]

More recently, however, new evidence has emerged that has challenged the fiery, boiling magma ocean depicted above. Scientists report the likely possibility that the early "Hadean" world of about 4.5 billion years ago "experienced far more dramatic swings in surface conditions than anything revealed in subsequent geologic history." Some of those swings probably did involve an ocean of liquid water.[9] Volcanic action caused great amounts of *outgassing*, releasing large amounts of water vapor into the atmosphere. When the air is saturated with all this water vapor, clouds and ice form, and the deluge begins. Even today, volcanoes continue to release water into the atmosphere, but now the water is recycled water that has made its way back into the Earth's molten layers.[10]

Adolescence and Adulthood
Whatever its origins, water has adopted many forms, attributes, and characteristics over the course of its history. The oceans comprise some 97.4 percent of the Earth's water. The remaining 2.6 percent freshwater lies in ice, permafrost, underground aquifers, rivers, and lakes. Less than 1 percent is accessible; the rest of the freshwater is underground or in the form of ice.[11]

Identity of the Parents
As far back as the sixth century B.C.E., the Greek philosopher Thales postulated that water was the most basic element of all reality. To Thales and those who followed in Greek thought, water in other compositions such as ice or vapor was no longer water but became "Earth" because solid or "air" because vapor. It remained to later Greek philosophers such as Empedocles in the fifth century B.C.E. to amend Thales's theory to include Earth, air, and fire as three other and equally important elements of all reality. Chinese thinkers posited *five* elements, Earth, metal, wood, fire, and water. By the time of Aristotle in the fourth century B.C.E. the theory of four elements composing the "matter" of the universe was "solid"; however, even Aristotle added a nonmaterial element, ether, which composes the heavens.[12]

With the rise of the scientific revolution in the West in the seventeenth and eighteenth centuries, the whole notion of "elements" was replaced by the smallest elements, "atoms," which themselves have been broken into their constituent parts. In our story, then, water became not an element but a compound of atoms, two of hydrogen and one of oxygen. The story of water's actual formula is a fascinating tale of scientists, researchers, laypeople and tinkerers, since it was not until the 1860s that our contemporary formula of H_2O was promulgated, and not even then fully accepted. Scientists now tell us that there are some thirty-three species of the compound.[13]

Water Cousins
Life emerged from the seas, from water. The search for extraterrestrial life begins with a simple question: is there water elsewhere in the solar system? The answer, say scientists, is "yes" on the one hand, but "not exactly" on the other. In a form of gaseous vapor, water pervades the universe. Even the Sun has bits of water, and water has been discovered in the atmospheres of stars. Yet the forms of water found in the solar system exist largely in the form of ice and permafrost below ground. For example, in 1996, on Earth's first cousin the Moon, the Clementine lunar prospector detected "ice deposits" that could have remained "in regions that have never seen the Sun for the past four billion years."[14] But the key to life beyond Earth is water as a liquid, not a vapor or a solid.

In March 2006, the Mars Reconnaissance Orbiter was launched to search for water on Mars. Assuming it survives the trip, it will spend two years searching for liquid water in an attempt to explain how Mars, apparently once wet and warm, became a chilly wilderness. There is ice on three of Jupiter's four moons, and on its moon Europa conditions exist that suggest its icy surface moved independently of its rocky interior, a phenomenon possibly explained by "a liquid ocean." This leaves us with the tantalizing question, if liquid water, possibly life?

Liquid water has also been discovered on two more of Jupiter's moons, Callisto and Ganymede. Even more recently, images from NASA's Cassini spacecraft have shown possible liquid water on Saturn's moon Enceladus. Geysers, some reaching 260 miles, may produce water and ice crystals. The combination of the water and heat from volcanic activity along with organic compounds presents the exciting possibility of life.[15] The search continues.

Character Patterns
Most of us know that water has three shapes: solid as ice, liquid as free flowing, and steam as vapor. The interaction of these three forms gives Earth its unique place in the solar system. As the rains fell all those millions of years ago, they formed not only the massive oceans, lakes, ice packs of the Arctic and Antarctic, rivers, and streams, but left footprints deep in the surfaces and

underground regions of Earth. Water's main, reliable routine forms what we know as the water or hydrologic cycle, its "life cycle": "Water comes from the sea as a vapor, travels for a time as a liquid, sometimes lingers as ice, and then returns to the sea again." In this process of precipitation from clouds, moving in, through, and around earthen forms and forming Earth, then condensation, and eventual evaporation back into clouds, water is "active and powerful, indeed more active and more powerful than the living things whose lives depend on it."[16]

Maggie Black in her key book, *The No-Nonsense Guide to Water*, provides a succinct summary of water's character traits: "At different temperatures and under different pressures, it changes form and weight and becomes different things: mist, snow, ice, steam, cloud, drops, spray, spume. It also blends with other substances, transporting them away, absorbing or dissolving into them, even corroding them, making something new. And it has extraordinary natural self-cleansing powers."[17]

The "Body": The Seas

While we land creatures tend to think of the Earth as ground on which we stand, it is more correct to visualize ourselves on a large raft floating on even larger waters. In the Western world it was not until the great voyage of the English *HMS Challenger*, as it circled the Earth from 1872 to 1876, that the seas themselves were first examined in detail.[18] Since then, we *groundlings* have learned a great deal about seas and land: half of the planet's "ground" lies below the seas from 1.8 to 3.6 miles below sea surface. Altogether the largest mountain range on Earth runs along the sea floor, totaling 46,600 miles in extent.[19] The oceans and seas cover 71 percent of Earth's surface, reach an average depth of 12,000 feet, and contain over 1,350 billion, billion liters of water; yet they still make up only 0.02 percent of the Earth's mass.[20] Half of the ocean water resides in the Pacific, while the Atlantic contains 23.6 percent and the Indian Ocean 21.2 percent.[21]

The "Heart": The Great Circulatory Pump

The waters of the oceans are not confined in one place but move in patterns around the Earth. Surface currents are blown about by winds, while the lower depths circulate because of differences in water temperatures. The waters move around as though on a "conveyor belt," "pumped" around the body. As the water travels northward from the tropics, it cools, becoming denser. At the same time, as the surface water evaporates, it leaves the salt of the sea behind, increasing the water's density.[22]

The denser current on the conveyor belt continues northward, gradually sinking beneath the water below to more than half a mile. This cool, salty body is then "conveyed" back toward the tropics and then into the Southern Ocean around Antarctica. There during the winter some of the saltier water freezes as sea ice and leaves the remaining waters even saltier and colder, sinking to the sea floor around Antarctica, the densest waters of any ocean.[23]

Global warming and melting ice can change the conveyor belt dramatically because temperature changes produce greater density or salinity. "According to computer simulations, even a modest dilution of the ocean's salt content—from increased melting of the Greenland ice sheet, for instance—could disrupt the cycle disastrously."[24] This is a troubling trend in light of the recent evidence of global warming.

Beneath the "Skin": Underground Waters

If you could visualize all the Earth's liquid surface water in lakes, rivers, and ponds, you would see only a portion of the Earth's waters. Sixty times as much water exists under the ground on which you stand, moving, channeling its way through massive forms of Earth, eating away at a slow pace. A portion of that water does its part in the water cycle, rising through the surface; part is captured in sediments, only slowly or perhaps never making its way to the surface; and another part is given off by molten rock, *magma*, forming lava, but locked in pockets never to "give" itself to the upper regions. Water has been found in Egyptian sandstones dating back some 40,000 years; and in the Pacific Northwest, "locked" water has been found in the Columbia River's basalt formations of Washington, Oregon, and Idaho dating back 32,000 years.[25]

Water also accumulates underground in large amounts forming basins called *aquifers* that serve as natural "reservoirs." There are several major aquifers on the North American continent such as the Strait of Georgia separating Vancouver Island from the rest of British Columbia, the Florida aquifer, and probably the most well known, the Ogallala, stretching from Nebraska to Texas.[26]

The "Skin": Surface Water

A substantial amount of the water falling in the form of rain, snow, or ice balls (hail) never reaches the ground to be soaked up. Of the amounts that arrive on the Earth's surface, its skin, physical and biological forces move water around by gravity and surface tension or by plants and trees seeking nutrients and sustenance, removing water from the soil and even within it. Only one-fifth of rainwater actually forms streams and rivers.[27]

Veins and Arteries

Rivers, indeed, are the veins and arteries, the vehicles for the lifeblood of the planet, as the Kogi believe. Streams, the capillaries, form when seepage develops in a depression and water feeds into it from miniature gullies, creating a permanent channel. Streams flow through their channels and come together to swell into a river; the complex interaction of waters forming the large rivers scour out the watershed, the basin that drains into the river.[28]

Rivers vary a great deal around the globe. The Amazon contains 16 percent of global runoff, while the Congo basin has a third of all the river flow in Africa. Whole systems emerge through mergers from tributaries and other, smaller rivers. For example, such mighty watersheds as the Mississippi, the Danube, the Ganges, and the Rhine basins cover hundreds of square miles. The Netherlands and Bangladesh are two countries whose very existence and cultures are defined by vast river deltas. Other rivers such as the Nile, the Niger, the Jordan, and the mighty Colorado receive waters from very remote sources, and their flow through rainless arid lands means huge losses in volume due to evaporation. Some rivers never reach the sea; called *ephemeral* rivers, they dry out after the rain.[29]

Behavior

Water in rivers, streams, rivulets, and tributaries behave in a variety of patterns. Layers of waters slide by one another: that perfectly cast fly moves more slowly near the bank, while debris on the bottom moves more slowly than leaves on the top. These flowing waters act like collectors, picking up sediment, sand, gravel, debris, pebbles, rocks, boulders, branches, logs and transporting them along the path leading to the ocean. At Rialto Beach on the Washington coast, for example, huge tree trunks and limbs line the shore, carried to the ocean down the river nearby and then cast high on the beach.[30] As rivers flow toward the sea, they enlarge and have less of a meandering pattern, flowing across a flood plain, which does indeed "flood" in times of heavy rains, as those of us who live in western Washington State witness yearly. Then finally the rivers deposit their last load, "stop," as they enter the sea in some form of delta, a series of networked channels.[31] Because of Hurricane Katrina along the Gulf Coast we are familiar with the Mississippi Delta, but that "delta" has been transformed by human engineering, a transformation partially responsible for the devastating floods in New Orleans and along the coast in 2005.

Lakes: The Eyes, Ears, Nose, and Throat

The planet holds some three million lakes, and the nineteen largest account for 38 percent of the total amount of water. The Caspian Sea is the largest lake, and Lake Titicaca on the Bolivian/Peruvian border is the world's highest at some 11,400 feet above sea level. The Great Lakes of North America remain the largest total concentrations of fresh, surface water in the world, constituting 18 percent of the Earth's supply. But how did they come to be? Lakes are formed in basins, but the basins come before the lakes, unlike the valleys scoured out by streams and rivers. The Great Lakes are an example of huge basins ground out of the Earth by the ice sheets of the last ice age. In addition to these "ice-front" lakes, formed from the glacial meltwater captured between the rising ground and the ice cliffs, the ice age is responsible for other forms that lakes take. "Kettle-hole" lakes are made from the ice blocks remaining from the ice crust that were buried by sediments and only slowly melted, creating pockets for rivers to fill. Moraines, such as those on Mt. Rainier and Mt. Adams in Washington State or Mt. Hood in Oregon, are basins that result from "boulders, pebbles, and clay, that the ice carried on its surface or froze into its base," leaving "numerous hollows ready to become lake basins."[32]

However, the oldest lakes in the world are formed in other ways, by movements of the Earth's crust, such as the lakes of the rift valleys of East Africa, Lake Tanganyika and Malawi, formed between 10 and 12 million years ago. Some of the youngest lakes are formed by craters of inactive volcanoes, such as Crater Lake, Oregon, formed about 6,700 years ago.[33]

Then there are the wetlands. Though they are seemingly less dramatic and important, E. C. Pielou notes that "[wetlands] are more productive, in terms of plant growth, than either agricultural land or natural grassland. They are storehouses of biodiversity, holding back floods in the wet season and gradually releasing the water later, in times of drought. They filter out pollutants and sediments from the water that passes through them."[34] Whether the wetland is constantly wet or at times dry, it constitutes a wetland because of the vegetation it supports, not by the water it holds, an important consideration when developers come along. Wetlands also occur in varieties. Those known as *peatlands*, which are permanently wet at some depth, are either *fens* formed by groundwater or slow-flowing surface water or *bogs* from rainwater, usually stagnant and lacking in nutrients. Then there are the nonpeat wetlands, the *marshes* and *swamps*, realities and symbols rich in mystery and a little fear. They differ only in their vegetation: swamps have trees and marshes have grass kinds of plants covering them. In marshes, potholes or sloughs are plentiful, small ponds in the center of small marshes.[35] Earth has "ears, eyes, nose, and throat" sunken in and spread over its skin or its outer surface.

Hair, Memory, and Breath

For all of its power as a liquid, the two other "personalities" of water, solid and vapor in the forms of ice and clouds, seem even more marvelous.

Although global warming is threatening the great ice packs of the South and North poles, at Antarctica and in the Arctic, ice remains one of Earth's most useful forms of water. These great ice packs reflect the Sun's rays back into the atmosphere, helping to cool the Earth. But as anyone who has filled a water bottle for hiking and put it into the freezer knows, water when it freezes has this peculiar phenomenon of expanding. "Once the temperature of a cooling body of water is nowhere higher than 4 degrees C, the coldest water—the water that will freeze first—is also the least dense and therefore collects at the surface."[36] As it expands, the ice floats on top of the water. Were it not for this peculiar behavior of water to float frozen above water below, the heat in water would radiate away, which would create more ice.[37] The last recent ice age peaked about 8,000 years ago, and sea level was then some 400 feet below its current level because so much water was in its solid form. The intervals between the advances and retreats of ice are at 21,000 and 40,000 years, and we can expect them to continue at that rate.[38]

Then there are the fascinating characteristics of "ices," a plural here since some twelve relatives of "ice" itself have been discovered, although most can exist only in laboratory conditions. For example, "water can freeze (to ice VII) at 212 degrees F" and "can be cooled at least 68 degrees *below* freezing point without solidifying to ice. Liquid water below its freezing point is said to be *supercooled*." In 1998 researchers reported the development of ice XII. Possibly more discoveries are in store.[39]

Ice can be said to provide water with "memory." Remarkably, the long accumulations of ice on the planet have preserved elements of water in snow and then ice over millions of years, and "some 420,000 years of these 'archives' have been deciphered." Ice samples reveal different amounts of hydrogen and oxygen atoms, which tell stories of atmospheric changes in terms of ice bubbles. These may contain desert dust from eons ago. Even the oceans contain some memory since it may take hundreds of years for ocean water to be renewed.[40]

Water also freezes below the ground. In northern climes this water is frozen all year round, producing *permafrost*, "permanently frozen ground." Alaska and approximately 60 percent of Canada have permafrost conditions. Some permafrost marvelously contains liquid water even below freezing since the "freezing level," 32 degrees F, refers to pure water; underground water is far from pure. Genuine aquifers of liquid water form among pores of underground rock, and in some cases water flowing below the frozen permafrost creates underground erosion since flowing water rapidly erodes frozen areas, whether aboveground or underground.[41]

Equally remarkable is the behavior of ice at the poles. Ice first appeared on Antarctica about thirty million years ago with a stable ice cap some five million years ago. The Arctic on the other hand only began to ice up three million years ago. Since then ice has come and gone in cycles. In the Southern or Antarctic Ocean, which contains 90 percent of Earth's ice nearly two miles thick, the water temperature is between 29.3 and 28.6 degrees because the saltier waters lower the freezing point. Antarctic fish can put off freezing their blood as long as the water does not go below the magic 28.6 degrees F.[42] Although underground ice is only a small fraction of the Earth's total ice, which itself accounts for 77 percent of Earth's waters, its behavior remains an integral part of the story.

In Peter Hoeg's fictional work, Ms. Smilla's Feeling for Snow, Ms. Smilla, a Greenlander Inuit woman, notes the different names in the Inuit language for ice that we Americans and Europeans only call by one word:

> Then frazil ice is formed, grease ice, and pancake ice, whose plates freeze together into floes. The ice separates out the salt, the seawater freezes from below. In the distance is hiku, the permanent ice, the continent of frozen sea.
>
> Everywhere . . . are different types of ice floes, hikuaq and puktaaq. . . . The surface of the ice floes is a wasteland of ivuniq, packs of ice forced upwards by the current and the collision of the plates; of maniilaq, ice knolls; and of apuhiniq, snow which the wind has compressed into hard barricades.[43]

Now on a vaporous note, imagining what animals the cumulus clouds make, or enjoying the "taste" of snow falling into an open mouth, feeling the "stickiness" caused by humidity on a summer day in the Midwest or the tropics—these sensations are all gifts from the legion of water forms. These gifts are the results of water vapor, water as a gas, as distinct from visible liquid droplets in fog, mist, and steam. Water "begins" its transformation to vapor as it evaporates from its liquid forms in lakes, streams, soil, and vegetation. For example, in my region of the United States, the Pacific Northwest, Douglas firs abound, and on each summer day, "a single hectare of Douglas fir forest spews out about 50 tons of water vapor . . . or about 235 bathtubs' full" within each hectare's boundaries.[44]

Some of those water molecules in vapor quickly fall back to the waters, seas, rivers, and ground by means of fog or clouds forming rain and snow. When the air cools at ground level, fog results. Clouds, on the other hand, form when the rising water molecules condense around tiny particles, such as smoke particles, dust, ash, bacteria, etc., always present in the atmosphere.

The particles make the sky blue; the condensed vapors wrapped around particles form clouds: *stratus* for layered clouds, *cumulus* for the fluffy clouds Charlie Brown watches, and *cirrus* for the high, thin clouds that indicate colder weather. And then there is *nimbus* for the rain cloud. But note that clouds do not contain much water; only "about 0.035 percent of the Earth's fresh water is floating around above us at any moment."[45]

When new, the vaporous clouds reflect the Sun and are thus bright white. As these young clouds "age" by gathering more droplets, the droplets of vapor coalesce, becoming larger, less in number, and spaced more widely; "old" clouds then become grayer. A raindrop forms and falls as vapor droplets bounce into one another, coalesce and grow; their "weight" makes them fall. Raindrops also form as the water droplets in a cloud condense as ice on surrounding ice crystals and grow in size. These big ice packs then become big raindrops as they melt.[46]

While rainwater disappears quickly into streams, the seas, or groundwater, snow remains around for our delight and for spring runoffs, helping many towns and cities continue to provide water supplies into summer, while bringing spring floods as well. As every skier knows, the snow of the western slopes of the Cascade Mountains of Washington, Oregon, and British Columbia means slogging, sluggish skiing compared to the fluffy powder packs of the Rocky Mountains.[47] The mild climates of the Pacific regions and the large amounts of rain produce heavy snowfalls. Between snowstorms the softening snowpack becomes more dense and meltwaters fill air spaces in the snow, refreezing as ice, producing slick conditions for skiing. However, in the colder and drier Rockies, the low temperatures keep the snow "light and fluffy."[48] Eventually the snow itself melts, water evaporates, and the cycle continues.

The Human Body

Our final section on water's story in the "body" Earth moves literally to water in the human body. We begin our lives in uterine water, amniotic fluid. When "the waters break," we are born. The human body is approximately 50 to 60 percent water,[49] ranging from 75 percent for babies to 46 percent for elderly women,[50] and the other liquid in the body besides blood, lymph, is watery and circulates throughout the body. Without water in our body, "Within days, the lips would vanish . . . , the gums blacken, the nose withers to half its length, and the skin so contracts around the eyes as to prevent blinking."[51] Even our blood, containing sodium like seawater, tastes salty.

Our body water also is salty yet tolerable, while the waters of the seas are poisonous, and drinking seawater kills by dehydration: "if the body fluids outside our cells become highly enriched in salts, osmosis depletes the cells of water."[52]

If the body contains up to 60 percent water, where is it? Water, as cytoplasm, is the fluid medium in all the body's cells. Neither the structure of this water nor its workings are clearly understood, but cell water does have its own unique structure and can incorporate higher as well as lower average densities more than in ordinary water. Water in the cell guides proteins in the cell to bind to the correct molecule, a critical function. Ball writes:

> It is hard to overstate the importance of this kind of delicate specificity of binding interactions for proteins . . . how easily might a protein pick up the wrong target molecule, unless its binding site is exquisitely tuned. Water has been co-opted during the course of evolution to help in that tuning; its propensity for forming hydrogen bonds that point in very specific directions makes this possible.[53]

The water in our blood "enables it to carry the nutrients necessary for the different cells and organs of our body, and to transport waste products to the appropriate organs of elimination, such as the kidneys."[54]

At the same time water helps maintain a constant cellular temperature in the body and so an overall constant body temperature. About 3 percent of the water in our bodies is replenished daily. Likewise giving off water in sweating is another tool in regulating body temperature. The body needs a regulated balance of water. At a normal room temperature of 68 degrees F, a typical male adult should drink at least 1,650 milliliters (approximately seven 8-ounce glasses) of liquid a day; on average he also consumes some 750 ml of water contained in food. The process of oxidation, which involves the breaking down of nutrients by the body, produces an additional 350 ml of water. Totaling 2,750 ml of water, some 1,700 ml is later excreted as urine, 500 ml is lost through perspiration, 400 ml is exhaled, and another 150 ml is contained in feces.[55]

Noted British Columbian ecologist and philosopher David Suzuki provides us with a dramatic illustration of the life of water in our body's water cycle: "Water enters our bodies, circulates through it to the rhythm of the heart, ceaselessly carrying food, fuel, and cellular and molecular detritus to and from various organs of the body. Water seeps through our skin, escapes from our lungs as vapour and exits every opening in the body. It then reenters the hydrologic cycle, trickling into the soil."[56] Water gifts our lives daily.

Conclusion

Throughout this "biography," contemporary science has revealed the many marvels of water in a manner that complements water's religious significance—its amazing adaptability as fluid, solid, or vapor, its powerful abilities for scouring out the Earth, the redirection of its energies, its inner structures and outer manifestations. The sheer magnitude of water is a wonder: some 30 trillion gallons "of fresh water are recycled every day—a yearly output of 9,500 cubic miles, or one-hundredth the volume of the Mediterranean Sea." However, two-thirds of this amount is floodwater running to the sea, while still other large amounts drain away in unpopulated areas. Overall, "just a quarter to a third of the total amount of recycled fresh water is easily available to us." Then we are faced, before we talk about human impacts on water, with the fact that 65 percent of natural water resources lie in only ten countries on the globe.[57] Water is not fair in its distribution.

In addition, this remarkable gift that furnishes all life is becoming and will become even more threatened in its purity and distribution, as we will investigate in the next chapters. In preparation for that discussion, let us note that since water use tripled between 1960 and 1990, if our use of water even doubles over the next 35 years, "the taps will have run dry." The reasoning here is simple: "Sustainable use of the world's water supplies at a level commensurate with population growth requires that water be used with restraint and efficiency, and this simply does not happen on the whole."[58] Coupled with the scarcity of fresh water in many countries of the globe, the requirements of sustainability demand concerted, strong programs and efforts at the national and international levels. The next chapters will show us critical aspects of this increasing scarcity and uses of water around the globe. While we humans tend to concentrate on our water needs, other living creatures and the planet itself have needs that challenge us even further in our water use.

Notes

1. David Alt, *Glacial Lake Missoula and Its Humongous Floods* (Missoula, Mont.: Mountain Press, 2001), 133–143.

2. Phillip Ball, *Life's Matrix: A Biography of Water* (New York: Farrar, Straus & Giroux, 1999), x.

3. Ball, *Life's Matrix*, 9.

4. Ball, *Life's Matrix*, 9–10.

5. Ball, *Life's Matrix*, 10.

6. Robert Kandel, *Water from Heaven: The Story of Water from the Big Bang to the Rise of Civilization and Beyond* (New York: Columbia University Press, 2003), 53.

7. Ball, *Life's Matrix*, 18.

8. Ball, *Life's Matrix*, 18–21.

9. Rebecca Lindsey, "Earth Observatory," publication of NASA's Earth Science Enterprise, 1 March 2006, 1–4.

10. Kandel, *Water from Heaven*, 27, 38. Physicist Louis Frank has proposed an alternative theory of extraterrestrial origins of water: small water comets containing water in ice form continue to bombard the Earth even today. See Louis W. Frank with Patrick Huyghe, *The Big Splash* (New York: Carol, 1990), 43ff.

11. E. C. Pielou, *Fresh Water* (Chicago: University of Chicago Press), 1–2.

12. Ball, *Life's Matrix*, 118–129.

13. Robert Bowen, *Surface Water* (New York: Wiley, 1982), 4.

14. Ball, *Life's Matrix*, 85–86.

15. John Johnson Jr., "New Evidence of Liquid Water Makes Enceladus a 'Better Bet,'" *Seattle Times*, 10 March 2006, 12.

16. Pielou, *Fresh Water*, 3–4.

17. Maggie Black, *The No-Nonsense Guide to Water* (Oxford: New Internationalist, 2004), 9.

18. Ball, *Life's Matrix*, 30.

19. Bill Bryson, *A Short History of Nearly Everything* (New York: Broadway Books, 2003), 178.

20. Kandel, *Water from Heaven*, 25.

21. Bryson, *Short History*, 273.

22. Although fresh water evaporates from the oceans constantly and leaves more salt behind, the oceans do not grow saltier. Deep-sea vents draw water down into the crusts where salts are separated from the water; the clean water is then blown back up the stacks into the oceans. The process can take 10 million years to clean an ocean. Bryson, *Short History*, 279–280.

23. Ball, *Life's Matrix*, 32–35.

24. Bryson, *Short History*, 267.

25. Pielou, *Fresh Water*, 2–6, 13–14.

26. Pielou, *Fresh Water*, 34–36.

27. Pielou, *Fresh Water*, 60–70.

28. Pielou, *Fresh Water*, 82–84. Interestingly enough, nearly three times as much water from streams and rivers flows into the Atlantic as the Pacific Ocean. Bowen, *Surface Water*, 10.

29. Black, *No-Nonsense Guide*, 18.

30. Pielou, *Fresh Water*, 97–113.

31. Pielou, *Fresh Water*, 119–140.

32. Pielou, *Fresh Water*, 152, 150.

33. Pielou, *Fresh Water*, 150–152.

34. Pielou, *Fresh Water*, 214.

35. Pielou, *Fresh Water*, 216, 222–224.

36. Pielou, *Fresh Water*, 185.

37. Bryson, *Short History*, 271. Bryson continues: "The current ice age started about four million years ago," with intervals of receding ice and progressing ice; further ice ages will continue in intervals (427–428).

38. Kandel, *Water from Heaven*, 76–77.

39. Ball, *Life's Matrix*, 203, 202. According to Kandel, these other forms of ice take a cubical rather than hexagonal shape, but only at high pressures and low temperatures (*Water from Heaven*, 6); *supercooled* water refers to water as "liquid droplets rather than ice crystals" (*Water from Heaven*, 139).

40. Kandel, *Water from Heaven*, 124, 125.

41. Pielou, *Fresh Water*, 193–200.

42. Kandel, *Water from Heaven*, 78; Bryson, *Short History*, 273; Ball, *Life's Matrix*, 210–213. Even blood freezes at 31 degrees F, not 32.

43. Peter Hoeg, *Ms. Smilla's Feeling for Snow* (London: Varvill, 1993), 363–364. Also available in Tiina Nunnally's translation, *Smilla's Sense of Snow*, published in the United States by Delta.

44. Pielou, *Fresh Water*, 238, 240.

45. Bryson, *Short History*, 263–265. There are actually some ten kinds of cloud types: "High cirriform cloud comprises ice crystals while stratiform clouds are layered, cumuliform ones having a heaped appearance. Medium level clouds carry the prefix alto- while low clouds carry nimbo-" (Bowen, *Surface Water*, 62).

46. Pielou, *Fresh Water*, 241–244.

47. In the Inuit language there are different names for the various kinds of snow: *qanik* for fine-grained powder snow; *pirhuk* for light snow; and *kangirhuarhuq* for freshwater ice (Hoeg, *Ms. Smilla's Feeling*, 79, 220, 242).

48. Pielou, *Fresh Water*, 244–246.

49. Cameron Woodworth, "A Clean Drink of Water: Choices and Responsibilities," *Sound Consumer*, August 2006, 1.

50. David Suzuki, *The Sacred Balance* (Vancouver, B.C.: Greystone Foundation, 1997), 59; Woodworth, "Clean Drink," 1.

51. *The Economist*, May 13, 2000, quoted in Bryson, *Short History*, 272.

52. Ball, *Life's Matrix*, 242–243.

53. Ball, *Life's Matrix*, 251–255, 264–265, 268.

54. Kandel, *Water from Heaven*, 5.

55. Nathaniel Altman, *Sacred Water: The Spiritual Source of Life* (Mahwah, N.J.: Hidden Spring, 2002), 7, 9, 11–12.

56. Suzuki, *Sacred Balance*, 62.

57. Ball, *Life's Matrix*, 338.

58. Ball, *Life's Matrix*, 338.

~

CHAPTER FOUR

Water and the Human Cycle

Shortly after Jim and Brooke Rufo-Hill arrived in their village in the Dominican Republic as Peace Corps workers in 2004, Jim began experiencing earaches. After a rash of such incidents, he was told by the Peace Corps doctor that his earaches resulted from contaminants in the water. The village where Jim and Brooke served was downstream from chicken and pig factories and a lot of agricultural runoff. Jim began introducing a water filtration system in several houses, including his own; the system filtered approximately 90 percent of the water's contaminants. Yet Jim and Brooke could still not drink the water safely.[1] To those with sinks and showers in their homes, water is often thought of as a pure, unlimited resource. In truth, in most parts of the world clean water is becoming more and more inaccessible.

The problem that Brooke and Jim encountered, pollution, is only one of the many threats to water at the beginning of the twenty-first century—global warming, dying rivers and rivers running dry, poor sanitation, water salinization, dam construction, and potential water wars, among others. In the next two chapters we will examine these threats to water in order to understand the enormity of the crisis and to examine the bases for a new water ethos that will provide principles to address these threats for a sustainable water world.

Beginnings

Marc de Villiers, water expert, outlines the seriousness of the situation:

> The trouble with water—and there *is* trouble with water—is that they're not
> making any more of it. They're not making any less, mind, but no more either.
> . . . People, however, they're making more of—many more, far more than is
> ecologically sensible—and all those people are utterly dependent on water for
> their lives. . . . Humans can live for a month without food but will die in less
> than a week without water. Humans consume water, discard it, poison it, waste
> it, and restlessly change the hydrological cycles, indifferent to the conse-
> quences: too many people, too little water, water in the wrong places, and in
> the wrong amounts.[2]

Since the emergence of our human ancestors water has remained a key to
survival, not just through drinking, but as a means of transportation and to
sustain crops. Hunter/gatherers could not establish settlements far from water. As the great civilizations of more recent times developed—Egypt along
the Nile, Babylonia along the Tigris and Euphrates, civilizations along the
Seine, the Thames, and others—the waterways were keys to development,
settlement, and trade. Their needs and desires to control waters have long
characterized human societies, especially through irrigation systems.[3]

By 3000 B.C.E. the Egyptians had developed drilling techniques. The
Chinese had deep wells by 1000 B.C.E. Early irrigation systems were developed in the Fertile Crescent lands of modern Iraq and Iran. Called *qanats*, a
shaft was drilled into the groundwater of the hills and low mountains, and
water flowed by gravity through the tunnel to its destinations. The *qanats*
provided water from Afghanistan to Egypt and are still in use today.

The great Roman aqueducts were built in the fourth and fifth centuries
all across Europe and the Near East. Eleven aqueducts brought water to
Rome, in channels some 100 kilometers long that were mostly a series of underground tunnels. Some Roman aqueducts are still used today, and while
many laud the ingenious architecture of the Romans, they actually learned
from the Assyrians, the great engineers of the ancient world.[4] Europeans did
not develop wells systematically until well into the twelfth century C.E. By
then Carthusian monks had perfected percussion drills and also initiated
such sanitary features as flow-through toilets and in-house sanitation.
Bruges in Flanders had a municipal water system by 1340, and in the sixth
century London had developed a system of pumps that furnished the entire
city.[5]

Despite—or in part as a result of—centuries of innovation in the ways we can use, store, and distribute water, the real situation in the world today is dire indeed for many countries where problems of water scarcity, pollution, and overpopulation threaten millions. A World Health Organization (WHO) report indicates that 1.1 billion people, one-sixth of the world's population, lack access to quality drinking water and 2.4 billion people, two-fifths of the world's peoples, lacked adequate sanitation in 2000.[6] For 2001, WHO estimated that there were over two million deaths from infectious diarrheal diseases attributed to water and sanitation concerns, which on average comes to 5,843 daily. Of those deaths 1.4 million were of children under the age of 5.[7] The numbers are increasing. Maude Barlow, coauthor of *Blue Gold*, estimates that by 2055, two-thirds of the world will be living in a situation of severe water scarcity. Already 75 percent of Russia's lake and river water is unfit to drink.[8] "Half the world's population does not have basic sanitation systems, and a quarter has no access to clean water. As a result, around 80 percent of all diseases and deaths in developing countries are the result of contaminated water," including such diseases as dysentery, cholera, typhoid, hepatitis, malaria, dengue fever, and guinea worm.[9]

Ethiopia in particular suffers from a lack of fresh water. By the roll of nature's dice it has the least available water in the world, and there are scarce resources for sanitation. As a result over 500,000 people die yearly from lack of available water or from a water-related disease.[10] The situation of the Hmong people of Vietnam and Burma illustrates the tragic effects of human intervention in natural systems. Driven from Vietnam by the wars there, they were then forced from Burma by the Burmese government to preserve the mountain forests which the Hmong were stripping to grow opium crops at high altitudes. The Hmong moved to the high mountains of Thailand where tribal people had never farmed. By the early 1980s, as a result of the Hmong's slash-and-burn farming techniques, the river waters poured down the denuded hillsides, stripping away the soil. The wild animals had disappeared, crops yielded only one-third of their pre-1970s levels, and toxin-producing grasses sprouted in the valley. The Hmong's story of displacement is a sad comment on compounded impacts of human activities on watersheds.[11]

Water as an Endangered Resource

Overpopulation, polluted waters, inadequate or no treatment, increasing demands of agriculture and industry, including especially the computer industry, global warming affecting Arctic and Antarctic ice, and changing water temperature—all these and more are contributing to what are several crises around water. The United Nations 2003 *World Water Development Report* puts the situation in sharp relief:

> Water consumption has almost doubled in the last fifty years. A child born in the developed world consumes thirty to fifty times the water resources of one in the developing world. . . . The number of people dying from diarrhoeal diseases is equivalent to twenty fully-loaded jumbo jets crashing every day, with no survivor. . . . As land is cleared and water demand grows for agriculture and other human uses at the expense of natural ecosystems, the appropriation of moisture by humans looks set to continue.[12]

The 2006 UN *World Water Development Report* concludes its extensive discussion by noting that in many parts of the world, 30–40 percent of water is lost to leakages in aging systems and illegal tapping. In developing countries the Food and Agriculture Organization estimates the efficiency rate of irrigated agriculture at 38 percent. Increasing demands and decreasing quality of water portend critical shortages—"one of the great challenges of this century."[13] For Alice M., a Cree elder, the culprit in the decline of the Earth's waters is self-evident: "I blame it all on the person who started destroying the land, the river. Now we do not have good drinking water, and a river that was once so strong and deep and that had provided for a lot of families is now all dried up and sad to look at."[14]

Pollution

In our discussion of pollution, we should first distinguish between pollution and contamination: for our purposes, *contamination* will refer to conditions in which water is "naturally tainted," and *pollution* refers to water "tainted by human activities," a distinction employed by E. C. Pielou in her excellent study, *Fresh Water*. In lakes some pollutants are fine in "natural" quantities. But in many lakes they occur in excess from sewage, runoff from feedlots, golf courses, parks, gardens, and fertilizer from fields.[15] These pollutants flush large amounts of nitrates and phosphates into waters producing excessive amounts of algae, and the results are very visible: a green scum on the water surface. The decomposing algae uses up the water's oxygen, resulting in the deaths of fish and some animals. Furthermore, when oxygen is diminished, bacteria produces methane, a "greenhouse" gas contributing to global warming.[16] Excessive sediments from landslides, logging, and construction work near lakes and streams also bring pollution. "Sudden, abnormal influxes of sediments can destroy an aquatic ecosystem within minutes by blanketing the bed of a lake or stream and suffocating all the bottom organisms," notes Pielou. Landslides often bring other contaminants like gasoline, solvents, oil, etc., causing suffocation of aquatic life.[17]

In much of rural India, excessive amounts of fluoride have been found in bedrock in deep wells. Farmers have been forced to dig deeper toward bedrock because of shortages at higher levels, and these are wells initially funded by UNICEF during the Water Decade of the 1980s. Likewise deep pumping has brought arsenic poisoning to large parts of Bangladesh. The plight facing people in the country's 68,000 villages and parts of adjacent India is described by WHO as "the largest mass poisoning of a population in history."[18]

Then there are the toxic pollutants we have heard so much about, such as PCBs, dioxin, mercury, lead, and others. Some come from industries discharging their effluents directly into the water. For example, until 2006 the beautiful city of Victoria, British Columbia, discharged its wastewater directly into the waters of the Strait of Juan de Fuca.[19] Other major cities around the world do the same. New York City's outfall pipes continue to dump sewage mixed with rainwater into the Hudson River, and Halifax, Nova Scotia, across the continent from Victoria, has no sewage treatment.[20] As Jim Rufo-Hill's story at the beginning of the chapter indicates, 98 percent of domestic sewage in Latin America flows raw into whatever waters are available, and 90 percent of people worldwide still drop their waste into water.

Industrial pollutants have been found increasingly in both lake and coastal waters. The tailings from mining have washed iron sulfide into streams worldwide, creating sulfuric acid. "The acidic effluent, called acid mine drainage, harms local ecosystems through both its acidity and its load of metal ions such as aluminum, zinc, and manganese." Iron hydroxide turns streams into orange waters, covering rocks with bright "yellowboy" residue, as it is called in the United States. Also, mercury pollution has been reported around the world. In Brazil, the gold-mining industry still deposits over 130 tons of mercury into the Tapajoz River. Other toxic metals released into the waters include "lead, arsenic, zinc, copper, tin, cadmium and cobalt."[21]

In India, effluent from industrial firms in many cities such as Vadodara in southern Gugarat state runs untreated into rivers on their way to the seas and is siphoned off with the river water along the way to grow crops in hundreds of fields. While recycling effluent may be a useful approach to water management, industrial effluent possesses untreated chemical wastes that can cause great harm to humans and animals and even destroy the fields that use them.[22]

Recently pharmaceutical drugs have been showing up in the waters of the United States. These include "antibiotics, anti-depressants, cancer treatments, birth control pills, seizure medications, tranquilizers," and others.[23] A recent report on National Public Radio noted that a new form of dual-sex fish is appearing in the Potomac River in Washington, D.C., most likely a genetic mutation caused by pharmaceutical pollution.[24] In Boulder Creek, Colorado, fish are showing up with male and female characteristics, from ibuprofen and acetaminophen in the water from treatment plants.[25] While WHO reports that these chemicals do not pose much of a health risk presently because their concentrations are low, the consequences for both animals and humans from long-term exposure are unknown.

Pollutants show up in groundwater and in overland flow. In the United States, "60% of liquid hazardous waste is injected into the ground and traces have turned up in aquifers in Florida, Ohio, and Texas. Worldwide 300–500 million tons of heavy metals, solvents, toxic sludge and other waste accumulate in water sources."[26] There is also the runoff from the "asphalt jungles" of shopping malls, businesses, roads, etc. By one estimate, when the rains come, a typical asphalt covering around a Wal-Mart superstore produces 413,000 gallons of contaminated water for every one inch of rain.[27]

Another source of human-made contamination of water comes from our desires, beyond our actual needs, for oil. In 1989 the episode of the *Exxon Valdez* pouring its cargo into Prince William Sound in Alaska caused many to awaken to the damage from oil spills. That spill released some 11 million gallons that killed approximately 400,000 seabirds. Yet every year 3.5 million tons of oil spill into the seas, most through oil tanker accidents. While it seemed like the response to the *Exxon Valdez* spill showed that oil can be "dispersed by evaporation . . . settling to the seabed and is eventually broken down by microorganisms," a decade later only 4 percent of the spill had been removed by natural *and* artificial methods. In addition, the results of oil spills go far beyond the visible seabirds killed and result in "the deaths of fish and marine plants, including bottom dwellers, and the destruction of algae, a crucial part of the marine food web."[28] Although all of these statistics and studies can be overwhelming, they necessarily show the massive scope of the problem.

Perhaps the greatest source of human-made pollutants in waters comes from agriculture. In addition to other concerns around agriculture, the use of artificial fertilizers to stimulate crops, pesticides in order to control crop attack, and herbicides to control weeds brings these chemicals into the water system as runoff. In 1998 the Environmental Protection Agency noted that "around 7 percent of all U.S. watersheds have sediments contaminated to a degree that poses potential health risks to people eating fish and wildlife," most from mercury and PCBs "released by organic-chemical manufacturers and pulp and paper plants."[29]

Banning such pollutants would be wonderful; however, they are already present in many waters. Dredging just means recycling, and while the pollutants may settle eventually and become buried in bottom sediment, any disturbance such as a passing storm, or even a ship, can stir them up again. These poison pods of pollution, ingested by lower forms of life, eventually make their way up the food chain, becoming more concentrated along the way. Pielou states:

> Persistent poisons, continuously accumulating, are a lasting threat to our freshwater supplies. They may persist for decades or centuries after being deposited. Poisons accumulate in a lake's water as well as in its sediments, especially in deep lakes with long residence times . . . whence they could become liberated by an unforeseen accident.[30]

Then there is *acid rain*. Rain becomes acidic when it mixes with industrial gases, fossil fuel in power stations, the vegetation burning during forest clearing, and car exhaust already polluting the air. The gases, mainly sulfur and nitrogen, dissolve in the falling rain, polluting the ground, streams, rivers, lakes, and vegetation on which the rain falls. The acid rain furthers the damage by combining with natural mineral compounds, which may be mildly toxic, making them even more toxic.[31] Acid rain is particularly acute in the eastern United States, Canada, the former Soviet Union, Scandinavia, and China. "By the early 1990s, around half of the lakes in the Adirondack Mountains of New York State and 20 percent of the lakes in Sweden no longer contained fish."[32] Ironically, the efforts to build taller smokestacks in power plants only made sure that the emissions traveled further to be washed out in the rain. "So it is that the remote natural environments of Scandinavia bear the brunt of the fumes from northern Europe and the former Soviet bloc countries."[33] The 2006 UN *World Water Development Report* indicates that there has been only modest improvement in the northeastern United States, and none in the Adirondacks or the Catskills of New York.[34]

No matter what our *activities* might produce, our body wastes themselves constitute increasingly difficult water problems. The situation is not new, only more serious given population increases. The great Roman aqueducts, so admired by students of antiquity and people everywhere, were in reality made necessary by the huge amounts of human excrement accumulating in cities as large as Rome and as small as Paris at the time. The cities originally did not need aqueducts. By way of contrast, the Japanese city of Edo, modern Tokyo, approached waste quite differently in the eighteenth and nineteenth centuries; the people of Edo composted their waste, using it in fields.[35]

India serves, again, as a tragic example; 80 percent of pollution in India's rivers is from untreated human waste. Costs of treatment—removing pathogens from the water—are very high and unrealistic for most countries in the world.[36] In this context issues of sanitation and sewage join with other forms of pollution and "continue to be the major source of waterborne disease and death in developing countries."[37] Fearful of such disease, people in the developed world flush with even more water in an attempt to rid our houses of the problem, creating the need for water treatments elsewhere.

Rivers

Rivers in the former Soviet Union are heavily contaminated from agricultural runoff, industrial and radioactive waste, and bacterial contamination. A 1997 study of the Czech Republic reported that three-fourths of that country's river waters were "severely polluted," and a third of surface water could no longer support fish. In China, 80 percent of the rivers no longer support fish life, and discharges into the Yellow River make it worthless even for irrigation. Even in Western Europe where regulation has been in place, many rivers are in dire straits. From the North Sea to the Baltic Sea to the coastal waters along the Mediterranean, pollution is "severe." The 1999 report of the World Commission on Water stated that the Amazon and the Congo are now the only major rivers in the world that are healthy. Over half of the world's rivers pose severe health problems.[38]

Further problems result when rivers are "channelized" by *straightening* the river. The adverse effects may outweigh the desired effect of reducing flooding by forcing the waters to flow more quickly. Erosion is increased; habitat diversity is reduced due to the increased flow, and the calm waters that fish need to rest or deposit eggs are gone. The Wild Bird Society of Japan reports that as rivers are channeled for flood control, birds are losing their natural habitats along the old banks that now turn dry, and smaller fish are decreasing which in turn means a decrease in the bird population.[39] Furthermore, when streams are channeled into another river through engineering projects, the ecosystem of both rivers is impacted, bringing new diseases and parasites into different waters. In conclusion Pielou dramatically notes that "What happens [when the waters of two rivers are combined artificially] resembles the decimation of indigenous people . . . when European explorers arrived bringing new epidemic diseases with them." Each stream's equilibrium is changed, and new diseases can enter the ecosystem.[40]

Yet that does not deter China from one of its most ambitious projects of water diversion: a transfer of water from part of the Yangtze in the south, the fourth biggest river in the world, to the empty Yellow River of the north. Two gigantic channels and a 65-mile tunnel are involved; two of the projects are already under construction. The three projects are estimated to cost close to $100 billion and will displace almost 1 million people. In spite of the social, financial, and environmental impacts that critics see ahead—more pollution, huge relocation costs, and ecological damage to floodplains among them— the project lives on and will produce water probably too expensive for its beneficiaries to buy.[41]

The Seas

In 1960 planners in the former Soviet Union increased use of irrigation water from the Aral Sea's two tributaries to boost the production of cotton, one of the thirstiest plants possible, in Uzbekistan and Kazakhstan. From the 1960s to the 1980s the area of irrigated land doubled, and fully 85 percent of the fields in the Aral Sea basin were growing cotton; other crops were simply dropped.[42] As a result the sea was reduced to half of its original size, and the waters became saltier as irrigation drained the sea. The area is now blanketed by toxic saline dust from the dry seabed.[43] Over 77 million tons of dust from the empty sea flows across the area yearly, containing chemicals such as DDT. The salt is worse: "It comes on the wind, down the irrigation canals, and through the pipes carrying drinking water from reservoirs. . . . Salt destroys the perilous productivity of the land, uses up precious water in flushing it out of soils, creates poverty, and ultimately kills the people themselves. . . . [T]he land and its people are being poisoned by salt."[44]

Today the soil has become waterlogged, and salt leaches to the surface. This requires farmers to use more water to grow cotton. That in turn brings about more salt, removed only by flushing with more water, and more flushing consumes more water than irrigation. The results are that 97 percent of women in the areas around the Aral Sea have anemia, which causes a large number to die from hemorrhages during pregnancy; 87 percent of the newborns are anemic. Infant mortality is the highest in the entire former Soviet Union, and rates from various forms of cancer, tuberculosis, kidney and liver diseases are unusually high.[45] Even though most recently, fortunately, part of the Aral Sea is returning,[46] the overall tragedy has left a lingering legacy— all over human attempts to engineer water to produce cotton.

Rising levels of carbon dioxide in the atmosphere from global warming are making all the oceans more acidic. Although the oceans absorb carbon dioxide and thus lessen the impact of global warming, the dramatic rise in carbon dioxide levels from automobiles and industrial uses has changed the pH levels. The lower the level, the higher the acidity. There is a possibility that by 2050 continued exposure to carbon dioxide, along with higher sea temperatures brought about by climate change, will mean that the coral reefs, plankton, and marine snails, central to other marine species, may not survive.[47]

The evidence of ocean pollution is all around, washed up on beaches, pouring from pipes directly into the seas. Chemicals poured into the seas poison living marine creatures, turning them into sponges for plastics and PCBs. The huge shipping fleets that constantly transport goods around the globe "spew as much greenhouse gases into the atmosphere as the entire profligate United States. . . . Filling, dredging, and polluting the coastal nurseries of the seas, we decimate coral reefs and kelp forests, while fostering dead zones." Already a quarter of all coral reefs have been bleached white or killed.[48] Cruise ships traveling the seas produce some 30,000 gallons of sewage and 19 tons of garbage *daily*. Most of that ends up in the sea, and at the same time the ships spew diesel exhaust equal to the amount of 12,240 automobiles per day.[49]

It is so important to remember the interconnectedness of natural resources. Mangrove forests have guarded the seacoasts of the continents for centuries. Mangrove forests "treat effluent, absorbing excess nutrients such as phosphates and nitrates, . . . and the ecosystems of which they are the linchpin have long provided a livelihood for coastal peoples."[50] They also protect coastal waters from flooding in the cases of hurricanes, typhoons, and the feared tsunamis. Recently, mangroves have been cut, dredged, removed to make way for commercial and industrial interests. The most dramatic recent effects of such mangrove losses were visible in the terrible destruction caused by the Asian tsunami of December 2004. The areas least damaged were those protected by mangroves; those areas decimated were areas where mangroves had been removed to make way for resorts with beautiful beaches.

Finally, perhaps the most long-lasting source of pollution in the seas comes from decades of dumping of nuclear wastes. The Farallon Islands off the coast of San Francisco, California, have been the site deluxe for thousands of 55-gallon drums of radioactive wastes. Other sites were used as well, but by the 1990s when the dumping stopped, more than 50,000 drums had been dumped at the Farallons alone. In addition, the other nuclear powers such as Russia, China, Japan, and European nations had been doing the same. As these drums, some pumped with bullets to let the water in ("and of course, plutonium, uranium, and strontium out"), corrode and decompose over time, we can only imagine what the results might be.[51]

Puget Sound

From the top window of my house, I have a slight view of Puget Sound, a large saltwater basin populated by ferries, cargo ships, sailboats, and tourist boats, a giant waterway from Tacoma in the south up to the Strait of Juan de Fuca leading out to the Pacific. But the Sound is not sound; it is in deep trouble from pollution. Dungeness crabs, the favorite for decades of locals and tourists alike, are dwindling and in some cases gone from their habitat. Near Tillicum Village, a tourist center, the crabs' locale has become an "underwater desert." Other sites are bare of fish, crabs, and even the lush eelgrass where crabs used to hide.

Along with the crabs, seabirds are disappearing, and salmon stocks are dwindling to only 10 percent of their historic high. Puget Sound's herring now contain "higher contamination levels than those in Europe's highly polluted Baltic Sea."[52] More recently the Washington State Department of Health issued its first-ever warning that eating Chinook salmon more than once a week or the resident blackmouth more than twice a month could be dangerous to one's health.[53] As a response to growing pollution orca whales often found in the Sound that feed on the once abundant sea life have been given the strongest protection for species close to extinction.[54]

The causes are not hard to find: heavy industrial pollution, residential stormwater runoff, semitreated wastewater, residue from boats of all kinds, leaking septic tanks, and a surging population that grows at the rate of 270 people per day. Water pouring off one of the two bridges crossing Lake Washington that eventually empties into the Sound was found to contain copper levels 15,000 times higher than what damages young salmon on their way to sea. Here the culprit seems to be car brake pads on the ever-crowded bridges. While there are bright spots in local government efforts to reduce these factors, the huge number of different legal jurisdictions involved makes the process painfully slow. There is strong resistance to tougher enforcement among residents, boat builders, the building industry and developers among others. The costs for cleaning up the Sound are over $12 billion.[55]

Conclusion

It is easy to glance over statistics and not register their meaning, but the facts and stories in this chapter are compelling in understanding the crises we face. We cannot say that agriculture, industry, and human consumption are evil, or that technological progress should stop, when these benefit people in many ways. Yet, we must begin to look at the consequences of the ways in which the water world has changed in order to give meaning to potential solutions for easing the water crises. In the next chapter we look at other dimensions of the complex water crises, such as dams, population increase, and increasing, competing demands for water, global warming, and conflicts over water. A glimpse at the potential here for "water wars" alerts us to the real dangers arising from different understandings of water, contrasting needs and purposes for water, and the race for clean water.

Notes

1. Personal interview with James Rufo-Hill and Brooke Rufo-Hill, 13 May 2006.
2. Marc de Villiers, *Water: The Fate of Our Most Precious Resource* (New York: Houghton Mifflin, 2000), 12–13.
3. Donald Worster, *Rivers of Empire* (New York: Oxford University Press, 1985), 19–21.
4. de Villiers, *Water*, 54–55.
5. de Villiers, *Water*, 54–57.
6. World Health Organization, WHO and UNICEF Joint Monitoring Programme, *Global Water Supply and Sanitation Assessment 2000 Report* (Geneva: UNICEF, 2000), 1.
7. United Nations, *Water: A Shared Responsibility. The United Nations World Water Development Report 2* (New York: Berghahn, 2006), 46.
8. Maude Barlow, speech, WTO demonstrations, Benaroya Hall, Seattle, 25 November 1999.
9. Phillip Ball, *Life's Matrix: A Biography of Water* (New York: Farrar, Straus & Giroux, 1999), 330–340.
10. Penny LaGate, "Ethiopia," *6:00 News*, CBS, 14 August 2005.
11. Kerry Brown, "In the Water There Were Fish and the Fields Were Full of Rice," in *Buddhism and Ecology*, eds. Martine Batchelor and Kerry Brown (London: Cassell, 1992), 91.
12. United Nations, *Water for People, Water for Life: The United Nations World Water Development Report* (Geneva: UNESCO, 2003), 5, 10.
13. United Nations, *Water: A Shared Responsibility*, 521–525.
14. Quoted in K. Ettinger, "A River That Was Once So Strong and Deep," in *Water, Culture, and Power*, eds. John M. Donahue and Barbara R. Johnston (Washington, D.C.: Island Press, 1998), 47.
15. E. C. Pielou, *Fresh Water* (Chicago: University of Chicago Press, 1998), 50, 181.
16. Pielou, *Fresh Water*, 181–182.
17. Pielou, *Fresh Water*, 182.

18. Quoted in Fred Pearce, *When the Rivers Run Dry* (Boston: Beacon, 2006), 51. There seems to be a similar pattern developing in the Red River delta of Vietnam, home to 11 million people, where tube wells are being drilled and arsenic levels are rising (Pearce, *When Rivers Run Dry*, 55).

19. Jonathan Martin, "Victoria Revisits Issue of Treating its Sewage," *Seattle Times*, 14 July 2006, sec. B.

20. de Villiers, *Water*, 89.

21. Ball, *Life's Matrix*, 353–354; de Villiers, *Water*, 89.

22. Pearce, *When Rivers Run Dry*, 231–233.

23. Cameron Woodworth, "A Clean Drink of Water: Choices and Responsibilities," *Sound Consumer*, August 2006, 1.

24. NPR News, KUOW Seattle, 9 a.m. news report, 6 September 2006.

25. Matt Jenkins, "The Wet Net," *High Country News*, 2 October 2006, 12.

26. Maggie Black, *The No-Nonsense Guide to Water* (Oxford: New Internationalist, 2004), 100.

27. Dashka Slater, "Big-Box Talk," *Sierra Magazine* 91, no. 6 (November–December 2006), 21.

28. Ball, *Life's Matrix*, 354.

29. Ball, *Life's Matrix*, 349.

30. Pielou, *Fresh Water*, 183.

31. Pielou, *Fresh Water*, 183–184.

32. Ball, *Life's Matrix*, 354.

33. Ball, *Life's Matrix*, 355.

34. United Nations, *Water: A Shared Responsibility*, 138.

35. Black, *No-Nonsense Guide*, 5–6.

36. Black, *No-Nonsense Guide*, 40–41.

37. Ball, *Life's Matrix*, 350.

38. de Villiers, *Water*, 87–89.

39. Yutaka Kanai and Furukawa Setsu, Wild Bird Society, Conservation Division, Tokyo. Personal interview, 17 October 2005.

40. Pielou, *Fresh Water*, 213.

41. Pearce, *When Rivers Run Dry*, 219–221.

42. Pearce, *When Rivers Run Dry*, 203.

43. David Holley, "A Rising Tide: The Aral's Return," *Seattle Times*, 26 May 2006.

44. Pearce, *When Rivers Run Dry*, 210.

45. Pearce, *When Rivers Run Dry*, 203, 210–211.

46. Holley, "A Rising Tide."

47. Quoted in Juliet Eliperin, "Growing Acidity of Oceans May Kill Corals," *Washington Post*, 5 July 2006, sec. A.

48. Julia Whitty, "The Fate of the Earth," *Mother Jones* 31, no. 2 (March–April 2006): 34–45.

49. Jonathan Stein, "Enemies of the Ocean," *Mother Jones* 31, no. 2 (March–April 2006): 50.

50. Black, *No-Nonsense Guide*, 92.

51. Bill Bryson, *A Short History of Nearly Everything* (New York: Broadway Books, 2003), 281–282.

52. Robert McClure and Lisa Stiffler, "Marine Life Is Disappearing from Puget Sound, and Fast," *Seattle Post-Intelligencer*, 9 October 2006.

53. Cherie Black, "New Alert on Eating Local Salmon, *Seattle Post-Intelligencer*, 27 October 2006, p. 1.

54. McClure and Stiffler, "Marine Life," *Seattle Post-Intelligencer*, 1.

55. Lisa Stiffler and Robert McClure, "Reality Already Is Soaking In," *Seattle Post-Intelligencer*, 11 October 2006, sec. A; "Saving Puget Sound Could Cost $12 Billion," *Seattle Post-Intelligencer*, 13 October 2006, sec. A.

CHAPTER FIVE

~

A Tenuous Relationship:
Human Need and Water Resources

The previous chapter outlined the many threats to water from pollution around the world waterways, all brought about through human activities. We briefly touched upon some of the principles necessary in addressing these threats, such as local participation in water management, equality among various users, and sustainability. Before we can develop such principles further and draw upon religious beliefs and practices in supporting ethical water use, we must pursue even further the major developments that are impinging upon water in our times. In this chapter, then, we will examine the impacts of dams as development tools, of growing population pressures upon competing demands, of global warming, and of actual and potential water wars. Each of these developments is a major contributor to the crisis, but together with the increasing pollution of the waterways, the compounding interaction of these factors leads to an accumulation of "tipping points" that could herald catastrophic changes unless addressed quickly and decisively.

Dams and Reservoirs

As a child, I felt dwarfed by the immense size of the Hoover Dam near Las Vegas, Nevada. Looking down the almost 700 feet to the waters below was a dizzying sight. At the time it was the first super-dam, completed in 1935 as a testament to the power of a nation emerging from the Depression. As an adult, I felt less dwarfed but more awed at the Grand Coulee Dam, awed by the sheer engineering feat required to tame the mighty Columbia River waters. These gigantic twentieth-century engineering marvels hold back Lake Mead and Lake Roosevelt, and along with Shasta Dam in California form the big trinity of dams in the United States.[1] Dams have been built for centuries, and even as the enthusiasm for dams in the States is declining, new dam construction is proceeding at a rapid rate in countries as diverse as China, India, Japan, and little Belize. As of 2000 the world's top dam builders are China with over 22,000, the United States with some 6,500, India with 4,300, Japan with 2,675, and Spain with 1,196. Asian countries alone have built over 31,000 dams.[2] These and other large dams hold more than 5.5 billion acre-feet of water.[3]

For centuries, since the first recorded humans made earth dams in Egypt about 4,500 years ago, dam structures have been used for a variety of purposes—water supplies, irrigation, flood control, hydroelectric power.[4] The thousands of acres of productive crops in eastern Washington would have been impossible without the Grand Coulee Dam, and the electrical needs of millions in Washington, Idaho, and Oregon have been met with the dam's help. Worldwide a fifth of the electricity needs of people are met by hydroelectric dams, with 95 percent of that energy from large dams.[5] In the twentieth century a large dam was built on the average of one per day.[6]

However, dams have costs. The great Aswan High Dam of Egypt, completed in 1971, meant the resettlement of over 100,000 people and increased salinity and the erosion of soil of the Nile River. By diverting some four-fifths of the water from the sea to farmland, the Nile no longer carries the upland erosion into the farmers' fields, as the old river did.[7] The fertile sediments now pile up behind the dam in Lake Nasser and will render the dam practically useless due to continued sediment buildup. Below the dam the slower river renders the "parasitic disease schistosomiasis . . . more prevalent." Finally, in the delta to the sea, the sea catch has dropped, and the reduced amount of minerals flowing to the Mediterranean impacts sea life.[8]

In the United States, perhaps no other Western river has engendered so much controversy over dam building as the Colorado River. Already by the 1950s the river's dams and the resulting reservoirs, such as Lake Mead behind the great Hoover Dam, had resulted in higher and higher salinity levels all along the way and especially in the waters that finally flow into Mexico. A huge drain was built to carry away the salty residues, but it discharges back into the Colorado just before the border. Another dam, the Glen Canyon Dam, was built over great objections by environmentalists and others and raised the salinity level higher. Finally, a series of diversion schemes, each expensive in itself, was devised to keep water flowing to Mexico according to earlier agreements, while decreasing salinity levels.[9]

China's huge Three Gorges Dam across the Yangtze Kiang River, completed in 2006, is the largest in the world and will reduce coal consumption "by forty million tons a year, will produce the equivalent electrical output of a dozen nuclear power plants," and will alleviate widespread flooding along the rivers. The impact is huge: 1.2 million people have been relocated, and farmers will have to till fields in higher, less fertile areas. The reservoir itself will be almost 400 miles long and 0.7 miles wide and possibly lead to extensive upstream silting.[10] These "costs" may not be calculated for years.

Japan is one of the top five dam builders on the globe. More than 2,650 dams have been constructed in a country smaller than California to provide irrigation and control flooding and to let the waters of that rainy nation flow rapidly but controllably to the sea as quickly as possible.[11] Because of Japan's steep terrain, water flows abundantly to the plains below where over 60 percent of the population lives. Thus the government argues that even more dams are needed. Recently, however, that strong government line, backed by the huge construction industry, has been challenged by growing opposition in the anti-dam movement, most notably by *Suigenren* (Water Resource Development Issue and Communication Network), a national anti-dam network. The Network has sued six prefecture governments over dam construction. One local mayor even passed the "Stop Dam Construction Law" in his city.[12]

In Belize, where I have spent a great deal of time over the past decade, a struggling, developing nation is attempting to harness its waters for its own electric production rather than depend on the irregular supply from neighboring Mexico to the north. The Chalillo Dam on the Macal River in western Belize, built in 2002–2005, was met with great opposition, and the newly proposed Vaca Dam has kept dam opposition alive, particularly from indigenous peoples, local environmental groups, and groups outside the country. Opposition to the Chalillo project brought together nine environmental and other groups under the umbrella organization BACONGO (Belize Alliance of Conservation NGOs). In spite of their efforts, which included several legal appeals and a final appeal to the Judicial Committee of the Privy Council of Great Britain, BACONGO lost their case in January 2004. However, road construction had already begun in January 2002, with groundbreaking in May 2003, despite the fact that the Belize House and Senate did not pass legislation supporting the dam until June 2003, and the appeal cases were still pending.[13]

The Chalillo Dam's negative impacts have reached other parts of the country as well. Electricity rates have increased, and the water quality has deteriorated downstream. At the dam site itself, water seeps under the dam because of the kind of soil involved, and mercury contamination in higher amounts than before the dam was built is present in the water and thus in the fish caught in the downstream waters. At the same time the government officials whom I interviewed in the Department of the Environment and the Ministry of Natural Resources and the Environment assured me that the dam was functioning well and held great promise for the people of Belize.[14]

For all their merits, it seems that dams have some great drawbacks, "costs" not factored into the original purposes or even costs of construction and proposed benefits. Recent studies of the impact of dams worldwide, begun in part due to dam opposition around the globe, reveal that "some 40–80 million people [have been] displaced by dams while 60% of the world's rivers have been affected by dams and diversions."[15]

India now has 3,300 big dams and a thousand more under construction. Bitter opposition has emerged over more dams on the sacred Narmada River. Arundhati Roy, internationally known novelist and environmental activist, in her small book *The Cost of Living*, takes on the arguments in favor of large dams, particularly on the Narmada, and shows the destruction in India caused by the dam-building industry over the past half-century. Far from delivering people from their poverty, as government, the World Bank, and others had postulated, India's big dams are "a brazen means of taking water, land, and irrigation away from the poor and gifting it to the rich. Their reservoirs displace huge populations of people, leaving them homeless and destitute. . . . They cause floods, waterlogging, salinity, they spread disease. . . . They last only as long as it takes Nature to fill them with silt."[16] These are strong charges that will be examined in the pages to come.

One of the most significant purposes of dams is to provide irrigation. Yet E. C. Pielou notes that if irrigation is the primary purpose of a dam, a great deal of water is lost due to evaporation from the surface of the reservoir behind the dam, and irrigation eventually leads to excess salts in the irrigated soil.[17] The evaporation from Lake Nassar behind Egypt's Aswan High Dam "could fill every faucet in England for a year," with evaporation of fully "a quarter of the average flow of the [Nile] river into the reservoir, approaching 40 percent in a dry year."[18]

The major problem with the reservoir created by the dam in comparison with a natural lake lies in the water's chemistry. Because they have flooded land and vegetation, the new reservoir contains dead plant material "which serves as a habitat for rapidly multiplying bacteria capable of absorbing any mercury that happens to be in the soil; they convert the mercury into a form that fish can ingest, and in this way mercury enters the food chain." This form of mercury is much more toxic than the original and becomes more concentrated on its trip up the food chain. Pielou notes that the Crees of the James Bay region of Quebec have mercury levels in their hair much higher than the upper limit recommended by the World Health Organization; fish in the reservoir had six times the legal level for fish in Canada.[19]

In addition to higher levels of mercury due to the decomposed vegetation, reservoirs release two greenhouse gases, carbon dioxide and methane, in large doses. As a consequence, a "reservoir powering a hydroelectric plant can sometimes give off as great a quantity of greenhouse gases as a coal-fired generator yielding the same electric power."[20] Half of the reservoirs of Brazil's hydroelectric dams "warm the planet more than an equivalent fossil-fuel power plant. The World Commission on Dams [said]: 'There is no justification for claiming that hydroelectricity does not contribute significantly to global warming.'"[21]

Another problem of dams involves the silt buildups in the reservoirs, as we saw in the case of Egypt's Aswan High Dam. Worldwide reservoirs are losing storage capacity at a rate of 1 percent per year, with those in China at 2 percent.[22] The report of the World Commission on Dams notes "more than 50% of active storage was lost . . . for 10% of the projects." One-fourth of the hydropower reservoirs in the United States have some sediment problems and over 9,300 of the 80,000 large and small U.S. dams are considered "high hazard," i.e., a failure of the dam would bring about serious loss of life and large property damage.[23]

A dam also affects the river above and below. Above, any organism dependent on air has been drowned, as well as homes, farms, even towns. The streams and rivers flowing into the reservoir have also changed, depositing sediments that would have flowed away. Downstream effects are more dramatic. The discharge of waters impacts the quantity and quality of aquatic life, at times raising or lowering the stream level and increasing or decreasing the flow speed. Such changes alter the seasonal flow of the stream or river, and the slower waters below the dam may lack the nutrients that remain behind the dam; these factors in turn affect all life as the stream flows to the sea.[24]

Finally, there are the human costs. The November 2000 report for the World Commission on Dams "estimated that between 40 and 80 million people have been displaced by large dams, although the actual figure may be much higher. Most receive pitiful compensation and end up impoverished."[25] Relocation is to different lands that may or may not be suitable for farming; most often indigenous people are the ones displaced with little care for their loss of ancestral lands and vital food sources from fishing.

The Commission's report lists several other negative impacts of large dams, such as the loss of species and ecosystems along rivers and watersheds related to dams, and problems that tend to occur during building such as delays, cost overruns, loss of economic profitability, and failure to meet targets. Yet the most critical remark of the report's authors concerns the consequences of dams on human living: "Perhaps of most significance is the fact that social groups bearing the social and environmental costs and risks of large dams, especially the poor, vulnerable, and future generations, are often not the same groups that received the water and electricity services, nor the social and economic benefits from these." This conclusion utilizes criteria of human rights and sustainable development in assessing the usefulness of dams.[26]

Then there is the cost no one examines as a whole: the numbers of lives lost from broken dams, waters released from dams to ease the pressure on the dams themselves, and water releases during flood times. When a typhoon hit Henan Province in central China in 1975, the Banqiao dam operators were ready, or so they thought. However, an upstream dam had burst under the pressure, and when the 97,000 acre-feet of water crashed into the Banqiao dam, it too gave way sending 400,000 acre-feet of now-muddy water downstream. Unofficial figures of the numbers of dead ranged from 80,000 to 200,000. Similarly and more recently when Hurricane Mitch breached the dams in Honduras in October 1998, the ensuing landslides and floods produced deadly walls of water in the country, killing an estimated 10,000 people. Deaths also occur when the dams release water downstream to prevent collapse. Ironically, ". . . dams designed to prevent floods often end up creating floods."[27]

The 2000 study of the World Commission on Dams did not call for tearing down all dams nor halting any more building. The chair of the commission, Kader Asmal, stated that dams can be justified if (1) they were shown to overcome the drawbacks and (2) they had the approval of those impacted directly.[28] In the final pages of the report, the twelve commission members summarized the major problems that dams present. While acknowledging the many benefits that the dams have contributed to human development, they conclude that too high a price has been paid to gain these benefits, particularly in social and environmental terms. A lack of equity in allocating the dam's benefits challenges the values of dams in addressing water needs, and dams too often result in "social injustice and environmental damage."[29] In short, dams, at least large dams, have become the dinosaurs of the twenty-first century—massive and cumbersome, wasteful of the surrounding countryside, outdated, and out of balance with the environment.

This lengthy discussion of the impacts of dams highlights a widespread twentieth-century approach to water supply for the variety of human needs. The commission's definitive study offers principles and criteria for evaluating any future dam building by emphasizing the importance of alternatives. That dimension of the report and the principles of sustainability, equity, participation, and social justice that the report utilizes will be developed in a later chapter.

Increase in Demand

Dams are built in response to the needs of large populations, and many of the major impacts on fresh water result from the dramatic increases in population and urbanization. Population worldwide increased by three times since the beginning of the twentieth century, with water demand growing six times in the same period, and the global population is expected to grow another 50 percent in the next fifty years with large numbers moving to urban areas. Usually urban dwellers demand more water use for household consumption than rural users, and demand even in the most developed nations is increasing even when the population remains steady or actually declines.[30]

The United Nations World Water Development Reports 1 and 2 document the rapid buildup of cities and "megacities" of over 10 million people; in 2000 there were 387 cities with over a million people, with 47 percent of the world's population. By 2010 more than half—51.3 percent of the world's population—will live in urban areas.[31] Water demand increases indirectly because as people move to the cities, their diet changes and they consume more meat, which places huge burdens on water. It has been estimated that if population growth continues at its present rate in the United States alone, another decade will see a 30 percent increase in meat consumption, with a corresponding increase in water use.[32]

As greater numbers of people are concentrated in large cities, not only do their basic water needs increase but their human wastes accumulate in greater amounts, and as the World Health Organization has indicated, when basic sanitation services and adequate water treatment are lacking, large cities and their surrounding areas become the world's most life-threatening environments. In addition, when water drainage is inadequate, more people are in danger of flooding and the further spread of disease. In parts of large urban areas inhabited by low-income populations, infant mortality rates have increased.[33]

Another consequence of increased demand is that the natural flow of fresh water into the sea slows as water is diverted for more irrigation for more food, for more industrial uses to meet consumer demands, and for daily water use. As a result salinity begins to intrude into the river systems. Problems with the salinization of fresh water have been particularly acute in parts of Western Europe, Japan, and the coastal United States.[34] A similar process of increasing salinity results from irrigation of hot, dry areas. Because of high rates of evaporation of the natural water used in irrigation, the groundwater becomes saturated with mineral salts. The consequence is that the salt content in the unevaporated water becomes greater than the crops can tolerate. The solution has been to "leach out such accumulated salts by additional irrigation which carries them, in solution, deep underground." This process in turn raises the water table, and the land, as in large areas of Pakistan, becomes waterlogged.[35]

Across the world with 10 percent of Earth's landmass under cultivation and 10 percent of that amount under artificial irrigation, increasing population growth puts more demand on agricultural sources and resources. Increasing industrial uses for water include water used for transferring heat and then cooling in nuclear reactors, the demands for computers that utilize huge amounts of water for manufacturing, and so forth. The demands for more water bring with them the need for more purification plants, better distribution systems, enlarged sewage systems, and then treatment plants.[36]

Increased demands for water puts pressure on the Earth's great aquifers as well. Current rates of extraction mean that water seeping back into the aquifer cannot replenish the source equally. This process then is really the *mining* of a nonrenewable resource. Problematically, when an aquifer is not sufficiently recharged, overdrawing the water can lead to desertification, turning the land above literally into desert.[37] Fred Pearce in his masterful study, *When the Rivers Run Dry*, reports that "Overall total pumping in India, China, and Pakistan probably exceeds recharge by 120 to 160 million acre-feet a year. . . . The consequences of the eventual, inevitable failure of underground water in these countries could be catastrophic."[38] A similar situation is occurring in Mexico, Argentina, Brazil, Saudi Arabia, and Morocco.

In the United States one of the most important aquifers is the Ogallala, stretching from Nebraska through the Midwest to Colorado, New Mexico, and into Texas. Some 200,000 wells bring irrigation from the aquifer to a third of the U.S. fields. The aquifer is not recharging well, and over large areas the water table is now 100 feet lower—it is totally gone in parts of Texas, Oklahoma, and Kansas. When the Ogallala is combined with the aquifers of the Central Valley of California and the Southwest, over 30 million acre-feet more is pumped out than is replenished.[39]

Bottled Water

As water quality deteriorates or becomes questionable in various parts of the world, many people, pushed along also by clever marketing and the desire for "perfect health," resort to bottled water. The world bottlers target their "pure water" to specialty, i.e., economically advantaged, audiences: "water for sportsmen and sportswomen, water for pregnant women, water for babies, water for growing children—all part of the contribution of bottled water in general to perfect health at every age and in all circumstances."[40]

In the United States the bottled water phenomenon began with the mass marketing efforts of Perrier water in 1978.[41] Since then, bottled water sales worldwide have risen dramatically from some 1 billion liters in the 1970s to 84 billion liters in 2000! Clever marketing of their water products as "pure water" taps into the dynamics of healthy lifestyles around the world. Coke's Dasani brand is tap water that has been purified and filtered; the same for Aquafina by Pepsi. Pressured by watchdog groups such as Corporate Accountability International, Pepsi agreed in July 2007 to label Aquafina as drawn from a Public Water Source.[42] Fiji Water really does come from Fiji "where 'rainwater filters through volcanic rock over hundreds of years. It's the way nature intended water to be, untouched.' In a plastic bottle?"[43]

In truth, bottled water may not be any purer than tap water. In 1999, the National Resources Defense Council reported on a four-year study of the bottled water industry, testing some 103 brands and concluding, ". . . there is no assurance that just because water comes out of a bottle that it is any cleaner or safer than water from the tap. In fact, an estimated 25 to 40 percent of bottled water really is just tap water in a bottle—sometimes further treated, sometimes not."[44] Of the bottled water sold in the United States, 60–70 percent is packaged and sold within the same state and so not subject to regulation by the Food and Drug Administration. Bottled water, as opposed to tap water that is tested several times per day according to regulations of the Environmental Protection Agency, is only tested weekly.[45]

Perhaps the most dramatic instance of the battles over bottled water has taken place in India in reference to Coke and Pepsi products there. In February 2003, the Centre for Science and Environment published a report which noted that not only were many of India's own brands of bottled water infused with pesticides, but Coke and Pepsi drinks in general had much higher levels of toxins than the European Community's limits. The Centre for Science and Environment's report was confirmed by a Parliamentary committee in 2004. Yet a further consequence of Pepsi's and Coke's industries in India is that, because the companies get their water from the groundwater at their plant sites, contamination and depletion of water used by locals for farming and drinking occur. Not only do the results indicate that groundwater, the major source of water for 90 percent of rural and 50 percent of urban customers in India, may be contaminated throughout the country, but regulation in these cases is deemed unaffordable.[46]

Furthermore, at Coke's India plants according to the company's own report "3.9 liters of water are needed to produce each liter of beverage" because of the need to wash bottles, floors, and equipment in addition to the water used in the drink itself. Coke has 50 plants in India, using "hundreds of thousands of liters of water" per day. Although Coke has used rainwater harvesting, most of the water is pulled from the aquifers, sparking complaints and protests from local farmers who state that the aquifers are drying up.

Then, in August 2005, the Kerala State Pollution Control Board found unacceptable amounts of cadmium in waste from a Coke plant and ordered the plant to stop production. Another Coke plant in Kerala used about 130,000 gallons of water per day on its 40-acre site and was refused a reissuing of its operating license due to opposition of the local village council.[47] In September 2006, the High Court of Kerala overturned the ban on the production and sale of Coca-Cola and Pepsi; however, seven states still have partial or full bans on Coke, Pepsi, and Spring drinks, and over 10,000 schools no longer allow the beverages to be sold.[48]

The bottles for bottled water require fossil fuels and energy use to produce; the plastic of plastic bottles can also leach chemicals if used over long periods or in hot environments. Once used, 86 percent of the plastic bottles in the United States end up in landfills. That figure amounts to some thirty million water bottles in landfills daily, and they can take 1,000 years to decompose. Bottled water packaging uses some 1.5 million tons of plastic per year.[49] In so many ways, water in bottles is a privilege of the wealthy, or of those of us seduced by the claim of "purity." The entire process is not sustainable, and the solution in developing countries lies not in buying bottled water, but in providing ways to ensure clean, drinkable water and clean sanitation that will continue over time.

Agriculture: Water for Food

Water for irrigation makes the most demands upon the Earth's meager 1 percent of fresh water, and the demand is growing. Although population and the rate of irrigation use remain steady in developed countries, further increases in irrigation are taking place in developing countries where population growth is increasing. This phenomenon in turn puts increasing pressures on other water uses.[50] Issues about water to drink are directly related to concerns about food to eat.

The extensive use of water for irrigation causes salinization of soil. In arid areas salts that accumulate in soil "turn the soil alkaline and caustic, inhibiting plant growth."[51] Seawater moving into groundwater from the lowering of the groundwater table and aquifers also brings salinization. The United Nations has estimated that fully a quarter of all irrigated land is now impacted.[52]

Another devastating water-based problem lies in *desertification*, the growth of deserts. Since the 1960s the Sahel area of northern Africa has seen the slow expansion of the African desert. Although some of this advance can be attributed to long periods of drought, the impact of human practices remains the major culprit, such as "overgrazing, overcultivation, and deforestation." With vegetation cover gone, the soil dries up, and its ability to hold moisture is compromised. Reduction of the soil cover "leads to a decline in air humidity, cloud formation, and rainfall. In other words, the land becomes trapped on a gradual decline toward desert."[53] As with salinization, the impact of desertification is tremendous. The United Nations estimates that 60 percent of land outside human areas is impacted by desertification, placing millions of livelihoods at risk.[54]

In Japan irrigation patterns have created a different problem. Rice paddies were once watered by streams and creeks flowing through the area. Diversions were set up to make sure the appropriate amount of flooding took place. The area was wet all year long. Today, the paddies are supplied with faucets that turn off the water supply during the nongrowing season. The result is that the paddies no longer serve as places for birds to nest and lay their eggs.[55]

Perhaps the most unlikely form of agriculture to impact water is lawn turf. Turf grass—on lawns, golf courses, everywhere—is the United States largest irrigated crop, "occupying three times more land than irrigated cornfields." The demand for turf is growing, especially in the expanding suburbs.[56] By spending some $40 billion a year to plant and care for their turf, U.S. residents and commercial interests send nitrogen-rich fertilizers into streams and oceans, "causing algae blooms, degrading water quality, and killing fish." In several cities of the arid West, such as Las Vegas, Phoenix, and Salt Lake City, watering turf can account for two-thirds of residents' water consumption. Even though agricultural irrigation still accounts for the largest water use, the new population increases in the nation's West and especially the Southwest are increasing more rapidly than agriculture needs.[57]

As urban populations increase and new industries arise in developing countries, a greater demand will be made on the waters used in agriculture; the proportions of water used by consumers, farmers, and industries will change. "By 2025 . . . water scarcity will be cutting food production by 385 million tons a year." Already in response to existing scarcity in many countries,

"Up to a billion people are today eating food grown using underground water [from aquifers] that is not being replaced."[58] The situation looks bleak.

Industry: Water for Production and Power

Industry and power plants are also demanding greater amounts of water, second only to agriculture. Plants generally return almost all of the water used
to the rivers. However, power plants return warmer water, and industrial
plants often return polluted waters, saturated with "detergents, hydrocar-
bons, heavy metals, and toxic organic matter."[59] Although great strides were
made in the United States and Europe to reduce emissions from industry especially after the Love Canal disaster of the 1970s and the sight of Cleveland's Cuyahoga River aflame with industrial waste in 1969, elsewhere in the
world "many waterways remain loaded with sulphurous and stinking contaminants as well as raw sewage." As industrial plants discharge their wastewater without treatment into open waterways, more water is polluted, and
contamination spreads to aquifers and other groundwater areas.[60]

The major industries contributing to contaminated water are first the
food and beverage industry, accounting for between 40 percent in developed
areas and 55 percent in developing areas, followed by paper and pulp at 23
percent and 10 percent, respectively, then textiles, metals, chemicals, wood,
and others.[61] Pulp industries in the United States use between 60,000 and
90,000 gallons of water for each ton of paper. Cotton remains one of the
most toxic industries using water because the bleaching process uses 48,000
to 72,000 gallons per ton with inadequate removals of contaminants.[62] The
auto and computer industries are also culprits. Some 2,800 gallons of water
are used to produce just the chips for one personal computer; building a
computer also uses over 700 chemicals, over half which are hazardous, and
some of those find their way into the groundwater. That explains why Santa
Clara County, California, the center of a high-tech industry, "has over 150
groundwater contamination sites and more Superfund sites than any other
county in the nation."[63]

One of the major impacts of globalization of the world's economies involves the transfer of industries from developed to developing countries. In
addition to concerns about labor and environmental impacts, these transfers
mean industries now compete for scarce freshwater sources in countries already water stressed. The 2003 UN World Water Development Report notes
that any economic benefits of lower costs entail greater stresses on local supplies and involve greater changes to water users.[64]

Global Warming

Although the full impact of human activities on global warming is debated, hardly any studies on global warming dispute the fact that humans have had a powerful impact on the environment through industrial and agricultural production, power plants, the automobile, and other uses. The Intergovernmental Panel on Climate Change's report in February 2007 acknowledges with a 90 percent certainty that the great majority of global warming has come from human-made greenhouse gases. Climate variation cannot explain the rising sea levels, warmer ocean waters, melting glaciers, and other factors witnessed in recent years; eleven of the hottest years on record have taken place in just the past twelve years. Global average temperature has risen approximately 1.2 degrees F from 1901 to 2005. Continued global warming will lead to greater acidification of the oceans, impacting marine life. Certainly the effects will alter species, food production, and human health. The report also states that global warming will result in greater droughts and heat waves and extremely strong storm surges bringing more intense flooding.[65] While more dramatic sea level rises occurred in the early formation of the Earth, today even this conservative estimate of rising temperatures would mean tremendous changes for many inhabited islands as well as lowlands such as the coast of Bangladesh and other countries. "This isn't a smoking gun; climate is a battalion of intergalactic smoking missiles" was the enhanced image of the report's coauthor, Andrew Weaver, a Canadian climate scientist.[66]

Possibly more serious for managing water resources are the changes in future "rainfall patterns and behaviors, in evaporation, and in amounts of runoff and moisture in the soil at different times of year." Studies of river basins show that there will be more intense rainfall and floods in China, Australia, the United States, and Switzerland while in Africa the decline by 17 percent of rain runoff has resulted in lowering soil moisture which may drastically contribute to greater food insecurity.[67]

Global warming has also meant less snow in mountain areas. The western mountains of the United States have seen an 11 percent shrinkage since 1950, and the Cascade mountains of western Washington, Oregon, and British Columbia have experienced a 50 percent decline in some areas. Less snow for a shorter period of the year results in streams filling earlier and drying out sooner in summer.[68]

With these facts in mind, what is the cumulative effect of global warming? Basically the whole hydrologic cycle intensifies. "A warmer atmosphere holds more water (6 percent for every degree Celsius), and the increasing cloudiness reduces daytime warming and retards nighttime cooling by blocking outgoing long-wave radiation." The results are more heavy rainfalls, more flash flooding, the drifting northward of semitropical plants and animals, "radical reductions in the number of zooplankton near the ocean surface," and "sharp declines in mid-ocean nutrient levels," creating food shortages for deep ocean creatures.[69]

The situation at the North and South Poles is critical. The Antarctic ice sheet is losing "up to 36 cubic miles of ice each year." At the same time, the Arctic ice pack was smaller in 2006 for the second year in a row; according to the National Snow and Ice Data Center winter ice reduction has been the largest in a century. So "instead of being reflected by ice, the sun's rays are absorbed by open water, leading to further warming."[70] Arctic seas are now breaking open much earlier, preventing native peoples from hunting the herds that provided them with sustenance. There are increasing incidents of skilled hunters falling through the ice, twelve incidents in Alaska in 2006. An August 2006 report by the National Aeronautics and Space Administration (NASA) confirmed that ice has been melting much faster than ever before: summer ice coverage was the smallest in 100 years, and winter coverage was 6 percent smaller than the average over the last 26 years.[71] Satellite imagery reveals an ice cap almost 30 percent smaller than 25 years ago.[72]

To understand the link among all the factors we have discussed so far, the work of John Schellnhurer, a science advisor at the Tyndall Centre for Climate Change Research in the United Kingdom, may provide some answers. In 2004 Schellnhurer proposed that if any of twelve tipping points were to trigger suddenly, then catastrophic changes would most likely occur. The twelve tipping points are in order and include changes that occur in or because of the Amazon rainforest, the North Atlantic current, Greenland's ice sheet, the ozone hole, the Antarctic circumpolar current, the Sahara desert, the Tibetan plateau, the Asian monsoon, methane clathrates, salinity values, El Niño, and the West Atlantic ice sheet. While the details of his theory are beyond our discussion, one example of the interrelationships involved will suffice. Global warming is expected to melt the snows of the Tibetan plateau "and uncover dark soils ideal for absorbing sunlight and warming the earth in a positive feedback loop." Then the warmer climate would impact the monsoons dramatically which in turn affect half the world's population. Already warming has released five times more methane than thought from the Siberian and Alaskan permafrost.[73] While some would call such talk alarmist and dismiss these analyses, the convergence of the tipping points is already present, and the 2007 Intergovernmental Panel on Climate Change report confirms much of Schellnhurer's prognosis.

Water Wars?

As nations compete over increasingly scarce supplies of water, tensions are bound to increase. This is especially true with waters that flow through several nations. There are some 264 rivers shared by two or more states with 40 percent of the world's population in shared river basins.[74] Turkey, for example, is building a huge complex of some 22 dams on the Tigris and Euphrates rivers, waters historically shared with lower-river Syria and Iraq. Robert Engelman of the Population Action Institute notes that as Turkey seeks to expand water resources for its growing population through dam projects over the next 20 years, Syria and Iraq will experience dramatic decreases in their fresh, river water supplies.[75]

Perhaps no dispute is as contentious on water issues as the continuing conflict between Israel and the Palestinians. When Israel seized the West Bank of the Jordan River during the Six-Day War of 1967, in part to prevent Jordan from diverting the Jordan River for its own purposes, it gained access not only to the headwaters of the river but also to the western aquifer, and thus increased its water supply by half. Israel now draws up to 75 percent of the upper Jordan River. So while Israelis use water for extensive irrigation as well as lawns and other consumer uses, Palestinians are dependent on water trucks to bring water past border crossings at high prices.

The Oslo Accords of 1995 held a promise that Israel would assist the Palestinians in finding new sources of water. However, in reality the Accords solidified Israel's lion's share of aquifer waters, providing a growing Palestinian population with 15,000 gallons of water per year while Israelis are allowed 65,000 gallons per year. In the words of Fred Pearce, "In 1964 Israel hijacked the waters of the Jordan River. There is no other way to put it." The Accords only certified the theft.[76]

The newly constructed wall separating Israel from Palestinian territories also cuts off Palestinian farmers from wells and pumped supplies they could rightfully claim, preventing Palestinians from accessing a quarter of the water previously taken from the western aquifer. In 2002 the average domestic water allowance per person per day for a Palestinian was 71 liters (18 gallons); for an Israeli, 350 liters (92 gallons). In the West Bank area, Palestinians have been forbidden to build new wells and hardly ever are allowed to repair old ones.[77] For the Israelis there is no talk of giving up water deemed "necessary" for a lifestyle worth defending—often conflated with survival. Martin Sherman, political scientist at the University of Tel Aviv, puts it this way: "Frequent showers, swimming pools, well-groomed private gardens, and public parks all involve water consumption, without which adequate standards of modern life cannot be attained."[78]

Other critical areas of conflict involve Bangladesh, India and Nepal, and Egypt, Sudan, and Ethiopia. The geographical features of so many cross-border rivers and water basins can easily become disputes between upstream and downstream users, and now between upstream and downstream states.[79] The flowing Mekong provides another case study. Largely due to the years of warfare in the regions around the Mekong—Cambodia, Laos, Vietnam, Thailand—the Mekong remained the least modified among the world's central rivers. Now a battle looms among the surrounding nations, including China, the source of the Mekong's waters. Dams, canals, and channels are built already, and more are being developed as countries see the fast-flowing waters as vast economic resources for river traffic, energy, irrigation, urbanization, and other "development" projects. Where once even the poor of Cambodia could survive the year because of the abundant fishing along the Mekong and its tributaries, fishing is dwindling. In the words of Chris Barlow of the Mekong River Commission, "The fisheries are a source of natural wealth for the poor. . . . But if the fisheries are destroyed, their only alternative would be a job in a factory in Phnom Penh making textiles for the West."[80]

If any conflict could be seen as a "water war" in the United States, it lies in the Western states around the Colorado River, which flows through seven states. The once-mighty Colorado—site of adventurers rafting down its waters in the Grand Canyon—now delivers almost no water to the sea, producing instead a shrinking river delta. In addition to the impact of dams discussed above, cities are taking an increasing amount of the Colorado's waters for urban and suburban users, and agriculture still consumes the largest portion of the river. Irrigation keeps the fields in the Imperial Valley and others in Arizona and California producing bumper crops for consumers and export. Yet because the farming with Colorado water is subsidized, waste is rampant through evaporation from reservoirs, ponds, and flooded fields, and water-thirsty crops such as alfalfa end up claiming remaining waters.

The lower states now contend that they have guaranteed entitlement rights according to "prior appropriation," i.e., whoever first puts the water to use has the right to future use of that amount,[81] no matter what the state of the river. The upper states are not happy to deliver their scarcer waters to cities such as Phoenix and Los Angeles instead of Denver and the farmers in their states—so they argue that the last users to come on line should give up their access in a crisis. In the words of one Denver newspaper, "It could stack up as the biggest water war in the West. Arizona could get shut off completely."[82]

The competition for water pits growing urban centers such as Los Angeles, Las Vegas, and Reno on the one hand against farmers on the other. For many farmers water has become a commodity worth more than their crops, and they have begun trading their water rights to cities.[83] But the ultimate doom for desert farming may result from salinization; water returning to the rivers from field use picks up increasing amounts of salt, approximately 10 million tons per year which never reach the sea.[84] Water won the West, but death by salt may be the ultimate price to pay.

Less intense but certainly no less important will be "wars" fought in courts or disputed in the international arena, contentions around public and private ownership, and most fundamentally, arguments about water rights. In a chilling report, eleven retired U.S. generals argued that climate change may prolong the war on terrorism and produce instability in several states which will further threaten security and stability. The report, commissioned by the U.S. government-financed Center for Naval Analyses, sees climate change as "a threat multiplier for instability in some of the most volatile regions of the world." This multiplier effect will worsen poor living conditions in many nations that may increase migrating and refugee peoples.[85] Potential water wars call for a "war" to combat climate change soon.

Conclusion

The past two chapters have discussed the current threats and future dangers to the waters of the world. Water is suffering—from continuing pollution, impacts of large dams and reservoirs, river diversions and contamination, population and consumption growth, agricultural and industrial demands, groundwater withdrawals, global warming, actual and potential water battles. Water, we are reminded, is renewable, a *gift* in the frame of religious traditions, but finite, and our human "footprints" have reduced the amount of fresh, clean water at a time when human demands are increasing. Our next set of discussions will involve the attempts of national and international organizations to address the global water crisis, issues surrounding water as a right, water rights, and the ethical questions surrounding water access, ownership, and distribution. Is water a right, a resource, a commodity, a tradable good? Who manages water and for the benefit of whom? To whom does water belong? Then in subsequent chapters we will look at the motivating powers of religious traditions in moving their adherents to take responsible, sustainable actions for the Earth's common good and finally at positive and hopeful steps that address the global water crisis.

Notes

1. E. C. Pielou, *Fresh Water* (Chicago: University of Chicago Press, 1998), 206.

2. Maggie Black, *The No-Nonsense Guide to Water* (Oxford: New Internationalist, 2004), 116.

3. Fred Pearce, *When the Rivers Run Dry: Water—the Defining Crisis of the Twenty-First Century* (Boston: Beacon, 2006), 134.

4. Pielou, *Fresh Water*, 205–206.

5. United Nations, *Water for People, Water for Life: The United Nations World Water Development Report* (Geneva: UNESCO, 2003), 255.

6. Kader Asmal, "Chair's Preface," in *Dams and Development: Report of the World Commission on Dams* (London: Earthscan, 2000), ii.

7. Robert Bowen, *Surface Water* (New York: Wiley, 1982), 9.

8. Robert Kandel, *Water from Heaven: The Story of Water from the Big Bang to the Rise of Civilization and Beyond* (New York: Columbia University Press, 2003), 196.

9. For full account see Marc de Villiers, *Water: The Fate of Our Most Precious Resource* (New York: Houghton Mifflin, 2000), 235–239.

10. Phillip Ball, *Life's Matrix: A Biography of Water* (New York: Farrar, Straus & Giroux, 1999), 359.

11. Black, *No-Nonsense Guide*, 116.

12. Yasuo Endo, *Suigenren* founder, Masa Ujiie, Atsuko Masano, reporter, personal interview, Tokyo, 14 October 2005.

13. For full discussion of the case and the actual court decisions, see *Belize Reporter*, 3 June 2001, and the web site of the Environmental Law Alliance Worldwide, which supported BACONGO: www.elaw.org/resources.

14. BACONGO flier opposed to the Vaca Dam, and personal interview with Sharon Matola, director, Belize Zoo, one of the BACONGO nine, 28 March 2006; personal interviews with Martin Allegria, Department of the Environment, and Ismael Fabro, chief executive officer, Ministry of Natural Resources and the Environment, Belize, 24 March 2006.

15. Executive summary, in World Commission on Dams, *Dams and Development: Report of the World Commission on Dams* (London: Earthscan, 2000), xxx.

16. Arundhati Roy, from "The Greater Common Good," in Arundhati Roy, *The Cost of Living* (New York: Modern Library, 1999), 14–15; see also the case against dams in India in Vandana Shiva, *Water Wars: Privatization, Pollution, and Profit* (Cambridge, Mass.: South End Press, 2002).

17. Pielou, *Fresh Water*, 206.

18. Pearce, *When Rivers Run Dry*, 141.

19. Pielou, *Fresh Water*, 207–208.

20. Pielou, *Fresh Water*, 208.

21. Quoted in Pearce, *When Rivers Run Dry*, 143.

22. Pearce, *When Rivers Run Dry*, 145.

23. World Commission on Dams, *Dams and Development*, 64, 66.

24. Pielou, *Fresh Water*, 211–212.

25. Executive summary in World Commission on Dams, *Dams and Development*, xxx.

26. Executive summary in World Commission on Dams, *Dams and Development*, xxxi.

27. Pearce, *When Rivers Run Dry*, 152.

28. Pearce, *When Rivers Run Dry*, 137.

29. World Commission on Dams, *Dams and Development*, 310, 319.

30. Michael Specter, "The Last Drop: Confronting the Possibility of a Global Catastrophe," *New Yorker* 82, no. 34 (23 October 2006), 64.

31. United Nations, *Water for People, Water for Life*, 160–162; United Nations, *Water: A Shared Responsibility. The United Nations World Water Development Report 2* (New York: Berghahn, 2006), 89–90.

32. Bowen, *Surface Water*, 23.

33. United Nations, *Water for People, Water for Life*, 168–169.

34. Bowen, *Surface Water*, 21.

35. Bowen, *Surface Water*, 22.

36. Bowen, *Surface Water*, 23–24.

37. Kandel, *Water from Heaven*, 157.

38. Pearce, *When Rivers Run Dry*, 57–58.

39. Pearce, *When Rivers Run Dry*, 59–60.

40. Ricardo Petrella, *The Water Manifesto* (London: Zed Books, 2001), 80–82.

41. Annie Shuppy, "Prime Numbers," H₂OU." *The Chronicle of Higher Education*, 3 Nov. 2006, A7.

42. "Aquafina Labels to Spell Out Source—Tap Water," CNN, at http://cnn.com. 16 June 2007 (accessed 7 August 2007).

43. Quoted in Paul Rauber, "Secrets of the Supermarket" *Sierra* 91, no. 6 (November–December 2006): 55.

44. Quoted in Cameron Woodworth, "Clean Drink of Water: Choices and Responsibilities," *Sound Consumer* (Aug. 2006), 4.

45. Environment, Health and Safety Online, "Drinking Water Information," at http://ehso.com/ehsohome/DrWater/drinkingwater.php#Overview (accessed 22 January 2007).

46. Black, *No-Nonsense Guide*, 102–103.

47. Pearce, *When Rivers Run Dry*, 44; Paul Jeffrey, "Wells Run Dry: Coke Faces Thirsty Opponents in India," *National Catholic Reporter*, 24 March 2006, 12–14.

48. "Around the Globe," *Seattle Times*, 22 September 2006, sec. A. Pearce notes that the amount of water taken by the Kerala plant is not a great deal: "A single local rice farmer with 25 acres could easily be using as much water as the Coca-Cola bottling plant. . . . [T]he state of Plachimara's wells [in Kerala] is not a gross example of a global corporation riding roughshod over locals but simply a typical story of what India is doing itself to its most precious resource" (*When Rivers Run Dry*, 44).

49. Woodworth, "Clean Drink of Water," 4; Sarah Nason, letter to the editor, *PCC Sound Consumer*, October 2006, 5.

50. United Nations, *Water for People, Water for Life*, 204.

51. Ball, *Life's Matrix*, 342–343.

52. Ball, *Life's Matrix*, 343.

53. Ball, *Life's Matrix*, 345.

54. Ball, *Life's Matrix*, 346.

55. Yutaka Kanai and Furukawa Setsu, Conservation Division, Wild Bird Society, Tokyo, Japan, personal interview, 17 October 2005.

56. Michelle Nijhuis, "The Lure of the Lawn: Can Westerners Get Over their Romance with Turf?," *High Country News*, 28 August 2006, 8ff.

57. Nijhuis, "Lure of the Lawn," 10, 12.

58. Pearce, *When Rivers Run Dry*, 306.

59. Kandel, *Water from Heaven*, 214.

60. United Nations, *Water for People, Water for Life*, 227.

61. United Nations, *Water for People, Water for Life*, 229.

62. Black, *No-Nonsense Guide*, 99.

63. B. J. Bergman, "The Hidden Life of Computers," *Sierra*, July–August 1999, 32.

64. United Nations, *Water for People, Water for Life*, 227.

65. Sandi Doughton, "Climate Scientists Surer Than Ever: Man's to Blame," *Seattle Times*, 2 February 2007, sec. A; Robert McClure and Lisa Stiffler, "Scientists Agree: Humans Causing Global Warming," *Seattle Post-Intelligencer*, 2 February 2007, sec. A.

66. Seth Borenstein, "Report on Climate to Include 'Smoking Gun' on Global Warming," *Seattle Post-Intelligencer*, 23 January 2007, sec. A.

67. Black, *No-Nonsense Guide*, 96, 98.

68. Michelle Nijhuis, "What Happened to Winter?" in *High and Dry: Dispatches on Global Warming from the American West* (Boulder, Colo.: High Country News, Summer 2006), 25–26, 28–29.

69. de Villiers, *Water*, 79–80.

70. Paul Rauber, "Signs of a Changing Planet," *Sierra* 91, no. 4 (July–August 2006), 17.

71. Howard Witt, "Arctic Town Isn't So Hot on Warming," *Chicago Tribune*, as reported in] *Seattle Times*, 6 October 2006, sec. A.

72. Doug Struck, "Scientists Say It's Just a Matter of When," *Washington Post*, 10 Nov. 2006, as reported in] *Seattle Times*, 10 November 2006, sec. A.

73. Julia Whitty, "The Thirteenth Tipping Point," *Mother Jones* 31, no. 6 (November–December 2006), 45–51, 100–101.

74. United Nations, *Water: A Shared Responsibility*, 525.

75. Quoted in Center for Defense Information, "Water, People, Land and Conflict," narrated by Rear Admiral Eugene Carroll; for a more general discussion of the potential for water wars, see Vandana Shiva, *Water Wars: Privatization, Pollution, and Profit* (Cambridge, Mass.: South End Press, 2002).

76. Pearce, *When Rivers Run Dry*, 161–162, 167–168.

77. Pearce, *When Rivers Run Dry*, 160.

78. Quoted in Pearce, *When Rivers Run Dry*, 171.

79. Black, *No-Nonsense Guide*, 19.

80. Quoted in Pearce, *When Rivers Run Dry*, 104.

81. Ball, *Life's Matrix*, 366.

82. Quoted in Pearce, *When Rivers Run Dry*, 197–198. For an intriguing discussion of water in the American West, see Marc Reisner, *Cadillac Desert: The American West and Its Disappearing Water* (New York: Viking, 1986).

83. Black, *No-Nonsense Guide*, 123.

84. Pearce, *When Rivers Run Dry*, 198–199.

85. "Climate Change May Worsen Instability," *Financial Times*, 16 April 2007, http://www.trughout.org/docs_2006.

~

CHAPTER SIX

Water Management: Privatization, Problems, and Resistance

The next critical resource in short supply will be fresh water, says James Trainor, managing partner of Newgate Capital, which specializes in emerging-market and natural-resource stocks. Lake, spring and glacier water fetch almost as much as refined petroleum. China, with 80 percent of its rivers too polluted for fish, is importing water from Alaska. That's just the start.[1]

As seen in earlier chapters, wastewater and sewage pose increasingly serious problems around the globe, especially around large population centers in developing countries. At the same time in the modern period, improved water and sanitation measures have ensured a healthier urban area and population throughout the world. Public health engineers rested their programs on the premise that, at least until recently, governments should provide clean water and sewage disposal. The governing principle for the International Drinking Water Supply and Sanitation Decade, established for 1981–1990, was: "access to water and sanitation services was a social right, justified on grounds of public health, to be provided principally at the public expense." The Decade failed from, first, the effort to transfer the sewage system model used in developed countries to the majority of the world's rural and urban populations.[2] Second, the shift to private companies as the main providers of water, which resulted in higher prices to ensure profits for shareholders, likewise ensured failure.

I argue that private or even public–private management of water and sanitation compromises people's rights to water, fails to provide adequate oversight, and ensures continuing water scarcity for vulnerable populations. If, as the 2006 UN World Water Development Report maintains, good management (not supply) constitutes the central concern for the twenty-first century,[3] then public management or public oversight of transparent private management is essential. Only then will the governing principles of a new water ethic, such as equity, transparency, participation, sustainability, and special provisions for the poor and marginalized, be ensured. This chapter investigates *how* we first arrived at privatization and highlights the forces behind the drive to privatize water. The remaining sections examine the resistance to privatization, a resistance that reveals the deep problems involved and points to the necessity of local, participatory, transparent, equitable management.

Privatization and Regulation

Historically, as urban centers proliferated in Europe and the United States in the nineteenth century, private companies supplied water to urban populations. However, because of transportation expense, poor water quality, the need for large-scale infrastructure investment, and the failure of private companies to supply poorer areas of cities and the countryside, the states and municipalities in these regions assumed water management and supply.[4] To this day, public agencies still supply over 80 percent of people in the European Union countries and the United States, with the significant exception of France, the leader in privatization.[5]

In the global South, however, in the twentieth century and now the twenty-first century, as urbanization increased rapidly in developing countries, private water suppliers provided water to the poor, which came in the form of jerrycans or tankers; however, their costs were several times that of water delivered by public services to the middle and upper classes.[6] Until the 1980s water was seen as a public issue, mainly at the municipal level, certainly in the developed and even in the developing world where inadequate supplies had to be supplemented by local private vendors.

In the 1980s, developing countries found themselves unable to meet their loan obligations, in part due to the rise in interest rates throughout the 1970s, but also due to internal corruption and other factors, such as wars, dictatorships, and civil unrest. As a consequence, international lending agencies, the World Monetary Fund and the World Bank, imposed rules forcing nations to open public enterprises such as water to privatization. For example, between 1988 and 1992 alone "US$1.6 billion in revenue was obtained by 'developing' countries from the privatization of public enterprises."[7] Lack of market competition also pushed states to open their resources and services to private companies. Finally, urbanization dramatically increased the pressure on public sources to provide potable water for millions around the globe and helped push the drive to privatization as part of needed reforms.

By the beginning of the twenty-first century, well over one hundred cities in developing countries had water supplies controlled by large multinational companies. Water management presented particularly difficult issues, such as updating broken and outmoded lines, making larger infrastructure investment, building or remodeling facilities, providing greater access to poorer economic groups, dealing with government bureaucracy and often corruption, experiencing long delays in gaining access to the water market, and the vagaries of the water market itself. These factors resulted in a swift reduction in water market players to ten. Two large French companies that control over 70 percent of the privatization process now dominate the market: ONDEO/Suez Lyonnaise des Eaux, now called Suez, and Vivendi/General des Eaux.[8] Suez operates in 130 countries, while Vivendi (recently renamed Veolia) is stationed in over 90.[9] The next largest group includes another French company, Bouygues-SAUR, the German–English partners RWE-Thames Water, the U.S.–U.K. partners, Bechtel and United Utilities, and until its demise, Enron-Azurix.[10] The remaining four players, three British and one American, are not yet capable of mounting an aggressive drive for markets against the leaders.

The basic assumptions behind water privatization increasingly value water "as a scarce commodity" and see that the failure to view water in this manner "lies at the heart of the water industry's problem."[11] The World Bank representatives to the World Water Forum at The Hague in 2000 spoke of privatization as "historically inevitable, using the phrase 'there is no alternative.'"[12] A July 2003 report in the *Economist* stated the reigning ideology succinctly, arguing that water must be treated "as a business like any other."[13] This ideology will be challenged by a new water ethic.

The World Bank views the problems surrounding water and sanitation, namely, the poor quality of the water supply and the lack of adequate supplies, as the results of state "overextension." Their remedy lies in moving water management from the public to the private sector to provide "cheaper services."[14] This premise understands water as a capital, tradable, profitable good rather than as a subsidized public service, in need of "cost-reflective pricing" and "commercialization."[15] There are important alternatives.

The World Bank, the International Monetary Fund, and donors have demanded that debtor countries sign water privatization agreements as a condition for debt relief and continued loans. In 2000 alone, the IMF required twelve nations, including eight in sub-Saharan Africa, to include water

privatization as part of their loan agreements.[16] A 1992 paper of the World
Bank, "Improving Water Resources Management," remarks: "When water services are reliable, the poor are willing to pay for them, and . . . when service
is not reliable, the poor pay more for less, typically from street vendors."[17]
These organizations interpret the very fact that poorer people pay higher
prices for their water as evidence that they are willing to pay higher prices.[18]

These international agencies argue, then, that the failure of governments
to meet water needs, the natural scarcity of water, the economic rather than
the public value of water, and the assumed "willingness" of the poor to pay
for water prove the need for continued privatization. They pay little attention to the methods utilized by localized rural and urban populations over the
centuries. There have not been significant challenges, until recently, to the
dominant ideology of privatizing water and transferring water management
schemes from the industrialized world to poorer regions.

International Regulations: NAFTA, WTO, and GATS

The World Trade Organization has instituted privatization through free trade
rules, pressuring lending agencies to privatize water as a solution to water
shortages and as a way to relieve indebtedness through structural adjustment
programs. The General Agreement on Trade in Services (GATS) focuses on
the deregulation of services such as water and opening those services to trade
among nations. However, under these guidelines governments cannot dis-
criminate between local service suppliers and foreign companies, regardless
of whether the local supplier is a community nonprofit and the foreign supplier is a large water corporation.[19] At the WTO Doha meeting in November 2001, the United States positioned water into the Ministerial Declaration, which refers to "the reduction or, as appropriate, elimination of tariff
and nontariff barriers to environmental goods and services," in other words,
water.[20]

According to the rules of the North American Free Trade Agreement
(NAFTA), water is defined as "a tradable good, obligating all levels of government . . . to sell their water resources to the highest bidder under threat
of being sued by private companies." Furthermore, under the Free Trade
Agreement of the Americas, "foreign investors will be able to sue and demand compensation from governments for any law or rule that affects their
profitability."[21] A recent study of loans to forty countries from the International Monetary Fund in 2000 reveals that "agreements in 12 [countries] included conditions imposing water privatization or full cost recovery," for example, in Tanzania, Rwanda, and Niger.[22] British Columbia now faces an

example of this rule. The U.S. company Sun Belt Water sued the Canadian government for a violation of investor rights according to NAFTA, after the company "lost a contract to export water from Canada to California due to a 1991 ban on bulk water export imposed by the government of British Columbia."[23] The case is yet unresolved.

In an effort to ward off such water privatization threats, in 1999 Canada banned all water exports by supertankers or pipelines. This proposal was necessary since the NAFTA treaty did not ban water exports, even though Canada's trade minister at the time of the NAFTA negotiations thought that water had been exempted.[24] The lawyer in British Columbia acting for Sun Belt Water stated that the export prohibition was actually immoral: "a cruel and inhumane response to the real needs of people throughout the world."[25] The corporate pressure continues for Canada's abundant waters.

Results of Privatization

The results of privatization are mixed at best, poor, unjust, and unsustainable at worst. Here is a quick summary of examples in both developed and underdeveloped countries. First, prices have risen in some cases drastically, and second, quality has deteriorated. In France, water privatization caused water quality to deteriorate and increased customer fees by 150 percent. The French government categorized the water received by 5.2 million citizens as "bacterially unacceptable."[26] A similar result occurred in England, along with an increase in customer disconnection. Rates increased dramatically (106 percent) and profits for the ten private English and Welsh water utilities jumped 692 percent.[27] In Germany, a 2003 study funded by the World Health Organization concluded that "major potential consequences of privatization include a tendency toward merely adhering to existing limit values rather than making [costly] efforts toward minimizing pollutants, and a higher risk of accidents that cause pollution of the water supply."[28]

The discrepancies between publicly and privately supplied water in the developing world are even more striking. For example, in Manila, the Philippines, the price of water has increased by 500 percent since 2001, and cholera has broken out.[29] In addition prices vary a great deal: the price for 1 cubic meter of water in Manila is US$0.11 for a household connection by the middle and upper classes, while the cost is US$4.74 from a vender for the poor. While not as extreme, the differences in Karachi, Pakistan, are $0.14 for connection versus $0.81 for vendor; in Phnom Penh, Cambodia, $0.09 versus $1.64; and in Ulan Bator, Mongolia, $0.04 versus $1.51.[30] These are only a few of the many cases around the world.

The Belize government privatized the water services to Cascal Company of the United Kingdom in 2000. Prices rose immediately. The company concentrated on increasing supply rather than on the need for greater access, water treatment, and sewage disposal. Then due to Cascal's failure to comply with the conditions of the privatization contract, in 2005 the government bought back the water works, but at a higher price than received in the original transaction.[31]

In Ghana some rural communities have had to pay 5 to 10 percent of capital costs for new wells and boreholes even prior to installation and must also pay for operation and maintenance costs. If they cannot pay, they do not have access.[32] There were "rampant water shortages," and private vendors sold water at 60 percent more than the original price. In addition, where illnesses from guinea worm, a water-borne infection, were almost nonexistent ten years ago, there has been "a surge in guinea worm infection."[33] Similarly, in South Africa a contract with Suez from 1994–1996 caused service costs to increase 600 percent, while costs of water connections rose 100 percent. Based on "cost recovery" policies, over ten million people were cut off. As a result, the cases of cholera rose, and pollution of waters increased due to uncontrolled effluents.[34] Under privatization, water availability will move "up" from poor rural communities toward wealthier urban markets. When markets set the limits on water, renewal of water and natural flows receives little to no consideration. The water crisis is worsening.[35]

Resistance to Privatization

A growing resistance to privatization has emerged in several regions around the world. In October 2004, in a popular plebiscite, Uruguayans approved by 64.6 percent a "constitutional reform that defines water as a good belonging to the public trust and guarantees civil society's participation in the management of the country's hydrological resources."[36] The constitutional amendment establishes the principles of public participation and sustainability, key principles in a new water ethic. Private provisions for water and sanitation were declared illegal, and a key declaration, *Z disposition*, relating to the private water transnationals, reads: "the compensation that could arise as a result of the entrance in effect of these reforms will not generate reparation for future lost profits, and only debts not gradually being paid off will be reimbursed."[37] As we will see in the case of Cochabamba, Bolivia, below, this is an important lesson learned in resisting privatization.

Numerous other examples of such resistance to privatization and efforts to support alternatives have occurred or are occurring around the globe: Porto

Alegre and Recife, Brazil; Olavanna, Kereala state, India; Penang, Malaysia; Grenoble, France; Atlanta, Georgia, Stockton, California, and before Hurricane Katrina, New Orleans, Louisiana, in the United States; Bogat, Colombia; Savelugu, Ghana; Buenos Aires, Argentina; Johannesburg and Cape Town, South Africa. The legislature of El Salvador is still debating a proposed new law that would open the now-public water company to privatization.[38] A 2004 law in Hamburg, Germany, forbids *any* form of privatization.

In the United States, in 2003, citizens in the city of Stockton, California, with mighty efforts opposed the privatization of the Stockton Water Company. They subsequently lost that effort, and Thames of England now manages Stockton's water supply.[39] In March 2006, the citizens of Barnstead, New Hampshire, voted to void the "personhood" status of corporations in order to prevent the town's public water supply from being usurped by industry bottlers.[40] Examples from all parts of the world abound.[41] At this point a case study will help clarify the issues involved.

Cochabamba, Bolivia

In 1999, Cochabamba, Bolivia's third largest city, and home to over 600,000 people within a surrounding area of 1 million, became a major test site for the controversial privatization of water facilities. In 1997, the World Bank suggested privatization of water utilities in Cochabamba, noting that benefits would include securing capital for water development as well as experienced water management. World Bank officials told then-president Gonzalo Sánchez de Lozada that privatization was a necessary stipulation in order for Bolivia to obtain $600 million in international debt relief.[42]

In September of 1999, Bolivian officials contracted with Tenari Water (*Aguas de Tenari*)—a consortium of the California engineering company, Bechtel, and Bolivian interests of the governing party—to lease Cochabamba's water until the year 2039.[43] Officials passed Law 2029 that stipulated that all community water projects were illegal; only Tenari could distribute water. People could not construct their own wells, and even water collection tanks were prohibited. Local townships could neither collect water taxes nor determine where wells could be dug.[44]

Within weeks of the law's implementation, Bechtel imposed rate increases of up to 200 percent on local families. The local minimum earning wage was $60 a month and Bechtel charged up to $15 per month for water in homes.[45] In November 1999, local factory workers, farmers, and environmental and other community groups formed a coalition called the Coalition for the Defense of Water and Life, *La Coordinadora*. In response to the rate increases the Coalition organized its first mobilization of over 10,000 on December 1,

1999, and called a strike in January 2000 that closed down the city for three days, forcing the government to sign an agreement to address water rates.[46] When the government failed to honor the agreement, La Coordinadora returned to the streets. The government of de Lozada's successor, the 1970s dictator Hugo Banzer, declared the march illegal and pledged to protect the contract. Some 1,200 heavily armed police and soldiers were sent to the march, wounding over 175 people with tear gas canisters and beatings. In February 2000, the government agreed to roll back rates for six months.[47]

When the government again failed to fulfill its promises, La Coordinadora called another strike in April for the complete cancellation of the Tenari contract. After two days, the government met with Coordinadora leaders with moderation from Cochabamba's Catholic archbishop. However, police bombarded the meeting and arrested the Coordinadora leaders, including spokesperson Oscar Olivera, and Banzar imposed a state of martial law.[48] The public immediately responded with continued protests. The local television station was on air as Bolivian army captain and graduate of the U.S. School of the Americas, Robinson Iriarte, fired rounds into a crowd of protestors and killed an unarmed seventeen-year-old boy, Victor Hugo Daza.[49]

After negative international response, Bechtel officials working under the auspices of Tenari were hurriedly removed from the country. Finally on April 9, 2000, the government canceled the contract with Tenari and turned over control to a publicly controlled water company, SEMAPA.[50] Then in November 2001, Bechtel filed a $25 million legal indemnity suit against Bolivia through the World Bank's International Centre for the Settlement of Investment Disputes (ICSID).[51] In the meantime the Bolivian Internal Revenue Service demanded 45 million bolivianos from SEMAPA.[52]

Finally in January 2006, the ICSID resolved the dispute, but each side interpreted the results differently. Bechtel notes on its web site: "the claims against the Bolivian government currently before the ICSID will be withdrawn. There will be no compensation paid by the Government of Bolivia or Aguas del Tunari [Bechtel subsidiary] for the termination of the concession and the withdrawal of the claim."[53] On the other hand, the Democracy Center, which had followed the case for years, reported that Bechtel abandoned the case "for a token payment of 2 bolivianos (30 cents)." The Center's report continues: "This is the first time that a major corporation has ever dropped a major international trade case such as this one as a direct result of global public pressure."[54] The long struggle of the people of Cochabamba has become a symbol both of resistance to privatization and of the actual realization of a democratic, participatory, socially responsible, and transparent public management system. In a later chapter we will explore the guiding norms that emerge from the Cochabamba story and that reflect principles of a new water ethic.

Privatization Processes

The actual reality of deregulation of public agencies and consequent privatization of water and sewage treatment is a complicated matter. Currently the major arguments *for* privatization concern the state's or municipality's inefficiency, waste, mismanagement, political interference, artificial subsidies of public agencies, and the need to meet the growing demands for clean and dependable sources of water. However, as Judith Rees notes in her analysis of regulation and private participation in water matters, a pure market solution and total privatization does not necessarily improve performance or meet other problems.

> There is no reason why private monopolies should be any more efficient or responsive to customer demands than public ones. They need not employ least-cost production methods, may have few incentives to innovate and will not necessarily provide the quantity or quality of water products for which customers are willing and able to pay.[55]

What is evident from Rees's study is that public regulation of some sort is absolutely essential for such a scarce resource as water. The precise way in which regulation by public agencies will actually interface with private initiatives varies a great deal. Rees points to two of several formats of privatization that are used most often: divestment and concessions. Divestment is a form of privatization that "transfers ownership of infrastructure assets into private hands as well as giving the private companies responsibility for all operations, maintenance, revenue raising and investment."[56] Rees argues that the more complete the divestment by the government agencies, "the more comprehensive are the regulatory needs."

Although there is little difference between divestment and concessions, the political climate often dictates that an alternative to divestment be used. Through concessions the water assets technically remain public, but the government "concedes" the water to a private company for a number of years, typically 25–30. The company then gains "usage rights over the assets and has complete responsibility for operations, system maintenance and new investments."[57] Although the concession system seems to introduce some form of competition that should produce greater efficiency and reduce the government's burden for regulation, Rees notes that there is still a strong tendency toward monopoly with its inherent economic inefficiency. The key again, she argues, is some form of public regulation,[58] a principle essential to a new water ethic.

Since 2000, companies are relying less on concessions and more on leases and management arrangements with public authorities. To avoid even the use of the unpopular term *privatization* such ventures are called *public–private partnerships* or *private sector participation*. However, these arrangements "still refer to the same kinds of contractual relationships with the private sector."[59]

Even major water companies such as Suez are questioning the existing models of water and sanitation privatization when attempting to service rural areas and poor areas in major cities. Suez recently announced that it is reducing its work in developing countries by up to one third, and SAUR reported to the water division of the World Bank that water to the poor cannot be delivered by the private sector. The risks are too high, and the needs too great.[60] The London International Institute for Environment and Development likewise agrees that however private companies are engaged in management of water and sanitation, privatization "should not be promoted internationally as if it provides the key to achieving the water and sanitation targets within the Millennium Development Goals," set at the 2002 Earth Summit in Johannesburg, of halving the numbers of people without water and sanitation by 2015.[61]

Women and Water Management

In her challenging and provocative analysis of Western forms of development in India and third world countries (forms she calls "maldevelopment"), Vandana Shiva, physicist, philosopher, and feminist, places the work of women at the forefront in the discussion of forests, rivers, and food production. Commenting on the UN Decade for Women, Shiva sees that the failure to include women in forms of development resulted from the very assumption that the pursuit of the Western forms of development would lead somehow to improvements in the lives of women. The cause for women's increasing "under-development" was rather "their enforced but asymmetric participation in [development], by which they bore the costs but were excluded from the benefits." Development projects, such as the large dams discussed earlier, "destroyed women's productivity both by removing land, water, and forests from their management and control, as well as through the ecological destruction of soil, water, and vegetation systems so that nature's productivity and renewability were impaired."[62]

As she develops her analysis of the impacts of development in such projects as dams, deep water drilling, and groundwater draining, Shiva describes as an example the efforts of women in the Doon Valley area to stop mining operations that were poisoning the local streams. Shiva quotes one of the leaders of the movement for a key question for our discussion: who manages the waters?[63] For centuries women have been the water managers until the colonial period, when Western, "hard" forms of development removed local, largely women's control of management.

In the long course of history women have gathered the wood, collected the water, produced the food in the fields necessary for village and town life. The dominant patterns of eighteenth- and nineteenth-century industrialization changed all that, replacing women with male-dominated managerial systems. As long as women's work in collecting water and other activities is deemed "unproductive" in today's global economies, we will continue to rely on a model of productivity, consumption, and development harmful to the waters of the Earth. As a hopeful sign, Shiva points to the role of women, along with others, in struggles all over—not just India but in other parts of the world—to reclaim water rights, oppose more dams and mining, restore streams and watersheds.[64]

In many parts of the world women still suffer great gender inequality, and this in turn influences their power and place in managing water issues. As water management became more centralized, modernized, and more technologically sophisticated, women lost their places to men in a hierarchical power structure. These developments are part of the larger patterns of contemporary development projects, based on importing models and practices from Western countries to developing nations.[65] In addition, the processes whereby women began to lose control over water management have become even more acute under various privatization schemes involving large, male-dominated corporations and management processes.[66]

At the same time, as Shiva and others point out, there is a resurgence of powerful forces throughout the Western world and in developing countries reasserting the roles of women in water. These range from the many protests against dam construction in India led by such people as Arundhati Roy, to well-dressing rituals in the United Kingdom to "reclaim" the powers of wells formerly dedicated to Celtic goddesses, then women Christian saints, to increasing numbers of women entering water engineering and science careers—spanning approaches from the religious to the scientific.[67]

Women are often defined as the main providers and users of water; they play many roles in the areas of water and sanitation, roles recognized at the World Water Forum of 2003. However, given the current operative economic models, women's "subordination and the consequent barriers to their active involvement in influencing water programmes are barely addressed. There is limited attention to women's rights to water and what these would mean in practice in poor communities where women's status is often very low."[68] The *United Nations World Water Development Report 2* of 2006 also recognizes the important and critical contributions of women; women are too often excluded from water management and "This exclusion inevitably makes water service provision . . . less responsive to real need."[69]

The assignment of water issues to women is a critical element in need of further exploration. If young girls must travel increasingly long distances to collect water and then are assigned the roles of water conservation and use in daily chores, what impact do these actions have upon their education, the proven ingredient for women's personal and collective advancement? Certainly the key principles of respect for the whole person, equality, and participation examined in the next chapter come into play here.

Conclusion

Private initiative and operations can often bring efficiencies to the acquisition, allocation, and distribution of resources such as water. Yet even the market conditions and circumstances in Rees's discussion illustrate the need for some form or forms of government-run public regulations to assure the ability to deliver a public good such as water to the public in a safe, efficient, accessible manner. However, in addition to these market approaches to the place of regulation, there are important ecological and cultural—social and *religious*—principles involved in such a scarce factor as water, an element of planet life that is the most fundamental and basic good to all life on Earth and to Earth itself. Even in the case of privatization, the 2006 *United Nations World Water Development Report 2* argues that "Successful water services privatization will require a clear set of rules that promotes both equity and efficiency in water distribution, effectively enforced by an independent government regulator adequately equipped with authority, finances and human capacities."[70] In addition the report recognizes that the actual potential for privatization was overstated in the 1990s, and there is now declining interest on the part of private companies and the World Bank. Here the factors of private regulation and private "ownership" shift to an additional dimension when the fundamental right to water, a necessary condition for the right to life, is placed alongside the ways in which water is currently being reduced to a commodity for consumers who have the financial means and mobility to secure it.

These contrasting views are well illustrated by speakers at the 2003 World Water Forum at Kyoto, Japan. Gerard Payen, CEO of Suez, argued that "the challenge here is to provide access to all earth's people at affordable prices. My experience as a water professional is that it is possible. . . . Public-private partnerships [PPPs] deliver huge results that can be win-win projects which benefit all parties." As Payen spoke, activists sitting in the auditorium held up large *lie meters* with the arrow at its highest level. On the other hand, Maude Barlow, chair of the Council of Canadians and author of *Blue Gold*, replied: "The political question really is who owns water and gets to control water. . . . On the one side are those who see water as an economic good to put on the open market for sale to the highest bidder. On the other hand, you are going to hear the voices of the growing civil society movement which have a vision of water as part of the global commons and treat it as a public trust for all time by governments everywhere."[71] Those civil movements have gained ground.

"Public–private partnerships," "economic good," "global commons," "public trust"—in the following chapter we will examine these different and contrasting approaches and the principles behind them. For precisely in that discussion the differences will emerge among principles, goals, and strategies surrounding water as a right with corresponding obligations on the one hand, water as a natural, some say sacred, resource essential for all the Earth, and water as a global, economic commodity useful for the benefit of the greatest number. This discussion will lead to a "new water ethos" and "new water ethic," that is, a perspective on water for the common good, the good of the commons, and norms for water use, distribution, and allocation, which in turn will guide practices and policies surrounding water for the twenty-first century.

Notes

1. Jane Bryant Quinn, "Investing Goes Back to Basics," *Newsweek*, 19 December 2005, 57.

2. Maggie Black, *The No-Nonsense Guide to Water* (Oxford: New Internationalist, 2004), 32–33.

3. United Nations, *Water: A Shared Responsibility. The United Nations World Water Development Report 2* (New York: Berghahn, 2006), 47–48, 520, especially chap. 6.

4. Karen Bakker, "Archipelagos and Networks: Urbanization and Water Privatization in the South," *Geographical Journal* 169.4 (2003): 328–341, 329.

5. David Hall, "Introduction," in *Reclaiming Public Water*, eds. Belén Balanyá et al. (Amsterdam: Transnational Institute and Corporate Europe Observatory, 2005), 22.

6. Hall, "Introduction," 22.

7. Bakker, "Archipelagos and Networks," 335.

8. Bakker, "Archipelagos and Networks," 330.

9. Maude Barlow and Tony Clarke, *Blue Gold: The Fight to Stop the Corporate Theft of the World's Water* (New York: New Press, 2002), 107.

10. Barlow and Clarke, *Blue Gold*, 107.

11. Bakker, "Archipelagos and Networks," 335.

12. Quoted in Hall, "Introduction," 16.

13. John Peet, survey, "Water," *Economist* (19 July 2003), quoted in Black, *No-Nonsense Guide*, 70.

14. Bakker, "Archipelagos and Networks," 335.

15. Bakker, "Archipelagos and Networks," 335.

16. Tony Clarke and David A. McDonald, "Water Privateers," *Alternatives Journal* 29.2 (Spring 2003): 10.

17. Quoted in Vandana Shiva, *Water Wars: Privatization, Pollution, and Profit* (Cambridge, Mass.: South End Press, 2002), 2.

18. Department for International Development, United Kingdom 1998 document, quoted in Bakker, "Archipelagos and Networks," 336.

19. Shiva, *Water Wars*, 94.

20. Shiva, *Water Wars*, 96.

21. Carmelo Ruiz-Marrero, "Free Trade and Water Privatization: The Wet Side of the FTAA," Americas Program, Interhemispheric Resource Center (December 2, 2004): 1–8, 4.

22. Black, *No-Nonsense Guide*, 74.

23. Shiva, *Water Wars*, 97.

24. Marc de Villiers, *Water: The Fate of Our Most Precious Resource* (New York: Houghton Mifflin, 2000), 247–249.

25. Quoted in de Villiers, *Water*, 253.

26. Vandana Shiva, "World Bank, WTO, and Corporate Control over Water," *International Socialist Review*, August–September 2001, 41.

27. Black, *No-Nonsense Guide*, 69.

28. Raner Fehr, Odile Mekel, Martin Lancombe, and Ulrike Wolf, "Towards Health Impact Assessment of Drinking-Water Privatization," *Bulletin of the World Health Organization* 81, 6 (June 2003): 408.

29. Carla Montemayor, "Possibilities for Public Water in Manila," in *Reclaiming Public Water*, eds. Belén Balanyá et al. (Amsterdam: Transnational Institute and Corporate Europe Observatory, 2005), 214.

30. Black, *No-Nonsense Guide*, 81.

31. Martin Allegria, Department of the Environment, Ministry of Natural Resources, Belmopan, Belize, personal interview, 24 March 2006.

32. Rudolf Amenga-Etego, "Stalling the Big Steal," *New Internationalist*, March 2003, 20.

33. Hassan Adam, "Against the Current: Community-Controlled Water Delivery in Savelugu, Ghana," in *Reclaiming Public Water*, eds. Belén Balanyá et al. (Amsterdam: Transnational Institute and Corporate Europe Observatory, 2005), 144–145.

34. Dale McKinley, "The Struggle against Water Privatization in South Africa," in *Reclaiming Public Water*, eds. Belén Balanyá et al. (Amsterdam: Transnational Institute and Corporate Europe Observatory, 2005), 182–184. See *Reclaiming Public Water* for other examples of increased costs in Indonesia, Malaysia, Bolivia, Mexico, and elsewhere.

35. Shiva, "World Bank," 41.

36. Ruiz-Marrero, "Free Trade," 225.

37. Quoted in Carlos Santos and Albert Villarreal, "Uruguay: Victorious Social Struggle for Water," in *Reclaiming Public Water*, eds. Belén Balanyá et al. (Amsterdam: Transnational Institute and Corporate Europe Observatory, 2005), 173, 178–179.

38. CRISPAZ, e-mail to Seattle Community in Solidarity with the People of El Salvador, CISPES, 24 November 2006.

39. "Thirst," produced and directed by Alan Snitow and Deborah Kaufman (Oley, Penn.: Bullfrog Films, Snitow-Kaufman Productions, 2004).

40. Barry Yeoman, "When Is a Corporation Like a Freed Slave?" *Mother Jones*, November–December 2006, 66.

41. For a complete discussion of these cases, see Belén Balanyá et al., eds., *Reclaiming Public Water* (Amsterdam: Transnational Institute and Corporate Europe Observatory, 2005).

42. Jim Shultz, "Bolivia: The Water War Widens," *NACLA Report on the Americas* 36.3(2003): 1.

43. Shultz, "Bolivia," 2.

44. Oscar Olivera with Tom Lewis, *¡Cochabamba! Water War in Bolivia* (Cambridge, Mass.: South End Press, 2004), 9.

45. Shultz, "Bolivia," 2.

46. Shultz, "Bolivia," 2.

47. Olivera, *¡Cochabamba!* 32–34.

48. Shultz, "Bolivia," 2.

49. Shultz, "Bolivia," 2.

50. Shultz, "Bolivia," 2.

51. Shultz, "Bolivia," 3.

52. Tom Lewis, "Directing SEMAPA: An Interview with Luis Sanchez-Gomez," in *¡Cochabamba!*, Oscar Olivera with Tom Lewis (Cambridge, Mass.: South End Press, 2004), 94, note 1. The Water War protests sparked popular protests on several other contentious issues, such as the Coca War, Tax War, and Gas War of 2003; see Tom Lewis, "The Legacy of the *Coordinadora*," 161–171, in Olivera with Lewis, *¡Cochabamba!* for further discussion. Of these issues Olivera states: "The real issue is that the rich of the world come to Bolivia to take away what little there is that could pull Bolivians out of misery. We need to stop this abuse whether it means defending water, gas, or the right to farm coca" (Olivera with Lewis, *¡Cochabamba!*, 176).

53. At www.bechtel.com/newsarticles.487.asp (accessed 6 December 2006).

54. At www.democracyctr.org/bechtel/bechtel-vs-bolivia-htm (accessed 6 December 2006).

55. Judith A. Rees, "Regulation and Private Participation in the Water and Sanitation Sector," TAC Background Papers 1 (1998), 10.

56. Rees, "Regulation," 16.

57. Rees, "Regulation," 18.

58. Rees, "Regulation," 18.

59. Hall, "Introduction," 16.

60. Quoted in Black, No-Nonsense Guide, 79.

61. Quoted in Black, No-Nonsense Guide, 85–86.

62. Vandana Shiva, Staying Alive: Women, Ecology, and Development (Trowbridge, UK: Redwood, 1994), 2–3.

63. Shiva, Staying Alive, 209.

64. Shiva, Staying Alive, 218–224; see also Shiva, Water Wars, 15, 63, 113, 123–124.

65. See, for example, the historical discussion of gender and water in Veronica Strang, "Taking the Waters: Cosmology, Gender and Material Culture in the Appropriation of Water Resources," in Gender, Water, and Development, eds. Anne Coles and Tina Wallace (New York: Berg Books, 2005), 21–38.

66. A. Grossman, N. Johnson, and G. Didhu, Diverting the Flow: A Resource Guide to Gender Rights and Water Privatization (New York: Women's Environment and Development Organization, 2003), quoted by Tina Wallace and Anne Coles, "Water, Gender and Development: An Introduction," in Gender, Water, and Development, eds. Anne Coles and Tina Wallace, 9.

67. Strang, "Taking the Waters," 35–37.

68. Wallace and Coles, "Water, Gender," 8.

69. United Nations, Water: A Shared Responsibility, 16.

70. United Nations, Water: A Shared Responsibility, 71.

71. Quoted in "Thirst," a documentary produced by Alan Snitow and Deborah Kaufman.

CHAPTER SEVEN

~

Rights to Water and a New Water Ethic

It is high time that we humans learned to control the pumping, storage, production, use, conservation and protection of water, on a basis of democracy and solidarity and at every level of the organization of society. . . . To create the conditions for everyone to exercise their fundamental right of access to drinking water—which is a right to life—is a matter of citizenship.[1]

Past failure to recognize the economic value of water has led to wasteful and environmentally damaging uses of the resource. Making water an economic good is an important way of achieving efficient and equitable use.[2]

Since ancient times water rules, regulations, and agreements have existed to provide access to streams, wells, oases, and other water sources. Water presents a very different problem than stationary land—namely, it moves. The systems developed then recognized that water has elements of common ownership, and while rulers and governments regulated, organized, and managed waters, the waters were not "owned." For example, the statutes of Roman emperor Justinian declared "that running water, like the air and the sea, was held in common and could not be owned." Medieval residents of Foxton, a shire near Cambridge, were fined "for widening or diverting the brook, their way of trying to take more than their share of water from the common stream," while the upstream villagers "had to be stopped from fouling the water with their livestock."[3]

From these and other disputes, rules emerged such as "polluter pays" and "riparian rights," which recognized the rights of the various peoples living along rivers and streamways to use the flow, provided they did no damage to other users. For the most part such agreements, regulations, and rules depended upon local control, resembling the systems that many today are calling "water democracies," of which Cochabamba is only one example. In past centuries, more often, community control characterized water uses from Africa, Asia, and Latin America, as well as Europe.

Now at the beginning of the twenty-first century, as clean water becomes more prized and competition for water more acute, water has been identified as a "scarce resource" and a "commodity" to be traded. With the majority of the world's fresh waters somehow managed by dams, diversions, and other means, the "owners" of those means have come to assert greater control, now seen as "ownership" over the waters themselves. In the late nineteenth and early twentieth centuries new principles emerged, gradually replacing the principle of "riparian rights" with principles of "prior appropriation," i.e., whoever arrived first and posted notice could claim rights, over land or water. In the United States, most Eastern states utilize riparian rights of reasonable withdrawals. However, in the Western states the great water battles have been and are being waged today on the principle of "prior appropriation"; water rights became the property of the holder. What has emerged from this principle is the reality "use it or lose it,"[4] not a policy for conservation.

As we saw in the previous chapter, by the 1980s the failures of public authorities to deliver and guarantee adequate fresh water and sanitation ushered in the era of privatization based now on principles of economic exchange. Water as a resource is viewed as a tradable good, and decisions about water are no longer governed by a sense of the common good of communities but rather by private property rights.[5] Private property rights have trumped riparian rights.

Water as a Basic Right

Given all the documents of the late twentieth century on human rights and the emphasis of international organizations such as Amnesty International, it may be surprising to learn that as late as the 1990s there were no explicit documents outlining water as a basic right. While all religious traditions see water as either a direct manifestation of divinity or one of God's free gifts, only the 1989 International Convention on the Rights of the Child asserted the *right* to drinking water and sanitation. Such a right could be *inferred* in the landmark United Nations Declaration of Human Rights of 1948 or the International Covenant on Economic, Social, and Cultural Rights of 1966, and even in the papal encyclical of Pope John XXIII, "Peace on Earth," of 1963; these documents outlined the rights to life, food, and well-being. Water could then be seen as basic to all these rights and so a right itself. However, even these documents and arguments only referred to water as "drinking" water, and "not to rivers, aquifers, or water in a livelihood context" such as fishing, or clean water for bathing or cooking.[6]

The first major conference on water itself was organized in 1977 by the United Nations at Mar del Plata, Argentina, where water was one of the major issues of concern. The UN promoted the International Drinking Water and Sanitation Decade in the 1980s to ensure that all had safe drinking water by 2000, yet the decade fell far short of its goals. The UN Conference on the Environment and Development in Rio de Janeiro in 1992 established the concept of sustainable development in relation to water and led to the institution of World Water Day on March 22 yearly. The World Bank worked with UN agencies to establish the World Water Council (WWC), which sponsors the industry-led World Water Forum. In January 1999, the WWC formed the World Commission on Water in the Twenty-First Century, committed to developing a vision and plans for water based on the work of the WWC.[7] The critical nature of the situation has not gone unnoticed.

Nations too have entered the discussions. In the 1990s the new South African constitution, written after apartheid was overthrown, became one of the first documents to recognize water as a human right, and the country's 1998 water law did state that meeting minimum human needs with an environmental reserve of water has first claim on South Africa's water resources. Other countries took up similar measures. Finally in 2002 the UN Committee on Economic, Social, and Cultural Rights explicitly obligated governments to "progressively extend access to sufficient, affordable, accessible and safe water supplies and to safe sanitation services."[8] However, here too, the document addresses only drinking water, not water for other needs of livelihood.

General Principles

International Statements
In the new century there has been a tremendous amount of activity by international agencies around water issues. The World Water Commission and the World Dam Commission issued a major report in 2000. The World Water Council, the Global Water Partnership, and the UN's Collaborative Council on Water Supply and Sanitation have been developed. There have

been five World Water Forums, in 1998 in Marrakech, 2000 at the Hague, 2003 in Kyoto, 2005 in Montreal, and 2006 in Mexico City. The first World Toilet Summit was held in Seoul in 2002. Also in 2002 the World Summit on Sustainable Development (WSSD) at Johannesburg, South Africa, highlighted water access and sanitation. The year 2003 was the International Year of Freshwater, and that year saw the publication of the first World Water Development Report.[9]

The 2002 Johannesburg summit issued key statements linking management of water resources with sustainable development, admitting that without basic water management sustainable development is just a dream. The preparation committee for the summit directly linked poverty eradication and water and agreed to endorse a new goal of sanitation. This theme was incorporated into the final vision of the summit itself, a major step in linking poverty eradication, water management, and health and social structures of countries. The summit's plan of implementation reads: "The provision of clean drinking water and adequate sanitation is necessary to protect human health and the environment. In this respect, we agree to halve, by the year 2015, the proportion of people who are unable to reach or to afford safe drinking water [as outlined in the Millennium Declaration] and the proportion of people who do not have access to basic sanitation."[10]

Then in the 2006 *United Nations World Water Development Report 2* an explicit definition of water emerged that reflects general Western rights theory: water rights are "authorized demands to use (part of) a flow of surface water and groundwater, including certain privileges, restrictions, obligations and sanctions accompanying this authorization, among which a key element is the power to take part in collective decision-making about system management and direction."[11] This important statement involving people's power for collective decision-making along with the general international approaches to water, integrated water resources, and sanitation management offers at least the beginning of realizable practices around new approaches.

These guidelines are important, but in some ways problematic. To be effective they have to be implemented within particular contexts and within the broader ethical framework about the very nature of water as a natural right, worth conserving for its own sake and not only for human use. All too often governments and other managers hand over responsibilities and even regulation of management to private companies with little incentive to conserve; they fail to examine the social and environmental impacts of water decisions for the long term. In April 2004, a group of international nongovernmental organizations (NGOs) strongly rebuked the Organisation for Economic Co-operation and Development (OECD) industrialized countries for their inability to take the world water crisis seriously and for falling short on their funding commitments.[12] The situation now is even worse.

Provisions in several of the documents view some aspects of water as an economic good, which may be problematic as we have seen. Nonetheless, water does have a place in local, regional, national, and international economies; in farming; energy production; industrial activities; and fishing. In fact, its economic aspect can lead to conservation approaches and new efficiencies in design. In addition, as we will discuss later, there is even a place for water tariffs, water pricing of some kind, and incentives to penalize "low-value" uses such as lawns, golf courses, swimming pools, while rewarding "high-value" uses like drinking water, sanitation, and pollution controls.[13]

The key issue in today's struggles over water usage is not nature's "unfair" sharing of water in water-saturated versus water-dry areas of the globe, but revolves around the management systems that tend to use global markets and international corporations in ways that end up increasing the gap between the water wealthy and the water poor. This stark reality prompted the United Nations in its 2006 *World Water Development Report 2* to focus on water management as the most promising approach to meeting the world's water needs and to include an impetus toward local, participatory management systems. However, new management forms must in turn by encased by new perspectives on water, a new ethos.

Before we move on to a discussion of a new water ethos, I would like to comment briefly on the language of the UN documents. The very use of words like *development*, *underdeveloped*, and other terms imply a reference to programs of the twentieth century that were based on an impositional model, i.e., the model of the so-called "developed countries"—the United States, Europe, Russia, Japan—which was taken to be *the* model to be utilized by so-called *developing* and *underdeveloped* countries. The model and the language privileged the wealthier countries of the North and emphasized sheer economic progress as the key to a country's success. As more recent United Nations documents reveal, there is currently a move away from such an imposition and an almost imperial sense of superiority. The 2006 *World Water Development Report 2* and even the first *World Water Development Report* of 2003 recognize the value of social and environmental factors, cultural dimensions, and the place of locally based management systems and ancient technologies. Several of these factors form part of the new water ethos we are examining.

A second issue revolves around the very meaning of *rights*. In the long history of the West, a *right* and doctrines of *rights* evolved from Greek and Roman classical thought through the medieval philosophers, and then were filtered through the theories of Rousseau, Hobbes, and Locke. It is beyond our work here to analyze the history of rights in Western cultural history; however, since the Enlightenment period, rights have come to be seen as residing in the individual rather than the community. A right is a demand that one can make upon another or upon a group, such as the state, based on some principles or guidelines. One has political, civic rights, for example, as a member of a particular state; some argue for economic and social rights, rooted in the dignity of the person. Many Western religious traditions secure rights in the notion of persons created in God's image. In the secular realm rights have found their way into constitutional and civil law. The UN documents, then, build upon this long tradition.[14]

However, my experience in Japan and in conversation with other Asian scholars and my reading of indigenous and Asian texts show that rights language, while it has become accepted as a mode of more universal communication, still often fails to take into consideration the dimensions of community. It is now becoming apparent in legal documents such as the amendment to the constitution of Uruguay and in recent UN statements that the communal nature of natural resources such as water and air has given rise to the recognition of communal rights, an idea never absent but often relegated to subordinate status in Western thought.

Philosophers and theologians too are expanding the meaning of rights to include rights of animals and other species, of the biotic community. James Nash begins his important discussion of rights with human rights, described as "those moral rights essential for human well-being." Rights are demands or claims that one makes on the basis of that claim to one's minimal flourishing. Nash continues that "these rights are the basic necessities—the minimal conditions—to which every member is entitled and which a society should strive to guarantee, in order to enable all to live in accord with their God-given dignity and to participate in social decision-making."[15] While the emphasis here is on the individual, there is room for extension of the basic concept. In the next few pages, Nash does exactly that and in concert with others such as John Cobb calls for a recognition of the rights of nature, biotic rights. Some might object immediately since rights are usually seen as entailing obligations; in fact, much of what is called deontological ethics rests on this correlation between rights and obligations. How can nature then have obligations on the one hand, and what obligations do humans have to nature on the other?

Certainly in some of the religious traditions we have examined, notably Judaism and Islam, we have seen that nature has, like humans, the obligation to reverence the Creator. Nash notes this consideration, responds to the objections against such a use of rights language for nonhuman entities, and attempts to establish a boundary line for biotic rights, namely, "conation," a drive or urge to be and to do, conscious or not.[16] Given Nash's development in the extension of rights language, I would go further in our discussions to speak of the *right* of water to *be*. I do not mean water rights, which directly concern humans' rights to water as basic to their well-being, but the *right* of water to its well-being. While initially this might seem merely metaphorically interesting, I will argue that such an idea, an ethical principle, finds a place in the traditions we have examined. Water has a right to its own flourishing, which translates to a right not to be polluted, not to be diverted from its natural flow, positively to contribute to nature's and humans' economies, to make demands upon humans minimally for respect and corresponding protection. The rights of water when in conflict with other rights, including basic rights of humans, may be overridden, but such an overriding demands fair adjudication. The story of water in its immediate, concrete context needs to be heard. While specifics around such a recognition of rights of water are yet to be formulated, the basic principle remains: water has a right to its existence in as natural a state as possible and water too has obligations to nurture the rest of creation. What is called for here is a balance of competing claims. Water's rights then are a key feature of a new water ethos.

A New Water Ethos

We "need a new ethos for water," says Fred Pearce among others, "—an ethos based not on technical fixes but on managing the water cycle for maximum social benefit rather than narrow self interest."[17] This new ethos must surpass the Millennium Goals of the United Nations to bring potable water and good sanitation to all peoples around the world. Among other things, such a water ethos must include major rethinking in the uses of water for agriculture, industry, and domestic consumption, must not impose water management principles from the developed world in terms of large, centralized or privatized projects, must rediscover the ancient practices of water conservation and employ high technology for local, small, community-based solutions. We first need to examine then the major principles and approaches, the ideological premises, around water. The solutions to our water crises lie in the recognition not only of the *right* of all peoples to clean water and adequate sanitation facilities but the *duty* to maintain water resources in such a way that those most impacted are involved and participate or are democratically represented. We need new norms and regulations based on foundational principles along with democratic management for the common global good of all.

Norms and Regulations

At present what are the international and/or ethical guidelines that guide or should guide the availability and use of fresh water, its purification and distribution? The question of a fundamental right to water not just as a scarce resource for humans but for the life of the planet itself clashes with the commodification of water as an economic good and its packaging, sale, and distribution as an item of consumption for those able to pay. Is water a natural right or a commodity to be exchanged on open markets? Do states and municipalities have obligations to subsidize such a basic need as that of water? Only in extreme cases? Who owns water? Can water be owned?

The following discussions examine approaches to these important questions in a variety of ethical traditions. There are multiplicities of ethical theories and even several variations within each theoretical approach, such as rule utilitarianism versus act utilitarianism, differences in Buddhist ethics, and so forth. Among the theoretical approaches are those put forth by culturalists (ethics is determined by cultural norms), relativists (each ethical approach is equally valid), pragmatists (ethics is what works), emotivists (ethics is what feels right), and naturalists (ethics derives from the workings of nature). There are also natural law theory, utilitarian ethics, divine right ethics, Kantian ethics, feminist ethics, environmental ethics, Buddhist ethics, Jewish ethics, Christian ethics, liberation ethics—and the list goes on.

While using definitions of ethics as expressed in the introduction to this book such as "the art/science that seeks to bring sensitivity and method to the discernment of moral values"[18] in Daniel Maguire's words, ethics is also encased in ambiguities of context and relationships, in the concrete dimensions of time, place, and body. Sociologist Mick Smith writes: "Ethics is then the flow of *things* in desire and wonder, it is the relation that lets things *be*, conserving and sustaining them in love and/or difference. . . . The ethical subject is . . . an eddy in the ebb and flow of a relational matrix of difference, a matrix that is, primarily, ethical."[19] Although Smith is speaking here of human relationships, I see here a useful analogy for our human-nature and human-water relationships as well. Ethics concerns not only objective analysis and the application of rules and principles, but also the subjective aspects of personal and group experiences, feelings, and the affective dimensions of life, ambiguity and discernment.

In this inquiry I am selecting ethical forms that I believe further the evolution of a new water ethic most directly and that in some manner have already appeared in the stories and crises outlined thus far: a utilitarian, cost/benefit view; a natural law perspective illustrated in the tradition of

Catholic social thought; a Buddhist ethic; and finally an ecofeminist and ecological approach. In these traditions, we begin with efforts to foster fair rules of pricing of water to a communitarian sensibility of water's place in the Earth community and include an examination of the importance of shaping attitudes around water use, ending with approaches calling for a wholly new way to envision human-nature relationships around water. These are not exclusive to one another; in fact, parts of each may well complement the others. At the same time we must recognize that there are a variety of interpretations and understandings within each of the traditions; I am choosing selective components that contribute directly to a new water ethic.

One final note concerns the use of the word *ethics* itself as well as the notion of an *ethos*. A Christian Japanese colleague of mine at Nanzen University, Nagoya, Japan, noted that the Western use of *ethics* implies a self-conscious individual reflecting upon his or her individual self in relation to other entities; the beginning is in the self. In contrast, Japanese and other Asians find this approach foreign to their experience; they are more apt to speak of an *ethos*, that is, a whole context of relationships that guide appropriate actions; the context involves aesthetic dimensions as much as rational and is focused on the import for the group rather than just the individual. Although I use the word *ethics* in the discussions to follow, I want to emphasize that the call for a new water *ethos* involves the whole complex of values, attitudes, practices, beliefs, sentiments to which my colleague referred.[20]

Utilitarian, Cost/Benefit

In his intriguing and challenging analysis of the ways in which water is valued as an economic resource, economist Robert Young states that the basis for most contemporary economic thought is a form of utilitarianism. He acknowledges that formal policy analysis is a normative matter, in which "questions of *ought* and *should* reveal dissatisfaction with the current state of affairs and identify a policy problem," while normative criteria "are a necessary basis for identifying an 'improved' policy. Policy analysis presupposes ethical principles that provide a standard of evaluation for existing and proposed policies." Called "welfare economics," mainstream normative economic analysis, says Young, is derived from a form of utilitarian ethics, which utilizes the maxim of "the greatest good for the greatest number" to decide policies.[21]

In general, utilitarian ethics is based on the premise established first by Jeremy Bentham and refined by John Stuart Mill that happiness is to be found in balancing the pleasure and pain involved in the conflicts of ethical choices. Mill states that ". . . actions are right in proportion as they tend to promote happiness; wrong as they tend to produce the reverse of happiness. By happiness is intended pleasure and the absence of pain." The criterion for decision-making then becomes that which promotes the greatest good.[22] In his analysis Young states that the translation of a utilitarian calculus into policy has evolved into the form of a cost/benefit analysis. The analysis involves weighing whether a policy's beneficial effects outweigh its negative impacts; both are expressed in monetary terms. Beneficial effects bring about positive usefulness or remove what causes a lack of usefulness, and costs are measured by increases in undesired effects or declines in desirable impacts.[23]

Some forms of cost/benefit analysis are key dimensions of decisions in almost every arena of modern life. However, the key word in Young's analysis is *monetary*; the benefit or cost is assessed in terms of its monetary value. From an economic perspective the monetary value outweighs all others. However, monetary value is not to be conflated to market values. In fact, the premise of Young's study is to assess the values of such nonmarket factors as the recreational and sports use of water; the benefits of reducing floods and of improving water quality; and the methods of utilizing water in industry, commerce, and agriculture.

Young notes that water's "unique attributes make it a classic example of the market's potential failure to achieve an economically efficient allocation."[24] This is especially true because of water's profound religious, cultural, aesthetic, and psychological value. Certainly water does command economic value, and the fair pricing of water is one of the bases of a new water ethos. However, from the 1960s onward Young's analysis finds that there has been a significant movement from seeing water's economic value as one of many values to declaring water a *commodity* to be bought, sold, and traded apart from its location in place and space and regardless of its withdrawal for questionable uses (private lawns and swimming pools, for example). He states that "Full-cost pricing, perhaps implemented with an increasing block rate structure, was proposed as an appropriate solution to many artificially created 'water shortage' problems."[25] This *commodification* of water helped bring us to the age of privatization and "full-cost pricing," usually with little increasing block rate structure.

Some form of utilitarian cost/benefit analysis can be helpful in arriving at decisions about the global water crisis and the policies and approaches to be used in water management. However, the narrow calculus of economic, even monetary value must be enlarged to include the *social and environmental costs* of water extraction and use. The calculus must include, for example, the many benefits of free-flowing river systems, wetlands (often deemed "wastelands" by another model), and deltas. Restoring river flows to their natural boundaries, providing water for estuaries and floodplains, allowing flooding to lands can all become a new economic tool for river management providing benefits to surrounding areas.[26] The following sets of discussions furnish further principles necessary for a holistic, sustainable water world.

Natural Law: Catholic Social Thought

Catholic social thought offers an entirely different approach to the utilitarian calculus. This tradition asserts that there is a basic right to water and that the primary role of government is to ensure that water is accessible with equity to all. The principles involved are not exclusively Catholic and are shared by many other Christian traditions, other religious traditions, and other schools of philosophy; they rest upon a philosophical base of a communitarian ethic, in which the basic dignity of persons and their entitlements to the goods of the created world are safeguarded by governments serving the *common good* of the community, even the global community.[27]

The notion of the *common good* is often used in Christian thought to evaluate the justice of a society and its particular policies and practices. Although the term had various meanings in the tradition of Catholic social thought, Pope John XXIII provided a substantive definition in his 1961 encyclical letter, *Mater et Magistra* ("Mother and Teacher"): the common good "embraces the sum total of those conditions of human living, whereby men [sic] are enabled more fully and more readily to achieve their own perfection."[28] Although that description would not immediately seem to include water, later in the same encyclical letter, Pope John speaks of some of "those conditions of human living" as "principal services needed by all," and specifically includes "pure drinking water."[29]

Pope John repeats that basic necessity in his next encyclical, *Pacem in Terris* ("Peace on Earth") of 1963, in which he asserts that the goal of government is "the realization of the common good" in which *all* members of the state are "entitled to share." The state then is to promote the "material welfare" of citizens by promoting the rights "of the human person."[30] Among these rights John lists the development of essential services such as water supply.[31]

In 1987 Pope John Paul II in his encyclical *Soliciduto Rei Socialis* ("On Social Concerns") again refers to the "availability of drinking water" as a key indicator of justice in relation to common goods. The guiding principle is "the fair distribution of the goods originally destined for all,"[32] a principle reiterated again and again in John Paul's thought.[33] When one of those public goods, namely, water, is so essential to the life not only of humans but also of the Earth itself, then the *use* (and access to) that good has priority over desires for or even efficiency of private ownership and distribution.

Finally, in his 1991 document commemorating the 100th anniversary of Catholic social thought, *Centessimus Annus* ("One Hundred Years"), John Paul continues the analysis with a reiteration of the "common purpose of goods" and their "original common destination as created goods." The state or some public regulations must defend public goods "such as the natural and human environments" that cannot be protected by market forces; these are collective goods, such as water, that belong to all.[34]

These documents provide a powerful set of principles and tools for analysis of the use, distribution, sale, and availability of water as a basic human good, an essential part of the common good of all. While these arguments do not rule out some forms of private ownership, they promote an understanding that water and other basic goods are not for the narrow, exclusive interests of particular groups such as corporations. It would seem essential, then, from these principles, that the state through some form of regulation and/or ownership be integrally involved in access, distribution, pricing, and sale of water. What the documents do not address is the essential nature of water as an absolute, not relative, good for the whole of the Earth, inorganic as well as organic.

Other principles from this tradition relevant to the discussion of the right to water and water management include the *right of participation* in decision-making; the principle of *subsidiarity*, i.e., acknowledging the limits of government and the corresponding delegation of decisions to local and bioregional levels; the principle of *stewardship* of the goods of creation, not ownership, a very strong emphasis against absolute private property rights; the principle of a *preferential protection* for the poor and marginalized; and principles of *equality* and of *solidarity* with others in their struggles.[35] While not exhaustive, these guides, too, like cost/benefit analyses, must be expanded and embrace the common good of the Earth, not just human common good.

Buddhist Ethics

Buddhist ethics provides us with further tools from a religious perspective. In the Buddhist cosmic view, all reality is interrelated, changing, and in flux. While Buddhist metaphysical views differ significantly from Christian views, there are many similarities in ethical codes that provide for a common vision in relation to the environment and in particular to water. As we saw in an earlier chapter, the initial view of Buddhism concentrates on the perspective that nature is an illusion. However, there is a further accent that compels Buddhists to be especially attuned to the natural world. In particular, a Buddhist view moves ". . . to a new way of looking at the world that emphasizes the satisfaction of basic needs rather than the pseudo desires created by modern consumerism, and encourages thriftiness in the use of natural resources, elimination of waste, co-operation, and the development of community and long-term global values."[36] At the heart of this perspective, found especially in Mahayana Buddhism, is the emphasis upon curtailing desires, preventing suffering of others, and a fierce mindfulness concerning one's actions and their impacts.

U.S. Buddhist author, Joanna Macy, points to the fundamental shift in a sense of self that can take place in forming a new understanding of human relationship with the Earth. There is no discontinuous, autonomous self in Buddhism. Identity is an "ephemeral product of perceptual interactions," and "the experiencer is inseparable from his or her experience" of the world. What results when we lay aside the conception of a competitive ego is moral behavior that elevates practices of nonviolence and generosity, which free us from the "dictates of greed, aversion, and other reactions which reinforce the delusion of separate selfhood." This shift in awareness to an ecological identification has the power to identify self with all others and to act on behalf of others and of the Earth. Although other Buddhist scholars will disagree with Macy's interpretation of Buddhism for an ecological age, she has posited a helpful view of the interrelatedness of the human-nature relationship necessary for the well-being of Earth.[37]

Ecofeminist Anna Peterson challenges Macy's emphasis due to the question of whether Macy's expansion of self to include the natural world is sufficient in itself for an ecologically healthy world. Because Macy does not believe that moral exhortation is sufficient to produce a just attitude toward the Earth, her call is for a much deeper sense of identification. However, for Peterson, there is no guarantee that such an identity could not be used for further exploitation through an identification of nature's identity with one's own, a reverse of what Macy intends.[38] Nonetheless, when combined with the mindfulness of each action that Buddhism demands and a focus on simplicity and curbing of desires through the practice of virtues, then Macy's expansion of identity to eco-identity will be very helpful.

Basic needs, thriftiness, elimination of waste, a communitarian approach—these values fit in well with the Christian social teachings just examined as well as the principles of ecofeminist and ecological ethics to follow. These involve the central value of attunement to nature through seeking a harmony between the human and natural worlds. Often in Buddhist traditions, this ethos is captured in an aesthetic rather than philosophical mode. For example, in the *Poems of the Elders*, the one seeking spiritual insights refers to the enjoyment of natural beauty, in this case the river Ajakarani:

> Whene'er I see the crane, her clear bright wings
> Outstretched in fear to flee the black storm cloud,
> A shelter seeking, to sage shelter borne,
> Then doth the river Ajakarani give joy to me. . . .
> Not from the mountain-streams
> Is't time today
> To flit. Safe is the Ajakarani
> She brings us luck. Here is it good to be.[39]

The nature of the relationship between humans and the natural world is reciprocal, and attunement is part of the path of enlightenment, achieved not through reasoned argument but through mindful awareness. Aware of the universality of suffering, Buddhist ethics calls for the moral principle of alleviation of suffering through compassion for all peoples, animals, plants, and the Earth itself.[40] Such mindfulness itself, as the very basis for a Buddhist analysis, requires a purification of the mind and a development of character through virtues not easily achieved, yet at the same time results in Buddhism's practical ethical stances. An ethic of discipline over water desires, a focus instead on real water needs, a prohibition against waste, and a mindfulness of action that reduces the world's sufferings provide a powerful and much-needed stream to the growing river of a water ethic.

Ecofeminist and Environmental Ethics

While Buddhist ethics can embrace a strong identification with the natural world, the complete absence of a distinctive self and its replacement with a self comprised of its relationships, and only of its relationships, present a particularly difficult dilemma for ecofeminists. Relationships and their ontological foundation are the basic ingredient of a feminist approach to the moral universe. However, over and against the dominant male structures of rational, individual selves and the subordination of women's identity to a self *only* in relation to others, usually male figures such as father, husband, boss, women struggle to assert their own sense of autonomy. At the same time, "feminist theory departs radically from Western, male-dominated versions of autonomy by insisting that the self, and human nature generally, cannot be understood outside of its history, context, and relationships." Although there is no one definition or form that feminism takes and arguments continue around the formative patterns of feminist thought, in general feminists argue that the notion of a separate, rational self acting out of self-interests with other equally separate, rational selves is a damaging idea.[41] The central concepts that feminist theory brings to our discussions of people and water are *relationality, context,* and *stories.* In that case, all our knowledge is partial, limited, subject to times and places. We have certainly seen that in the case of twentieth-century methods of centralizing, privatizing, and limiting water management to corporate groups dominated by males and masculine modes of thought and removed from the actual realities of water users, who are usually women in most parts of the world.[42]

Ecofeminist theory goes a step further and extends these concepts to the natural world. We are in intimate relationship with the natural world, in a variety of settings that must be taken into account in developing ethical actions, and each context includes the story of the people in place with their histories as well as the *stories,* the *biographies* of every aspect of nature, in our case the water world. Water has important stories to tell, and we have obligations to hear those stories of many water places and to learn. The story of Cochabamba offers an example of ethical insights emerging from the particular relationships of people to their region and their waters. Many times women in the area were the leaders and organizers of the resistance, joining with others in opposing the movements of the male-dominated agencies of government and the international corporations. These particular experiences of a people and a water region have formed essential parts of the ethical discourse around water.

Finally, an equally important aspect is the feminist theme of *embodiment,* i.e., being at home in one's body and citing the body, particularly women's bodies, as valuable dimensions of ethical discourse. Being at home in one's body is a key to being at home in the natural world, argue several ecofeminists.[43] Our relationships with nature constitute our very moral selves. Such *at-homeness* is at the heart of ecology itself, for the word derives from the Greek words *oikos,* home, and *logos,* study, "the study of the home." We are one with the Earth-home.

These elements of ecofeminist thought coincide with ecological principles operative in the discussion of water. As with other ethical approaches, environmental or ecological ethics covers a broad range of theorists from *deep ecologists* to *naturalists, constructionalists* and several others.[44] Profound divisions arise over topics such as animal rights, the extension of rights language to nonhuman, even nonanimal species. Yet regardless of persuasion a foundational ecological principle, *sustainability,* provides grounding of an environmental ethic. In the case of water, sustainability is rooted in our knowledge of water in a particular, local context and the relationship of a river, stream, or well to the region and to the future. The question is whether current practices and policies ensure not only that there is sufficient quantity and quality of water for the Earth and all inhabitants but that there will continue to be sufficient quantities and qualities in the future. Aldo Leopold, a pioneer in the environmental movement, postulated an ecological categorical imperative: "A thing is right when it tends to preserve the integrity, stability, and beauty of the biotic community. It is wrong when it tends otherwise."[45] Leopold also adds another significant ethical consideration when he insists that we extend our moral concerns and relationships to the regional Earth communities of which we are part. In this way, issues of "rights" and even the categories of "intimacy" and "love" can legitimately extend to the Earth. The question then is not just about water rights for humans but the right to water of Earth itself.

Sustainability implies an essential ecological principle, *subsidiarity*. That is, decisions about water, water access, water management, water control must increasingly be made at the local and bioregional rather than global, or even at times national, level. Environmental ethicist Larry Rasmussen writes: "But subsidiarity also means massively deconstructing what is now globalized. Food, shelter, livelihood, and other needs that can be met on a community and regional basis, with indigenous resources, talent, and wisdom, should be met there."[46] In that list of needs we can include water.

Another, equally important principle is *accountability*. Dependence on bottled water transfers authority and power from local control through public or public/private ventures with full accountability to large corporate powers with little accountability. As the struggle in Cochabamba, Bolivia, reveals, when there is little accountability to the public at large, great injustices can occur.[47] The principle of *equality* ensures that every human being has a right to access potable water, so basic to the right to life. Measures that overuse such a scarce resource for the benefit of a small group, especially that group which exercises some control over the access to water, violate such a principle.

The principle of *participation* dictates that all those involved in a decision be represented by some agency acting on behalf of their interests, whether a private corporation, a nongovernmental agency, government, or citizens themselves. As Vandena Shiva notes in discussing the plights of developing countries already in debt, "With communities bypassed, the World Bank [or some other agency] and indebted governments are making frantic deals with corporations to own, control, distribute and sell our scarce water resources."[48] Local communities have a right to present their needs, and through some agency the Earth itself must be given voice to declare its needs.

A grounded ecological ethic also includes a principle of *sufficiency*. That involves ". . . a commitment to meet the basic material needs of all life possible," including human, plant, and animal life.[49] We take what we need and leave the Earth, its waters, intact. This means living within limits and setting boundaries to consumption and irresponsible use of water.

Vandana Shiva also notes two rules used at the UN Convention on the Law of the Non-Navigational Uses of International Water Courses in 1997 for sharing international waters: "the rule of equitable and reasonable use and the no harm rule." Equitable use "referred to water sharing on an equitable basis among multiple users, and the no harm rule referred to not causing harm to co-riparian states."[50] Here conservation becomes an important ecological guideline. The principles of equitable use and no harm can also apply to other areas of water concerns, such as access, development, and production.

In her succinct analysis of water uses and privatization, Shiva works these principles together in her thesis that water sustainability can only come from another basic principle, the *democratic* control of water resources.[51] Water is a community resource, and Shiva's main argument against public–private partnerships surrounding water is that the agreement fundamentally disguises the fact that such "arrangements usually entail public funds being available for the privatization of public good."[52] As a consequence, water services shift from a view of publicly provided free services as a right to services provided to a consumer who has access through payment.[53]

Rules and Regulations

We have already seen some of the principles that have guided water allocation and use in earlier discussions of regional water conflicts. Thus upriver states are quick to assert territorial *sovereignty* and ownership of water in their territories, both above and below ground, with the concomitant right to any desired use. Downriver states, however, assert the principle of territorial *integrity* with the right to benefit from the "natural, uninterrupted and undiminished flow of watercourses originating in other countries." Since these two principles are often at odds, other principles have emerged for application.

These are: *the principle of a community of interests*, according to which no state may use the waters on its territory without consulting other states to achieve integrated management based upon cooperation; and *the principle of fair and reasonable use*, according to which each state has a right to use the waters of the respective basin by being awarded ownership and control of a fair and reasonable share of the basin's resources.[54]

The conflicts along the Colorado River in the western United States have been resolved utilizing the principle of fair and reasonable use. It is time to see these principles and others discussed in actual operation: we return to the story of Cochabamba.

Cochabamba Revisited

In the struggles surrounding privatization versus public ownership of water in Cochabamba in the late 1990s, the Coordinadora's slogan became "The water is ours." One of the guiding principles of the organization was "social property," that is, a social compact among SEMAPA, the public company in greater Cochabamba, and the 100-plus water committees in the surrounding areas. All citizens own shares and through consumer groups have representation on the board of SEMAPA: "the ambition was to convert SEMAPA into a socially owned and self-managed enterprise in which its property form would transcend existing legal provisions in order to make room for new means of management, decision-making, citizen participation, and social control." Such a process allows not only for recovery of the "social wealth" of water but also for community involvement in articulating the very meaning of the common good.[55]

Four basic norms devised by the Coordinadora guide the management and implementation of the "social wealth" of Cochabamba's water for the "common good": (1) *efficient* delivery of services; (2) *transparent* operations; (3) *socially responsible* decision-making; (4) *accessibility* for all.[56] These norms emerge as an alternative set to those that supported what Oscar Olivera calls the two forms of privatization, that of *transnational* corporations and the *state*. Olivera comments that the question here is one of organizing people to "take into their own hands the control, use, and ownership of collective and communal wealth," thus reflecting the broader principles of participation, equality, preferential treatment of marginal people, and subsidiarity discussed earlier.[57]

Around the globe, alternatives to both state ownership and privatization have grown dramatically since 2000. Based on the principle that water is a basic right, cities and even nations have fought to secure the grounding of this right in specific, what we might call *intermediate*, principles that reflect the broader principles outlined earlier. We have already seen the people of Uruguay amend their Constitution to secure the principle of water rights.

The people of Grenoble, France, claim "that water is a public good, but it should be a right for all."[58] Speaking of water and other basic services in Colombia, Hildebrando Velez writes: "Services [water and sanitation] must be considered to be the fundamental right of every person."[59] These stories of citizens engaging in struggles to protect waters and articulate their rights to water have given rise to many of the ethical principles mentioned above and reflect those principles in action.

Conclusion

In his compelling work grounding the basis for a world water contract, Ricardo Petrella argues in the absence of worldwide rules for a World Water Contract that would involve "(1) fundamental work on constitutional law [world water legislation] to facilitate (2) effective action for 'peace through water' and (3) the introduction and/or promotion of democratic management of water by local communities, involving, among other things, the creation of 'water parliaments.'"[60] Far from being another statement *about* water, the contract is meant to provide a dynamic foundation for *action* based on the premise that water is a global common good. While I would extend this principle to include the entire planet, and indeed Petrella does talk of water as a "*planetary asset*," the foundational statement provides an "intrinsic finality" to water, an intrinsic purpose, "based on *solidarity* and *sustainability*."[61] From this grounding any talk of *rights* of access to clean water and sanitation and *obligations* to provide such access begins.

What follows from these principles is that

> . . . each organized human community has the right to use water for its vital needs and for the social and economic welfare of all its members [and] must guarantee access and use to other human communities which share or do not share the same aquiferous basin, according to the modes of solidarity and sustainability agreed for this purpose.
>
> *The inalienable rights and duties with regard to water are collective rights and duties. . . . Control and supervision of priorities in the exercise and enjoyment of those rights and duties should take place at the level of each community, on behalf of and as a trust from the rights and duties of the world human community, which remains the primary subject of the common water heritage.*[62]

Building upon the premise that water is a fundamental right, struggling peoples, citizens, academics, and a host of NGOs are birthing *a new water ethos*, characterized by a set of guiding principles. While each struggle and development may express these differently, the principles begin with the understanding that water is a public good and each person, each citizen, has a right to access to clean water and sanitation. In sum, the new ethos involves: (1) community *participation*; (2) *transparency* in the dealings of management; (3) *accountability* to the public; (4) a sense of *social justice* in rates and delivery; (5) *efficiency* and ecological *sustainability* throughout the system; (6) local and national *support* by political authorities while preserving principles of *subsidiarity*; (7) *responsible*, committed, and trained management; (8) a basic respect for the inherent *dignity* of each person and all persons in the system—managers, engineers, users, citizens; and (9) something approaching a *preferential option for the poor*, or at least a system of cost-recovery that addresses the needs of the poor unable to pay. These principles can be summarized as "a commercial outlook with social obligations."[63]

The final chapter of our discussion moves to exciting developments in water use and management that embrace these principles. However, before we turn to the practical questions of implementation of a new ethos based on such ethical principles, we return once more to the powerful world religions. From our *cosmologies*, our worldviews, we derive our ethical guides to action. These religious traditions in their multiple varieties provide the basis for asserting the *intrinsic value* of water and the consequent *responsibilities* of humans to care for the waters in their *religious responses, duties*, and *worship* of divinities, God, or Allah, the objective grounding of all value.

In her incisive analysis of ecological ethics and the place in particular of religious ethics, Anna Peterson argues that the saliency of religious ethics in relation to the environment lies in the "solidarity of the religious community, the emotional and aesthetic satisfactions of rituals, and intellectual agreement with the logic of religious rules and values." The *content* of religious beliefs carries particular weight. "While faith without works may well be dead, for many religious people works without faith are empty," concludes Peterson.[64] We now return to those traditions.

Notes

1. Ricardo Petrella, *The Water Manifesto: Arguments for a World Water Contract*, trans. Patrick Camiller (London: Zed Books, 2001), 109.

2. "Principle No. 4," *The Dublin Statement on Water and Sustainable Development*, International Conference on Water and the Environment, Organized by the United Nations; Dublin, Ireland, January 1992.

3. Maggie Black, *The No-Nonsense Guide to Water* (Oxford: New Internationalist, 2004), 110.

4. Sandra Postel and Brian Richter, *Rivers for Life: Managing Water for People and Nature* (Washington, D.C.: Island Press, 2003), 93–94.

5. Black, *No-Nonsense Guide*, 117, 119.

6. Black, *No-Nonsense Guide*, 120.

7. Petrella, *Water Manifesto*, 25–27.

8. "A Right to Water: A Step in the Right Direction," WaterAid (www.wateraid.org.uk/), quoted in Black, *No-Nonsense Guide*, 121.

9. See Black, *No-Nonsense Guide*, 130–131, for a fuller listing.

10. Quoted in United Nations, *Water for People, Water for Life: The United Nations World Water Development Report* (Geneva: UNESCO, 2003), 28, 20–21.

11. United Nations, *Water: A Shared Responsibility. The United Nations World Water Development Report 2* (New York: Berghahn, 2006), 61.

12. Black, *No-Nonsense Guide*, 134.

13. Black, *No-Nonsense Guide*, 135–136.

14. For a fascinating discussion of the bases for the assertion of human rights, see Elizabeth M. Bauer and Barbara Darnett, eds., *Does Human Rights Need God?* (Grand Rapids, Mich.: Eerdmans, 2005). The discussions involved show the vigorous debate that still carries on in the fifty-plus years since the Universal Declaration was issued.

15. James A. Nash, *Loving Nature: Ecological Integrity and Christian Responsibility* (Nashville, Tenn.: Abingdon Press, 1991), 168.

16. Nash, 174–178.

17. Fred Pearce, *When the Rivers Run Dry* (Boston: Beacon, 2006), 308.

18. Daniel Maguire, *On Moral Grounds* (New York: Crossroad, 1991), 34.

19. Mick Smith, *An Ethics of Place: Radical Ecology, Postmodernity, and Social Theory* (Albany: State University of New York Press, 2001), 184.

20. For an interesting discussion of a particular cultural ethos, see Takei Sugiyama Lebra, *Japanese Patterns of Behavior* (Honolulu: University of Hawaii Press, 1976), particularly ch. 1, "Social Relativism as a Japanese Ethos."

21. Robert Young, *Determining the Economic Value of Water: Concepts and Methods* (Washington, D.C.: Resources for the Future, 2005), 17–18 (Young's italics).

22. Quoted in Karen Lebacqz, *Six Theories of Justice: Perspectives from Philosophical and Theological Ethics* (Minneapolis, Minn.: Augsburg, 1986), 16; see ch. 1, "The Utilitarian Challenge: John Stuart Mill," 15–32, for Lebacqz's analysis of the strengths and weaknesses of utilitarianism. There are a number of variations of the utilitarian calculus such as rule utilitarianism and act utilitarianism, each with its own understanding of utility and justice.

23. Young, *Determining Economic Value*, 18.

24. Young, *Determining Economic Value*, 22.

25. Young, *Determining Economic Value*, 27.

26. Postel and Richter, *Rivers for Life*, 168.

27. The phrase *Catholic social thought* is generally taken to mean a series of documents published by the Roman Catholic popes and by regional conferences of bishops, beginning with the publication of Pope Leo XIII's famous pronouncement of 1891, *"Rerum Novarum"* ("On the Condition of Labor"), an *encyclical* letter, on the situation of labor in Europe in the wake of the horrors of the Industrial Revolution.

The encyclical builds upon a tradition of philosophical thinking that traces its origins to Aristotle and its development to the Dominican theologian Thomas Aquinas, who rediscovered Aristotle for European scholars in the thirteenth century. The foundations of this tradition have been carried forward and continually developed ever since. Subsequent popes since Leo XIII have in turn added and further developed principles to guide social, political, and economic policies in light of changing times. See David O'Brien and Thomas Shannon, eds., *Catholic Social Thought: The Documentary Heritage* (Maryknoll, N.Y.: Orbis, 1998) for an introduction to this school of thought, and Edward P. DeBerri and James E. Hug, *Catholic Social Teaching: Our Best Kept Secret* (Maryknoll, N.Y.: Orbis, 2005).

28. O'Brien and Shannon, *Catholic Social Thought*, 94, para. 65.

29. O'Brien and Shannon, *Catholic Social Thought*, 105, para. 127.

30. "*Pacem in Terris,*" O'Brien and Shannon, *Catholic Social Thought*, 140–141, para. 55–62.

31. "*Pacem,*" in O'Brien and Shannon, *Catholic Social Thought*, 140, para. 64.

32. O'Brien and Shannon, *Catholic Social Thought*, 400, para. 10

33. O'Brien and Shannon, *Catholic Social Thought*, 413, para. 28; 408, para. 22.

34. O'Brien and Shannon, *Catholic Social Thought*, 461, para. 30; 469, para. 40.

35. William J. Byron, "Ten Building Blocks of Catholic Social Teaching," *America*, 31 October 1998.

36. Padmasiri de Silva, *Buddhism, Ethics and Society: The Conflicts and Dilemmas of Our Times* (Clayton, Australia: Monash University Press, 2002), 152.

37. Joanna Macy, "The Ecological Self: Postmodern Ground for Right Action," in *Readings in Ecology and Feminist Theology*, eds. Mary Heather MacKinnon and Moni McIntyre (Kansas City, Mo.: Sheed & Ward, 1995), 262–267.

38. Anna Peterson, *Being Human: Ethics, Environment, and Our Place in the World* (Berkeley: University of California Press, 2001), 207–208.

39. Th iv:196, quoted in de Silva, *Buddhism, Ethics and Society*, 155.

40. Donald Swearer, Sommai Premchit, and Phaithoon Dokbuakaew, *Sacred Mountains of Northern Thailand and Their Legends* (Chiang Mai: Silkworm Books, 2004), 5.

41. Anna Peterson, *Being Human*, 142. See also Vandana Shiva, *Water Wars: Privatization, Pollution, and Profit* (Cambridge, Mass.: South End Press, 2002); Mary Heather MacKinnon and Moni McIntyre, eds., *Readings in Ecology and Feminist Theology* (Kansas City, Mo.: Sheed & Ward, 1995); and Vandana Shiva and Maria Miles, *Ecofeminism* (London: Zed Books, 1993).

42. Peterson, *Being Human*, 138–140.

43. See Peterson, *Being Human*, 200–202; Sally McFague, *The Body of God: An Ecological Theology* (Minneapolis, Minn.: Fortress Press, 1993); Carolyn Merchant, *The Death of Nature: Women, Ecology, and the Scientific Revolution* (San Francisco: HarperCollins, 1983).

44. For an intriguing analysis of the varieties of environmental ethics found in a variety of religious traditions and the development of the central place of religious

traditions in an ecological ethic, see J. Baird Callicott's *Earth's Insights: A Survey of Ecological Ethics from the Mediterranean Basin to the Australian Outback* (Berkeley: University of California Press, 1994).

45. Aldo Leopold, *A Sand County Almanac* (New York: Oxford University Press, 1989), 201ff.

46. Larry Rasmussen, *Earth Community, Earth Ethics* (Maryknoll, N.Y.: Orbis, 1996), 337.

47. Vandana Shiva lists as one example among many Subic Bay in the Philippines, where the giant water company, Biwater, increased fees by 400 percent; see *Water Wars*, 98–99.

48. Shiva, *Water Wars*, 67.

49. Rasmussen, *Earth Community*, 172.

50. Shiva, *Water Wars*, 76.

51. Shiva, *Water Wars*, 127.

52. Shiva, *Water Wars*, 89.

53. Shiva, *Water Wars*, 90–91.

54. Petrella, *Water Manifesto*, 46–47.

55. Raquel Gutierrez-Aguilar, "The Coordinadora One Year after the War," in *¡Cochabamba! Water War in Bolivia*, eds. Oscar Olivera with Tom Lewis (Cambridge, Mass.: South End Press, 2004), 54, 60, 62.

56. Tom Lewis, "Direction SEMAPA: An Interview with Luis Sanchez-Gomez," in *¡Cochabamba! Water War in Bolivia*, eds. Oscar Olivera with Tom Lewis (Cambridge, Mass.: South End Press, 2004), 93.

57. Olivera, *¡Cochabamba!* 156.

58. Raymond Avrillier, "A Return to the Source: Re-Municipalisation of Water Services in Grenoble, France," in *Reclaiming Public Water*, eds. Belén Balanyá et al. (Amsterdam: Transnational Institute and Corporate Europe Observatory, 2005), 65.

59. Hildebrando Velez, "Public Services in Colombia: A Matter of Democracy," in *Reclaiming Public Water*, eds. Belén Balanyá et al. (Amsterdam: Transnational Institute and Corporate Europe Observatory, 2005), 103.

60. Petrella, *Water Manifesto*, 88.

61. Petrella, *Water Manifesto*, 91.

62. Petrella, *Water Manifesto*, 91–92 (Petrella's italics).

63. Quoted in Charles Santiago, "Public-Public Partnership: An Alternative Strategy in Water Management in Malaysia," in *Reclaiming Public Water*, eds. Belén Balanyá et al. (Amsterdam: Transnational Institute and Corporate Europe Observatory, 2005), 58. The principles, highlighted in italics with reference to the general principles discussed earlier, are enunciated in a variety of ways by the authors of twenty-one recent case studies of alternatives to privatization in *Reclaiming Public Water*.

64. Peterson, *Being Human*, 219–220.

CHAPTER EIGHT

~

"I Like Fountain Flow": Religion Revisited

The nineteenth-century English poet Gerard Manley Hopkins, a Jesuit priest, saw the natural world as a manifestation of the divine presence in all reality. Writing at the height of the Industrial Revolution in the mid-1800s, Hopkins often described his relationship to the divine in symbols of nature. In one poem he writes of his origins and livelihood in the divine waters: "Thee God I come from, to Thee go / All day I like fountain flow."[1] In our age of a technological revolution, we are much in need of Hopkins's sensibility, religious insight, and eco-Identity.

Sets of national and international laws and proclamations tell us what we are bound to do legally. Science informs us of the impacts on waters created by overuse, pollution, drought, global warming, population pressures, and increased demands in industry, agriculture, and domestic, particularly urban, consumption. Ethical frameworks examine what we "ought" to do. We have learned solutions to water problems, but we suffer a motivational *drought* to take the necessary actions to meet the current and coming water crises. Why we must act does not seem to have stirred religious leaders, excited state or other powerful leaders, presidents, or prime ministers, while activists, local leaders, NGOs, indigenous peoples, and many others have not only heard the call but have imbibed the message in the cells of their bodies. We need a bodily and spiritual transformation on the deepest levels of our watery selves, not only in the cells and plasma of our inner lives but at the deepest abyss of our unconscious, namely, in the realm of the symbolic.

155

The challenge to religions in their response to the environmental challenge is formidable. Former chair of the World Wide Fund for Nature (formerly World Wildlife Fund), Russell Train, expressed his puzzlement in 1990 that the lack of responses from religions ". . . has been nothing less than extraordinary. Here we have issues that go to the heart of the human condition, to the quality of human life, even to humanity's ultimate survival. Here we have problems that can be said to threaten the very integrity of Creation. And yet the churches and other institutions of organized religion have largely ignored the whole subject."[2] The good news is that there have been major strides in Christianity, and in other traditions, toward incorporating an ecological perspective into the heart of Christian teachings and practices. For example, by 1994 the World Council of Churches at the international assembly in Kuala Lumpur, Malaysia, reflected a new theological framework:

> The Spirit is God's uncreated energy alive throughout creation. All creation lives and moves and has its being in this divine life. This Spirit is in, with and under 'all things' (ta panta). . . . We not only reject a view in which the cosmos does not share in the sacred and in which humans are not part of nature; we also repudiate hard lines drawn between animate and inanimate, and human and non-human.[3]

From the perspective of a more scientific framework, David Suzuki has written in a manner that still roots water in the sacred: "We are water—the oceans flow through our veins, and our cells are inflated by water, our metabolic reactions mediated in aqueous solutions. . . . As air is a sacred gas, so is water a sacred liquid that links us to all the oceans of the world and ties us back in time to the very birthplace of all life. . . . It is the tide of life itself, *the sacred source*."[4]

The development of a "new water ethos" and a "new water ethic" called for by Pearce, Black, and others lies in part in restoring water to a central place in the world's religions and in our conscious spiritualities. In relation to our fundamental interchange with the water world in which we dwell, such a religious consciousness can provide the meaning and motivation to work for changes that purify our waters and our consciousness. A new consciousness would recall and recast the ancient respect for and intimacy with water—whether as divine in itself; as an essential manifestation of the divine in the world so that we flow like a fountain; as a basic part of the created; or even as an aesthetic mode of appreciation, value, and respect for all of the natural world so dependent on water. If there is no water, there is no nature to appreciate.

We must, as Phillip Ball states, "retain and even enhance the reverence that we feel for its [water's] mythical embodiment."[5] Maggie Black too has concluded: *"Perhaps water will manage to redeem the sacred status it has enjoyed since life appeared on earth, and magically divest itself of the commodity-driven character which is, after all, only a recent incarnation."*[6] Such a new consciousness demands a break with the tenacious hold of technological, large-scale, *hard* approaches to water issues and a breakthrough to more communitarian, people-based, democratic, local, and technologically *soft* movements based on valuing, respecting, even revering the water on our Earth.

Many who study the global water crises also see that religion and symbolic meanings must play a key role in shaping policies regarding water. In *Reflections on Water*, political scientists Joachim Blatter and Helen Ingram argue that researchers discussing water must understand the *meaning* of water in different times, places, and among different peoples. Their approach challenges bureaucratic management and the technological and scientific methods also criticized by Shiva, which reduce water to an economic resource. They advocate complementary approaches from the humanities that explore the diverse meanings of water. While studies in the life sciences have been welcomed in discussions on water issues, no such acknowledgment has been made for cultural studies, such as the place of religion, in providing meaning systems.[7] Thus we have several reasons for looking to religious traditions for providing both understandings of water's reality and the motivations to undertake action to protect water. Not only are these reflections important for those involved in religious traditions, they are essential for policy makers, managers, corporate leaders, activists, and researchers.

We return to the religious nature of our quest for new visions not only about the distribution of water to a thirsty and polluted world, especially in developing countries, but about the nature of water itself in our individual and collective consciousness. Religions provide cognitive meanings and understandings and bring *emotional* investments and motivations in our cosmologies of the world. While we need a cost/benefit analysis, the principles of a Christian social teaching, and a convincing ecological ethic of sustainability, we must also incorporate the insight of Buddhist ethics that a practical stance toward nature must proceed from our inner selves, purifying the mind and forging our character.[8]

I will examine each tradition studied earlier in terms of its contribution toward a new water ethos and for exemplary water practices currently taking place. The discussion is by no means exhaustive, but it will hopefully provide the basis for thought and action. In addition, if religions contribute to a new water ethos, then ways of interreligious cooperation are important for future progress. So let us begin this discussion.

Indigenous Traditions

The current struggles of the Hopi peoples of the southwestern United States provide a vivid example of the interrelationships between a religious consciousness of water's sacred reality and actions to preserve the purity of waters. Since 1969, Peabody Coal Company has strip-mined for coal on Black Mesa, an area sacred to the Hopi and to the neighboring Navajo peoples. By 1970 Peabody used mesa waters to push the coal through a long slurry pipe to a generating plant in southern Nevada. On the one hand, revenue from the mining has been the largest single income source for the Hopi, and the company hires hundreds of Hopi and Navajo. On the other hand, the company pumps some 1.2 billion gallons of water a year from the mesa's Navajo aquifer that feeds the springs, and the springs are drying up. Peabody claims drought is the culprit and that its long-term use will not harm the aquifer. However, the U.S Geological Survey reveals that median water levels have decreased by over 17 feet.

To Hopi activist Vernon Masayesva, the shrinking springs result from the broken covenant with the Spirit to respect the waters. Where science concludes that the decline in water in the West is due to climate change, "Hopi spirituality concludes that careless use of water is causing climate change. . . . 'You never waste water,'" says Masayesva. "'If you do, the rains are going to stop coming.'"[9]

During March of 2006, in an effort to bring the water crisis on the land to the attention of others, Masayesva and other Hopi runners gathered around a spring on tribal land for a water-blessing ceremony. The blessing marked the beginning of a 2000-mile, 14-day relay from the mesa land in Arizona to Mexico City, site of the 5th World Water Forum. The runners passed a gourd of the sacred water from one to another to deliver the message at the forum of the need to protect and conserve water. Masayesva had to return home due to a family emergency. On his way back it began snowing thirty miles from his house, and it snowed and rained for three days, breaking the longest recorded dry spell in Arizona's history. In Masayesva's view it snowed and rained because the runners made it happen. Ironically the Hopi runners and trip organizers, carrying out a Hopi tradition by running, were not allowed into the forum. But they were warmly received by Mexico City's mayor and traditional community leaders. For Masayesva, "Our traditions, our beliefs, aren't dead. We are rain people trying to convey water's message."[10]

This contemporary story tells us of the strong relationships in indigenous cultures among people, land, and water, and the divine. Humans are in dynamic relationship with the divine and the Earth. Thomas Berry, a "geologian" as he names himself, calls for such a rich identity and sense of *intimacy* in our dealings with nature to overcome our cultural *autism* in relation to the natural world.[11] Such an intimacy would go far in reestablishing human presence in humble acknowledgment of gifts, such as water, which God bestows.

The cosmologies of most indigenous traditions embrace an environmental ethic of sustainability, reverence, and respect for water and nature in general. In addition, indigenous traditions have learned to live in close relationship with nature. Most importantly, indigenous cultures have "rituals of reciprocity and respect for nature that enable them to leave an especially small environmental impact."[12] Indigenous traditions can provide important moral wisdom for our approaches to water in the twenty-first century.

Hinduism

Many environmentalists view Hinduism, and its Buddhist derivative, as antithetical to a worldview that embraces a strong concern for the material world, for waters. For example, J. Baird Callicott writes: ". . . the philosophies of the Indian sub-continent seem to share a pragmatic emphasis on either personal transcendence of or a detachment from nature. . . . That autistic indifference to natural phenomena does not provide, to my mind, the sort of affirmative, actively engaged moral attitude toward nature required for a proper environmental ethic."[13] Yet, we have seen in Hinduism perhaps the most powerful identification of water with divine manifestations and goddesses. Primordial water is divine and creates the world.[14] These beliefs support a strong ethic around water.

However, our study of Hinduism in chapter 1 pointed to the problem involved in the contradiction between ritual purity and cleanliness of waters, particularly in the case of the Ganges. Anil Agarwal has pointed to the individualistic nature of Hinduism, with an emphasis on one's own behavior. "In the absence of sewage systems, . . . some people just shut their eyes to the problem and concentrate on keeping themselves clean in a dirty environment."[15] Hindus, he writes, must "reexamine, ruthlessly, their religion. . . . There is a vast reservoir of tenets, practices, and beliefs that can help Hindus to reform Indian society."[16] Others call for an examination of sacred texts and an emphasis upon the many rituals involving pilgrimages to sacred shrines along rivers, bathing in waters for purity of soul, and connecting that purity with the cleanliness of the water, the goddess herself.[17]

While some view water pollution, as in the Ganges, as a sign of society's moral decay, many see cleaning the waters of rivers as respecting Mother Ganga and the goddesses associated with rivers and water sites. For example,

Dr. V. B. Mishra is a hydrologist concerned with water purity in the Ganga. He is also a priest of an important temple in Varanasi, one of the most holy cities in India. Founding a secular campaign to clean up the river, Dr. Mishra has employed religious advocates as well as civic groups. With care to understanding the distinctions between ritual purity and material cleanness, the campaign has been very successful in joining Hinduism and science.[18] Although many believe environmental activism in India will grow from nongovernmental activists before religious groups join the cause, Dr. Mishra's efforts and the various campaigns across India to oppose dams, restore wetlands, utilize traditional technologies to collect rain, and other activities reveal that change can be substantially strengthened by support from religious sources. In the meantime, the Hindu cosmological view, which sees waters as divine—not just the abodes of goddesses but as goddesses themselves—can serve as a powerful symbol of the great respect, even love we must have for waters, another important contribution to a new water ethos.

Buddhism

Buddhism's contribution to the new water ethos lies in its nondualistic vision of the connection between the human and natural world; the cosmos is a whole, and each part of the cosmos is part of all else. Everything is interrelated. Recall that Vietnamese Buddhist monk Thich Nhat Hanh believes that water itself is "a good friend, a bodhisattva, which nourishes the many thousands of species on earth."[19] In Zen Buddhism in particular, the oneness of all reality can lead to a sensitivity and piercing awareness of creation's suffering, particularly of the suffering of the waters. Through contemplation in Buddhism one can arrive at an awareness of water's sufferings that would lead to active engagement to relieve that pain.

Examples of such Buddhist engagement exist around the world. In Thailand, using both teachings and rituals, Buddhist monks have organized to preserve mangroves, to oppose shrimp farming and dam construction, and since trees were very important to Buddha, to preserve forested areas that protect watersheds. Building on the Buddhist doctrine of the interrelatedness of all things, Thai monk Prhaku Pitak organized a powerful movement to protect trees, employing a ritual in which a large tree was "ordained" a monk and clothed with a saffron robe. By linking conservation with spirituality, Pitak was able to involve local people in significant restoration work.[20] Such an approach could be extended to water conservation and preservation.

Another example involves the Buddhist Sarvodaya Shramadana movement in Sri Lanka. Begun as a student movement in the late 1950s and imbued with Gandhian and Buddhist worldviews, the movement has grown dramatically, particularly among poorer villages on the island. Steeped in the notions of self-help and decentralization, local villagers are involved in their own development process. The process involved shared labor, education, reforestation, and water works, eventually leading to markets for the sale of goods and other income-producing activities.[21]

American Zen Buddhists have developed nature retreats, "mountain and river" *sesshin* sessions, for greater awareness of the human place in the natural world. Groups have established rituals such as the Council for All Beings, and the central concept expressed by American Buddhist Joanna Macy of "eco-identity" frames a new consciousness with the planet. Internationally, Buddhists have formed chapters of the Nuclear Guardianship Project that targets radioactive waste. The activist mode of "green Buddhism" builds upon traditional Buddhist ideas now with a global reach, a social engagement, and strong support of women.[22]

For example, at the Green Gulch Zen Center, north of San Francisco, California, water conservation is a mandatory component of life at the center. Through the use of low-flow toilets and showers along with drip irrigation, the locally maintained water system of five reservoirs, three tanks, and a well suffice for the community's year-round needs. Buddhist practices of frugality are evident at meals when people wash their bowls in less than a cup of water per meal.[23] Such centers offer models for water conservation and mindfulness not only for other Buddhist centers but for other religious traditions as well.

One of the major contributions of Buddhism resides in the mindfulness in Buddhist meditation. While other traditions involve practices of meditation and contemplation, Buddhist mindfulness can inculcate a deep awareness of the natural world. The simple recital of *gathas*, or mindfulness verses, leads to a heightened awareness of every activity. These meditation forms make participants more aware of what is going on within oneself in terms of selfish desires and of what is going on in the world. A simple water *gatha* reads:

> Water flows from high in the mountains.
> Water runs deep in the earth.
> Miraculously, water comes to us
> And sustains all life.[24]

In reducing egoism, fostering empathy, deepening an appreciation of one's surroundings, and leading to a sense of oneness with the universe, such meditation can provide a powerful method for water awareness as we drink slowly, bathe or shower, and wash with greater awareness of the precious drops of water in and around our bodies.

Taoism and Confucianism

The key to understanding these two traditions lies in the concept of *ch'i*, energy. To block the flow of *ch'i* is to impede energy, whether in oneself or in the universe. That simple formula reveals the power of Taoism and Confucianism to contribute to a new water ethos and ethic. In Taoist thought, the principle of holism of Heaven, Nature, and the Human establishes our basic interconnections with one another. Second, the principle of *ch'i,* of life force or energy, is intrinsic to being, not subordinate to a transcendent force such as God in the Western traditions. The third basic principle central to a new ethos lies in the dynamic of balance in *yin* and *yang*. These principles form in turn an interrelated and holistic view of reality; everything possesses energy, exchanges energy, and depends upon energy.[25] There is a particular place in Taoist thought for water, often compared to *ch'i* in terms of flow. Thus forcing water against its natural flow, as in channeling rivers, in massive reservoirs, in diverting water uphill against its flow to irrigate fields—all these activities only block *ch'i* and thus impede the dynamics of the entire universe, resulting in harmful consequences.

In Confucianism *ch'i* is a spiritual force and a material force. With its focus on kinship with all beings in the natural as well as the human world, Confucian thought emphasizes active engagement in the world in order to harmonize Heaven, Earth, and Nature, and practical questions of ethical conduct are of great concern to Confucians. Special preparation in virtuous living characterize anyone who would involve himself or herself in ordering nature to bring about harmony. Since everything is united, one must become friends with the natural world, with mountains, with rivers, with animals to preserve one's own harmony and the harmony of the universe. If the Confucian emphasis upon harmony with one's surroundings in the social order is extended to the order of nature, then "each individual person and mankind [sic] as a whole are defined, exhaustively, by our respective individual and collective relationships to the natural environment. . . . The well-being of mankind [sic] and the well-being of the environment . . . will be inconceivable apart from one another."[26] In addition to allowing *ch'i* to flow through "effortless action" of Taoism, humans must engage in managing that *ch'i* so that no barrier can block the energy needed to establish harmony among Heaven, Earth, and Humans.

Judaism

For the three religions of the Abrahamic tradition (Judaism, Christianity, and Islam), the challenge to develop cosmologies and ethical practices for a new water ethos will be quite different. For each tradition, far from viewing the human as an integral part of the natural order, has developed strong divisions between the human and the divine and between the human and the natural world, especially in Christianity. Much work has been done in each tradition to overcome these historical biases, but it would be too simplistic to overlook that tension.

Judaism's main contribution to the discussion on water lies in the biblical primacy of creation from the waters and the subsequent covenant God makes with humans to care for the Earth and all that is in it. In the richness of the Jewish tradition, God is not separate from the creation, but is deeply present within. The Psalms often refer to the ways in which animals, rivers, streams, or other natural phenomena praise God by their activities—returning to God the divine presence within each. What follows from this sense of God's presence is the injunction that just as one may not take the *name* of God in vain, so one may not "take the endless material gifts with which we are blessed any more casually. We may not take the One's great gift of holy *water* in vain."[27] The strong admonition to respect God's creation as one respects God's name is a key point of understanding Jewish concern for the environment.

Jewish traditions, less influenced by Platonic distinctions between matter and spirit than Christianity, have always placed strong emphasis on working in this material world. For this reason, Jews have been active in the promotion of human rights everywhere in the world and in the civil rights movement in the United States. This provides a basis for preserving and conserving God's creation as "stewards" of the resources God has entrusted to humans. God *owns* creation. This understanding of God's ownership runs through the injunction not to sell the land into perpetuity because it belongs to the Lord or the provision not to farm the land in the seventh year. The weekly Sabbath rituals emphasize God's ownership and stress restraint in stewardship. The Sabbath involves three primary elements: "we create nothing, we destroy nothing, and we enjoy the bounty of the Earth."[28] Each element emphasizes that God is supreme, and God is the source of the Earth's bounty.

Judaism's insistence of God's ownership of creation with humans as God's responsible stewards might imply that the purpose of creation is to serve human interests, even if modest. However, the biblical materials also note that all creation worships God, not only humans. While this position neither identifies God with creation nor adopts the position of sacred reverence and noninterference with nature suggested in some Eastern and indigenous traditions, it does emphasize the respect for nonhuman life and natural phenomenon required in a theocentric view. Thus not only is the Sabbath a day of rest for humans, it is a day of rest for the animals as well.

We see these important themes in the following passage by a Jewish scholar:

> In numerous . . . passages, the earth as a whole, certain lands in particular, the soil, vegetation, and animal life are depicted as vibrant, sensitive, responsive, and reactive to the good and evil wrought by God and man [sic]. They enter into moral and even legal obligation. They can be obedient or disobedient to God. These facts confirm the impression . . . that a quasi-human, moral "life" pervades all of nature—earth and seas, mountains and valleys, stars and planets.[29]

Thus in Jewish traditions and rituals involving water examined earlier, the foundation exists for the development of concern for and commitment to water integrity. Due to God's creative power and abiding presence in creation, water has an intrinsic value independent of its use by humans. The universe is a creation of a caring God, and thus the natural order, including water, has a presence that demands respect, even obedience.

These themes have enabled Jewish leaders to engage in various environmental organizations and practices. Ellen Bernstein, a river rafting guide and environmental studies graduate, formed one of the first Jewish environmental organizations, Shomrei Adamah, "Keeper of the Earth," in 1988. In the introduction to her work *Ecology and the Jewish Spirit,* Bernstein writes that from her studies, ". . . I was convinced that the spiritual and ecological dimensions that I discovered for myself had the potential to enrich Judaism and provide meaning for my generation and those to come. . . . *Shomrei Adamah* developed programs, publications, and curricula to illuminate Jewish ecological values and enhance Jewish spirituality."[30] Bernstein is only one of many Jewish environmentalists.

Mark Jacobs, former executive director of the Coalition on the Environment and Jewish Life (COEJL), writes that Jewish environmentalists have successfully defined the environment as a Jewish issue. An early 1992 statement of COEJL reads: "For Jews, the environmental crisis is a religious challenge. As heirs to a tradition of stewardship that goes back to Genesis . . . , we cannot accept the escalating destruction of our environment and its effect on human health and livelihood. . . . The ecological crisis hovers over all Jewish concerns."[31] Jewish environmentalism can contribute powerful voices to the issues surrounding water in the coming challenges on policy and practice.

Christianity

Christianity inherits a rich Jewish tradition supportive of action on water issues. At the same time the long historical dualism within Christian thought and practice between the physical and the spiritual and between humans and the natural world, has inhibited engagement in ecological action. However, within the past several decades major new areas of Christian thought have argued not just for a retrieval of a greater sense of stewardship in human-nature relationships, but also for entirely new ways of thinking about those relationships. Through their explorations of such traditional beliefs as the Incarnation of God in the person of Jesus, the Resurrection of the material body, the Crucifixion of Jesus, and Salvation/Liberation, theologians such as Sallie McFague, Larry Rasmussen, Thomas Berry, Leonardo Boff, and others have extended Christian doctrine to embrace a more intimate sense of God's presence in creation, the crucifixion of the Earth itself, and the awaiting of all creation for liberation from oppression.[32] The Roman Catholic Church, the World Council of Churches, and in the United States the National Council of Churches have made water protection and accessibility a major theme of their reflections and statements.

Orthodox Ecumenical Patriarch Bartholomew speaks of committing a crime against nature, against waters as "a sin": "For humans to cause species to become extinct and to destroy the biological diversity of God's creation . . . for humans to degrade the integrity of Earth by causing changes in its climate, by stripping the Earth of its natural forests, or destroying its wetlands . . . for humans to contaminate the Earth's waters with poisonous substances . . . these are sins."[33] The Patriarch's words contain a powerful indictment of human actions.

Pope John Paul II's address to the world for the Lenten season of 1993 recalled the passages from Matthew's gospel in which Jesus speaks of water: "Whoever gives to these little ones even a cup of cold water, I say to you, he [sic] shall not lose his reward" (Matthew 10:42), and "Come, blessed of my father . . . for I was thirsty and you gave me to drink" (Matthew 25:34–35). These passages form the basis for his words to remember the sufferings of those who are experiencing desertification and lack potable drinking water: "We are deeply worried to see that entire peoples have been reduced to destitution and are suffering hunger and disease because they lack drinking water."[34] This concern was echoed in the statement by the Vatican's Pontifical Council for Justice and Peace at the 3rd World Water Forum in Kyoto, Japan, March 2003, linking water and poverty: "Many people living in poverty . . . daily face enormous hardship because water supplies are neither sufficient nor safe. Women bear a disproportionate hardship. For water users living in poverty, this is rapidly becoming an issue crucial for life." The statement views the problem as one of "distribution and resources." Here there is clearly a link between ethical and religious principles and water: "Access and deprivation underlie most water decisions. Hence linkages between water policy and ethics increasingly emerge throughout the world." The key principle supporting this premise is that of *solidarity* with others in meeting basic needs. The document also refers to the common good and the preferential attention to the poor.[35] At the 5th World Water Forum in Mexico City, March 16–22, 2006, the council declared that wasting water is unacceptable and noted the role water plays in peace and security issues, citing a harsh drought in southern Africa which increases tensions there.[36]

Similar statements and study commissions exist also among many Protestant denominations, the National Council of Churches, and the World Council of Churches, especially through the WCC's theme of "Peace, Justice, and the Integrity of Creation." The NCC marked World Water Day, March 22, 2007, with the announcement of a new water steward resource, "Water Stewards: A Toolkit for Congregational Care of Local Watersheds." Noting that there are over five hundred references to water in the Bible, Cassandra Carmichael, director of the NCC's Eco-Justice Programs, stated: "As Christians, we have a moral obligation to care for God's gift of water and protect our nation's waterways."[37] In its appeal to "Governing Bodies and Concerned Citizens" issued in early 2007, the NCC argued that water is a gift from God for all people and not a commodity traded for profit; consequently, "It is our religious responsibility to preserve fragile ecosystems in wetlands, creeks, and other riparian habitats."[38] One denomination of the NCC, the Evangelical Lutheran Church in America, developed a program to raise funds for deep tube wells in Bangladesh, deep enough to avoid the arsenic contamination in the shallow wells. These and other efforts at the international level of the World Council of Churches offer great promise of a more profound valuation of water in these faith traditions.[39]

The World Council of Churches has made water a central concern of several of its studies and works. In May 2005, the three hundred forty member churches around the world affirmed a statement establishing the Ecumenical Water Network that relates the work of the member churches to the broader water movement around the world. Specifically emphasizing the spiritual aspect of water, the network's brochure focuses upon the right to water and the development of community-based initiatives. At its Ninth Assembly in Porto Alegre, Brazil, February 2006, the WCC took the further step of adopting a statement, "Water for Life," which aimed not only to promote awareness for the preservation and protection of water, but also to undertake advocacy to guarantee the legal right to water, support further community-based efforts, monitor disputes in river basins, and contribute to the International Decade for Action, Water for Life (2005–2015) by "highlighting the ethical and spiritual dimension of the water crisis."[40]

The Roman Catholic bishops of the US Pacific Northwest and British Columbia, Canada undertook a lengthy study of the waters of the Columbia River through a series of conversations with the many users of the river—farmers, loggers, barge owners, indigenous peoples, recreational groups, commercial fishermen, miners, engineers, and ordinary citizens. Their study produced a document, *The Columbia River Watershed: Caring for Creation and the Common Good*, which articulates a vision of the river as a sacred trace of God's creation that must be respected by its multiple users:

> timber harvesting is done responsibly, with minimal disturbance to the land and water. In the vision fish populations are abundant. People realize the interconnectedness of rivers and ocean. Where feasible, farmers produce organic crops that safeguard water quality. . . . Water is carefully conserved through innovative irrigation techniques. . . . [Mine owners] assure that mining processes do not endanger waters and aquatic life.[41]

Using the philosophical and theological tenets of Catholic social teaching around the common good, the bishops intend their letter to serve as the basis for larger and ongoing discussions about the future of this important waterway to the international region.

These statements and others made by Christian organizations reference scripture or outline a theological argument, but they do not evoke the motivation necessary for engagement in change. This is particularly true in Christianity, because Christianity lacks the restrictions found in other traditions, especially Judaism and Islam, which prohibit someone from abusing nature and water use. No comparable statements exist in the Christian scriptures, and until recently they were absent from church documents. This makes the statement of Ecumenical Patriarch Bartholomew that calls the violation of nature a *sin* a powerful challenge to a Christian. Pope John Paul II joined in this condemnation in his 1993 Lenten address when he called pollution and desertification "criminal" actions. Such strong language helps root a new water ethos and ethic.

Exemplified by other religious traditions, ritual practices are vital resources for developing a new consciousness around water and new commitments to action. For Christians, the primary ritual is baptism: the death of the old and the rebirth of the new *in the waters*. No other medium so powerfully conveys the meaning of baptism as birth to a new life. The waters of baptism must be as pure and undefiled as the new life into which one is called. Other rituals involving holy water are also occasions for enhancing a sensitivity to the sacred character of water. In relation to well rituals, Irish ecological theologian Sean McDonagh suggests that, at least in Ireland, parishes should revitalize their holy wells. In that way the water quality in the well will be the measure of groundwater quality in the area.[42]

Finally, Christianity incorporates consumption practices that involve "virtual water." Blessings before meals, abstaining from meat on Fridays and from meat during the entire Lenten season, fasting during Lent at certain meals of the day, although no longer practiced, can be revived with a greater intentionality around the "virtual" water in the products we consume so easily, moving away from beef production which uses so much water in the process. When combined with forms of Christian meditation, these practices are capable of creating the kind of mindfulness we see in Buddhism.

Christians of various denominations are involved in a variety of environmental organizations. Evangelicals have formed the Evangelical Environmental Network; other specifically Christian groups include the North American Conference on Christianity and Ecology and the Au Sable Institute.[43] Similar groups of active Christians exist in almost every mainline denomination, sometimes in small numbers, but growing through continued work by theologians as well as practitioners.

Islam

In a manner similar to the Jewish tradition, Islam views the sovereignty of Allah and Allah's merciful rule over creation as the basis for all laws and all reflections on the relationships between humans and the natural world. As in the Jewish texts, humans must care for the world; they will be judged on how well they carry out that task. Although humans have "functional authority" over creation in their role as vicegerents, they have great obligations toward the environment.[44] We saw earlier that abuse of the Earth violates Allah's commands, and the many prohibitions surrounding such abuse make that clear in Muslim teachings.

Nature in Islam is integrally related to the human order: the human and the natural world together reflect the divine creator, and both are called on to praise Allah. Water, too, praises Allah. This perception of the human and natural world places water as a public good, available to all who need it, even in times of scarcity. While giving water to others, especially strangers, is a matter of Islamic charity, it is also a matter of Islamic law.[45]

The Islamic rituals we studied earlier remind us of the integration of daily life with one's beliefs as a Muslim. Further, the very architecture of cities where Muslims dwell also point to the central place of water: fountains in homes and markets are present not just for bodily refreshment from the hot sun, but also as places for spiritual renewal. Islamic scholar Hashim Ismail Dockrat, founder and director of the Institute for Human and Environmental Development, writes of this interconnection: "Hence this homogeneity between the body and soul—material and spiritual—has its own architectural expression. . . . This architecture is determined by the simplest of human activities, such as how to wash, how to sit on the ground, how to eat from a single platter, how to behave in the family and toward the stranger."[46] Even buildings are built with the integration of the physical and the spiritual in mind.

Islamic water laws provide explicit directions for water use that serve as a model for water regulation around the world. The ancient *hadith* in which the Prophet chastises Sa'ad for wasting water when performing ablutions, or cleansings, from a river instructs Muslim actions toward water. The water ablution here does not involve money, does not harm nature, does not take time; no pollution results, and no living things are harmed. The ablution is only necessary for prayers. Yet it is wasteful, and the wastefulness is prohibited. Wastefulness is further to be prohibited when water use takes time or expense, pollutes the water, harms living things, and impacts future users.[47]

The proper uses of water involve a hierarchy of water rights based on the overall theological premise that water is a gift from Allah meant for all: water is a good held in common, cannot be privately owned in its natural state, and must not be wasted. Furthermore in the hierarchy of rights to water, water for people has highest priority, then for livestock, and next for agriculture. This approach favors those who consume the least and have the least impact on water. Rules govern upstream and downstream water use. Well owners have senior rights but must not pollute nor drain the aquifer, causing other wells to fail.[48]

In general, water use should benefit all who share the waterways, and no harm should come to other users. A partnership exists between humans and water, which is part of the "general human partnership in all the sources of life."[49] Another important institution governing water in Islamic law is the *haram*—a sacred area, eventually extended to cover environmental areas.

Such zones are protected from intrusion and are most often associated with water sources in wells, springs, rivers, and underground.[50]

Islamic law serves as the basis for regulations and laws governing water use in many countries of the Near East. Such measures include water tariffs that increase as consumption increases, leakage control measures, recycling treated wastewater from mosque ablutions, water scheduling for agricultural uses, well regulations, aquifer protections, recycling industrial wastewater, closed water cycling at several industrial plants, and the reuse of wastewater effluent for irrigation. All these measures, guided by Islamic laws, have helped Saudi Arabia meet the growing demand for water with effective water management.[51]

Islam has also established several environmental organizations to build sustainable policies and practices, not only around water but on a host of others issues. "BoomIran," founded in 1980 in Iran, has developed a program, "Save Our Rivers," to protect polluted rivers and discover the origins of the pollution. Other environmental organizations include the Green Front of Iran, which organized sea coast cleanups; the Iranian Society of Environmentalists, primarily an academic organization for research; the Wildlife and Nature Conservancy Foundation of Iran; the Mountain Environment Protection Committee; and the Esfahan Green Message. After a severe drought in 1999–2001 that impacted twenty-five of Iran's twenty-nine provinces, over one hundred forty NGOs focused on the environment were established.[52] On an international level the Aga Khan Development Network, established by the spiritual leader Aga Khan III, Imam of the Ismai'li Muslims, has developed a large organization and fund dedicated to environmental issues, and particularly issues on water and development, based upon principles of Islamic law.[53]

One of the most successful examples of integrating Islam into ecological issues involves the island of Misali in the Zanzibar archipelago, surrounded by some of the most important coral reefs in the Indian Ocean. When overfishing by international trawlers decreased fishing yields, local fishermen began dynamiting the coral reefs. In spite of efforts by government and international organizations, including a ban on dynamite fishing, the dynamiting continued. In 2000, the World Wide Fund for Nature and Care International asked the Islamic Foundation for Ecology and Environmental Sciences (IFEES) to apply Islamic principles to conservation and development projects to ensure sustainability. The IFEES set up intensive educational workshops incorporating teachings from the Qur'an. As a result, they have established a conservation area, and fishermen are using sustainable fishing practices that bring improved fish catches.[54]

Islam, then, provides us with important contributions to a new water ethos in its integrated view of the human-nature relationship, the communal sense of water as a public good, the prohibition regarding water's purities, the rituals used in Islam for inner as well as external purity, and the sophisticated legal bases for establishing water rights and proper uses. All of these can contribute to a greater awareness of water usage and conservation, especially in the arid regions of Islam's homelands.

Conclusion

In all of these traditions, water has a profound meaning whether as divine in itself or as a manifestation of the divine. Abuse of water in any form is an abuse of the divine, a sinful and criminal act. This character of water is rooted in texts, stories, and rituals in which water is believed to purify inner stain just as it cleanses outer stain. Yet, as Russell Train recounts in one of the reflections earlier in this chapter, so many adherents of these traditions fail in their respect and care. This is both a problem and an opportunity for leaders in these traditions and for those concerned about the environment who may not share these religious convictions.

As of 2001, there are some five billion adherents to the world's religions, covering 82 percent of the world's population. Christianity with over two billion members, Islam with 1.2 billion followers, and Hinduism with 752 million adherents are the most prominent, followed by Chinese religions, Buddhism, and indigenous traditions with approximately 390 million, 360 million, and 230 million, respectively.[55] If even a small percentage of those 5 billion became knowledgeable of the place of water in their own traditions and motivated to take action in personal practices and public policies, who can imagine what changes might occur?

Education in the traditions, scriptures, cosmologies, and spiritualities is central. Such an educational program also demands an appreciation of the ways in which scientific understandings complement religious insights and even contribute to a sense of wonder for the marvels of water. In addition to education of the mind, there must also be education of the heart through rituals, prayers, meditation, and mindfulness practices. If every time we used water, we envisioned the water flowing from fountain, spigot, stream, river, or other source, then the abuses of water might cease, and water would not be wasted. Such mindfulness can then lead to creative ways to use water that retain its bounty and purity. Already drought, pollution of the waters, and scarcity force some to think in this manner. However, others among the five billion can be challenged through their traditions to become water-carers instead of water consumers.

The new ethos we have examined calls for many components in practice. Among these are:

1. Water identity—we *are* water people, born in amniotic water with bodies composed of great amounts of water. We take in water daily. We are nourished with water. We are intimate with water.
2. Water consciousness—if we are water people, then water awareness must penetrate our consciousness in small and large practices, daily and long term.
3. Water sin and ignorance—abuse of water is a crime against others and against the Earth. The principle that "polluter pays" must take on new meaning here. We must no longer tolerate ignorance of the consequences of actions inhibiting water's flow.
4. Water asceticism—in every tradition, no matter how pronounced, there is the basis for a discipline against waste and extravagance, for a reduction in our consumption of water and virtual water products.
5. Water spirituality—balancing asceticism is celebration; water festivals, well dedications, and other festivities that celebrate water's place in our lives.
6. Water rituals—a renewal and revival of existing water rituals and the creation of new rituals are essential in connecting us on deep psychological, symbolic levels to the current water crises.
7. Water solidarity—we join together with others around the globe in nongovernmental organizations, community groups, workers, to create a World Water Contract and local and regional contracts on water uses.

Religions have the capacity to provide new understandings, meaning systems, worldviews, and ethos to create communities across ethnic, political, social, and economic boundaries, as well as the power to inspire and bring moral authority to issues of great significance. In addition, religious traditions possess tremendous resources in organization, finances, and person power. In the antiwar and civil rights movements in the United States, Europe, and elsewhere, religions were shown to have the moral and spiritual bases to call forth responsive actions for greater justice. Similarly, religious traditions need to resort to their prophetic powers to call for needed changes in water use and management, not only in powerful, prophetic statements but in such actions as boycotts, letter-writing campaigns, protests similar to the struggles of the people of Cochabamba, Bolivia, or Stockton, California, and dam protesters in India. At the same time religious traditions can utilize their spiritual resources to inculcate habits of simple living, of material asceticism in the drive against a rampant consumption of scarce resources. The amount of "virtual water" used in the production of consumer goods for multitudes cries out for cutting back, buying less, recycling, and reusing. A religious discipline of meditation, mindfulness, or contemplation forms the necessary groundwork for sustaining efforts in personal and public struggles for a sustainable world.

These elements are not exhaustive, nor easily implemented. The transition from sacred texts, ritual practices, and observances to responsible actions toward the environment and water are mediated by individuals and groups who themselves must be committed to intimacy with Earth and water. Yet the elements above are essential not just for the credibility of religious traditions, but also for their contributions to the new water ethos and ethics. As Saadia Khawar Khan Chishti, educator and the only female member of Pakistan's Council of Islamic Ideology, states "A purely secular approach to establishing a paradigm of sustainable development has not and will not cure the root cause of the illness [of the water crisis]: the absence of an individual desire to learn and understand and the absence of an individual sense of responsibility for the holistic consequences of one's actions."[56] Water's place in religious traditions reveals the powerful dynamic that in preserving the resource of water we are not only promoting corporeal sustainability for future generations, but spiritual sustainability as well.

Notes

1. Gerard Manley Hopkins, in *Gerard Manley Hopkins: A Selection of His Poems and Prose*, no. 63, ed. W. H. Gardner (Harmondsworth, England: Penguin Books Ltd., 1964), 82.

2. Quoted in John Haught, *The Promise of Nature* (New York: Paulist Press, 1993), 2–3.

3. Quoted in Wesley Granberg-Michaelson, "Creation in Ecumenical Theology," in *Ecotheology: Voices from South and North*, ed. David G. Hallman (Maryknoll, N.Y.: Orbis, 1994), 100.

4. David Suzuki, *The Sacred Balance* (Vancouver, B.C.: Greystone Books, 1997), 75 (my italics).

5. Phillip Ball, *Life's Matrix: A Biography of Water* (New York: Farrar, Straus & Giroux, 1999), 372.

6. Maggie Black, *The No-Nonsense Guide to Water* (Oxford: New Internationalist, 2004), 140–141 (my italics).

7. Joachim Blatter, Helen Ingram, and Pamela M. Doughman, "Emerging Approaches to Comprehend Changing Global Contexts," in *Reflections on Water: New Approaches to Transboundary Conflicts and Cooperation*, eds. Joachim Blatter and Helen Ingram (Cambridge, Mass.: MIT Press, 2001), 1, 4, 16.

8. Padmasiri de Silva, *Buddhism, Ethics and Society: The Conflicts and Dilemmas of Our Times* (Clayton, Australia: Monash University Press, 2002), 159.

9. Quoted in Marilyn Berlin Snell, "The Rainmaker: A Hopi Leader Champions Clean Power in Indian Country," *Sierra*, January–February 2007, 16, 19.

10. Quoted in Snell, "The Rainmaker," 20.

11. Thomas Berry, *Dream of the Earth* (Mystic, Conn.: Twenty-Third Pub., 1989), chap. 1.

12. Gary Gardner, *Invoking the Spirit: Religion and Spirituality in the Quest for a Sustainable World* (Washington, D.C.: Worldwatch Institute, 2002), 18.

13. J. Baird Callicott, "Conceptual Resources for Environmental Ethics in Asian Traditions of Thought: A Propaedeutic," *Philosophy East and West* 37, no. 2 (April 1987): 125.

14. Mircea Eliade, ed., "Water," *Encyclopedia of Religion*, vol. 15 (New York: Macmillan, 1987), 352–353.

15. Anil Agarwal, "Can Hindu Beliefs and Values Help India Meet Its Ecological Crisis?" in *Hinduism and Ecology: The Intersection of Earth, Sky, and Water*, eds. Christopher Key Chapple and Mary Evelyn Tucker (Cambridge, Mass.: Harvard University Press, 2000), 172–173.

16. Agarwal, "Hindu Beliefs," 172–173.

17. See chapter 1.

18. See Gardner, *Invoking the Spirit*, 36–37, for a fuller account.

19. Thich Nhat Hanh, "Look Deep and Smile: Thoughts and Writings of Thich Nhat Hanh," in *Buddhism and Ecology*, eds. Martine Batchelor and Kerry Brown (London: Cassell, 1992), 105–106.

20. Gardner, *Invoking the Spirit*, 32–34.

21. A. T. Ariyaratne and Joanna Macy, "The Island of Temple and Tank," in *Buddhism and Ecology*, eds. Martine Batchelor and Kerry Brown (London: Cassell, 1992), 83–86.

22. Kenneth Kraft, "The Greening of Buddhist Practice," *Cross Currents* 44, no. 2 (Summer 1994): 169ff.

23. Stephanie Kaza, "American Buddhist Response to the Land: Ecological Practice at Two West Coast Retreat Centers," in *Buddhism and Ecology: The Interconnection of Dharma and Deeds*, ed. Mary Evelyn Tucker and Duncan Ryūken Williams (Cambridge, Mass.: Harvard University Press, 1997) 231–232.

24. Quoted by Hanh, "Look Deep," 105.

25. Callicott, "Conceptual Resources," 122–123, 125.

26. Callicott, "Conceptual Resources," 127.

27. Arthur Green, "A Kabbalah for the Environmental Age," in *Judaism and Ecology: Created World and Revealed Word*, ed. Hava Tirosh-Samuelson (Cambridge, Mass.: Harvard University Press, 2002), 12.

28. Eric Katz, "Judaism and the Ecological Crisis," in *Worldviews and Ecology*, eds. Mary Evelyn Tucker and John A. Grim (Maryknoll, N.Y.: Orbis, 1994), 59.

29. Quoted in David Kinsley, *Ecology and Religion: Ecological Spirituality in Cross-Cultural Perspective* (Englewood Cliffs, N.J.: Prentice Hall, 1995), 116–117.

30. Quoted in Mark X. Jacobs, "Jewish Environmentalism: Past Accomplishments and Future Challenges," in *Judaism and Ecology: Created World and Revealed Word*, ed. Hava Tirosh-Samuelson (Cambridge, Mass.: Harvard University Press, 2002), 452.

31. Quoted in Jacobs, "Jewish Environmentalism," 457.

32. See Sallie McFague, *The Body of God* (Minneapolis, Minn.: Fortress Press, 1993); Larry Rasmussen, *Earth Community, Earth Ethic* (Maryknoll, N.Y.: Orbis, 2001); Thomas Berry, *Befriending the Earth* (Mystic, Conn.: Twenty-Third Pub., 1991); Leonardo Boff, *Ecology and Liberation* (Maryknoll, N.Y.: Orbis, 1995).

33. Quoted in National Council of Churches, "God's Earth is Sacred: An Open Letter to Church and Society in the United States," at http://www.ncccusa.org/news/ 14.02.05theologicalstatement (accessed 10 April 2006).

34. John Paul II, "Water Is Sacred: Protect It," *National Catholic Reporter*, 19 February 1993, 32.

35. Quoted in "Global Water Crisis: A Test of Solidarity," *National Catholic Reporter*, 30 May 2003, 32. The full text of the council's statement is available at www .vatican.va/roman_curia/pontifical_councils/justpeace.

36. Quoted in "In Brief," *The Tablet*, 25 March 2006, 41.

37. Quoted in *News from the National Council of Churches*, at www.nccusa .org/news, 14 March 2007.

38. National Council of Churches, "Water: The Key to Sustaining Life—An Open Statement to Governing Bodies and Concerned Citizens," at www.nccecojustice .org/waterltr.htm, 2 May 2007.

39. National Council of Churches, "Help Bring Clean Drinking Water to Africa in 100 Days, at www.nccecojustice.org (accessed 26 April 2007); "Safe Drinking Water for Those Who Are Thirsty—Wells in Bangladesh," at www.nccecojustice.org (accessed 23 April 2007).

40. World Council of Churches, "Water for Life: Introduction," at www.oikoumene.org/index.php?id=2612 (accessed 3 May 2007); World Council of Churches, *Statement on Water for Life*, at www.oikoumene.org/index.lpho?id=1955 (accessed 3 May 2007).

41. Catholic Bishops of the Region, *The Columbia River Watershed: Caring for Creation and the Common Good* (Seattle: Columbia River Project, 2001), 12–13.

42. Sean McDonagh, *Dying for Water* (Dublin: Veritas, 2003), 100.

43. See Gardner, *Invoking the Spirit*, and Laurel Kearns, "Saving the Creation: Christian Environmentalism in the United States," *Sociology of Religion* 57:1 (1996): 55–70, for more information.

44. See Roger E. Timm, "The Ecological Fallout of Islamic Creation Theology," in *Worldviews and Ecology*, eds. Mary Evelyn Tucker and John A. Grim (Maryknoll, N.Y.: Orbis, 1994), 86.

45. Anne Coles, "Geology and Gender: Water Supplies, Ethnicity and Livelihoods in Central Sudan," in *Gender, Water, and Development*, eds. Anne Coles and Tina Wallace (New York: Berg Books, 2005), 90–91.

46. Hashim Ismail Dockrat, "Islam, Muslim Society, and Environmental Concerns," in *Islam and Ecology: A Bestowed Trust*, eds. Richard C. Foltz, Frederick M. Denny, and Azizan Baharuddin (Cambridge, Mass.: Harvard University Press, 2003), 364.

47. Ibrahim Ozdemir, "Toward an Understanding of Environmental Ethics from a Qur'anic Perspective," in *Islam and Ecology: A Bestowed Trust*, eds. Foltz, Denny, and Azizan (Cambridge, Mass.: Harvard University Press, 2003), 14–15.

48. Othman Abd-ar-Rahman Llewellyn, "The Basis for a Discipline of Islamic Environmental Law," in *Islam and Ecology: A Bestowed Trust*, eds. Foltz, Denny, and Azizan (Cambridge, Mass.: Harvard University Press, 2003), 204–205.

49. Mawil Izzi Dien, "Islam and the Environment," in *Islam and Ecology: A Bestowed Trust*, eds. Foltz, Denny, and Azizan (Cambridge, Mass.: Harvard University Press, 2003), 118.

50. S. Nomanul Haq, "Islam and Ecology: Toward Retrieval and Reconstruction," in *Islam and Ecology: A Bestowed Trust*, eds. Foltz, Denny, and Azizan (Cambridge, Mass.: Harvard University Press, 2003), 144–145.

51. Walid A. Abderrahman, "Water Demand Management and Islamic Water Management Principles: A Case Study," *Water Resources Development* 16:4 (2000): 465–473.

52. Richard C. Foltz, "Islamic Environmentalism: A Matter of Interpretation," in *Islam and Ecology: A Bestowed Trust*, eds. Foltz, Denny, and Azizan (Cambridge, Mass.: Harvard University Press, 2003), 264–265.

53. Tazim R. Kassam, "The Aga Khan Development Network: An Ethic of Sustainable Development and Social Conscience," in *Islam and Ecology: A Bestowed Trust*, eds. Foltz, Denny, and Azizan (Cambridge, Mass.: Harvard University Press, 2003), 478ff.

54. Fazlun M. Khalid, "The Application of Islamic Environmental Ethics to Promote Marine Conservation in Zanzibar: A Case Study," January 2003, at http://ifees .org.uk/index.php?option=com_content &task=view&id=40&Itemid=55.

55. Cited in Gary Gardner, *Invoking the Spirit*, 17.

56. Saadia Khawar Khan Chishti, "*Fitra*: An Islamic Model for Humans and the Environment," in *Islam and Ecology: A Bestowed Trust*, eds. Foltz, Denny, and Azizan (Cambridge, Mass.: Harvard University Press, 2003), 79.

~

CHAPTER NINE

Where Do We Go from Here?

The central focus of the work here has been both to outline the challenges and to provide ethical and religious considerations to the global water crisis in the hope that such explorations will lead to personal, local, regional, and even global actions in concert with others. At the same time the challenges presented in earlier chapters are daunting. At the end of our water journey, then, it is important to note the hundreds of actions, practices, policies, programs, and possibilities undertaken around the globe, especially those that reflect and incorporate some of the religious insights, principles, and sensibilities around water in a new water ethic. While the following discussion will not provide *the* definitive answers to the crises and will certainly not address all the issues, these are some of the efforts we look to in order to foster and continue the development of a global ecological consciousness and sustainable water practices.

The recent November 2006 report of the United Nations Development Program (UNDP) argues for a "soft path" to water resource development. The report both acknowledges and criticizes the "hard path" approach followed for the past half-century. The dam–reservoir combination not only harms the environment as we have seen, it concentrates power in the hands of the rich and powerful in society. The report calls for decentralized, small-scale technologies: "Getting more crop per drop, rather than more water to the fields, is becoming the central concern."[1] The report recommends that the group of 8 leading industrialized nations designate a minimum of 1 percent of gross domestic product for sanitation and sewage where needed

around the globe. There is also a call for both new technologies and the revival of old technologies. The author of the report, Kevin Watkins, stated
that "No other investment could bring greater benefits."[2]

Also in 2006, the United Nations World Water Development Report 2,
Water: A Shared Responsibility, calls for similar readjustments. In particular
this report reaffirms the important links between water access, poverty, and
development and argues that there must be a necessary and critical shift from
water supply to water management, greater emphasis upon local participation, democratic decision-making processes, increased involvement by
women, and an emphasis upon whole water ecosystems as "socio-eco-hydro-
logical systems." In addition, the authors emphasize that nonmarket valua-
tions, such as catchment preservation, must complement market-driven,
benefit-cost analysis.[3]

The calls from these and other sources for a new "water ethos" are
premised on several of the key principles enunciated in the previous chapters. Such principles focus on local, community-based approaches to water
management, with maximum participation by those most affected, with pref-
erences for poor and marginal communities, in solidarity with democratic
management practices. Given that billions lack access to potable water and
adequate sanitation, the world simply cannot afford conventional Western,
first-world approaches to water access, management, distribution, and cost
measures. Furthermore, all these efforts must be connected to reductions in
world poverty. If water now flows uphill to the wealthier urban dwellers, then
the new ethic must embrace a downward flow to those most in need.

Already we know that water demand for agricultural, industrial, and domestic needs will rise by nearly two-thirds by 2025. When the World Bank
at the 2002 World Summit on Sustainable Development in Johannesburg
promised to provide water for half of those without water by 2015, the model
was based on solutions such as large dams and reservoirs, more pipes and
sewer systems. Yet the costs for these twentieth-century approaches preclude
easy solutions. In the twenty-first century the issue concerns not only the
scarcity of water, but more importantly water management with new approaches that ensure that the access to water, a basic human right, is possible for all.

This is at the heart of the demand for, in Fred Pearce's words, "a new ethos
for water—an ethos based not on technical fixes but on managing the water
cycle for maximum social benefits rather than narrow self-interest."[4] Or put
differently, water must be seen as a social good for the human commons, not
primarily as an economic commodity. The principles involved, then, demand

low-cost, practical technologies centered around communities of people participating in transparent decision-making and management for sustainability. Pearce contends:

> The new thinking means going with the grain of nature. To insure our water supplies and protect against damaging floods . . . we will often have to tear down dams and dykes, recharge the underwater reservoirs, and remake the rivers . . . pour less concrete. . . . The twentieth-century view that the world can feed itself only by artificial irrigation of huge areas of the developing world will also have to go.[5]

Unfortunately, as Black notes, privatized utilities and their international backers generally transport the industrialized world's water engineering models lock, stock, and barrel to much poorer cities around the globe, with only minor consideration for their technical, financial, or managerial suitability. Reaching the Millennium Development Goals requires a much greater investment than transnational private institutions can provide.[6]

Strategies, Techniques, and Technologies

In his work *The Water Manifesto*, Ricardo Petrella looks at the ingredients for a substantive change in our perception of water and the meanings we ascribe to water. The first involves viewing water as a public good and natural right rather than an economic commodity, in fact, as "the first global *res publica* [public good] of societies calling themselves technologically and economically global: this is the first necessary change, and one that will certainly be difficult to achieve." The second key change is the necessity to "de-statize" water, i.e., freeing water from the control of state-centralized bureaucracies. This change calls for a community/cooperative form of ownership of a public good, similar to the efforts taking place in Cochabamba and other areas of the world, which incorporates the basic principles of subsidiarity, solidarity, the common good, equity, and the dignity of all persons.

The third conceptual and symbolic change "concerns the logic—inimical to solidarity and sustainability alike—that currently prevails in the global organization of agriculture," namely, the movement from peasant agriculture to industrial agriculture/agribusiness. We have already discussed the negative results of industrialized agriculture—pollution of waters both above and below ground, the huge expenditures of energy, the taming and rerouting of rivers. At the same time the mega-cities of the developing world cannot sustain increasing numbers of people moving from farms to cities.[7] New, less intensive forms of agriculture are now required.

Marc de Villiers guides us in a discussion similar to Petrella's. In his 2000 work, *Water: The Fate of Our Most Precious Resource,* de Villiers proposes four ways of meeting the global water crisis: (1) getting more water; (2) using less; (3) limiting population growth; (4) stealing water from others. We will now examine each of the four possibilities.

Getting More Water

De Villiers discusses proposals such as shipping water on huge tankers from water-rich areas to water-poor areas, carrying between 1 million and 1.5 million tons of water. An agreement on such possibilities was attempted between water-rich Turkey and water-poor Israel in the 1990s but failed at the political level. Other unlikely proposals include encasing arctic ice or even towing ice to water-poor areas, piping water from Alaska to California, or transferring water from water-rich British Columbia.[8] However, as we have seen with large dams, huge projects often have huge unforeseen consequences, and the sustainability of tankers and other such proposals seems unlikely.

A more serious proposal involves increased desalination processes. Globally some 7,500 plants are in operation, and two-thirds of those are in the Middle East with another 12 percent in Latin America. Israel and Jordan are extensively using desalination techniques. Whether the process is cheaper than reverse osmosis or water diversion, each with variations and advantages, basically each demands a tremendous output of energy sources, emitting even greater amounts of greenhouse gases, which makes the technologies suspect for meeting global water needs.[9]

Nevertheless, desalination is catching on, especially in the Gulf states of the Middle East. Saudi Arabia alone makes up 10 percent of desalination facilities and in 2004 proclaimed that plans were under way for six more plants. A number of islands, from Malta and some Greek islands in the Mediterranean to Caribbean islands, have used desalination to meet the increasing demands of tourists. While most of the plants utilize distillation, more recently reverse osmosis has gained popularity. Costs have come down, and cities such as Tampa Bay, Florida; Houston, Texas; Cape Town, South Africa; and Perth, Australia have adopted reverse osmosis technology. In Spain the government is building twenty reverse-osmosis plants, and China is entering the field. But the problems remain: excessive gases released from burning fossil fuels, enormous amount of energy required, and especially the salt waste and chemicals that often flow back into the sea. "[I]t is a supply-side solution to a demand-side problem,"[10] notes Pearce.

Cloud Seeding, Dew Collecting, and Fog Harvesting

Another approach involves a variety of techniques and technologies. Cloud seeding, a process of stimulating clouds to produce rain, results in the replenishment of aquifers through winter flows. Then there is the possibility of "dew" collecting in arid regions. In the Negev Desert, fog-drip irrigation is used for small-scale agriculture.[11] In England dew ponds still dot the landscape and, once abandoned, are being revived. The ponds are dug on a hilltop with waterproof lining so the water does not escape. Straw is placed beneath the clay earth, acting as insulation and keeping the clay colder than the soil beneath; stones placed on top shed heat at night and lower the temperature. Then because rising air cools, especially at night when temperatures drop, the ponds catch the low clouds and fog. Similar dew ponds are found on Croatian islands in the Adriatic.[12]

A similar approach involves fog-catching screens. From the Pacific coasts of Latin America to desert countries such as Yemen and Oman to Haiti, Namibia, Eritrea, and Nepal, large plastic sheets of mesh are erected to capture moisture from fog. The tiny droplets accumulate on the mesh to form large drops that run into a trough. Such a device provides 4,000 gallons of water a day for the small town of 350 people in Chungungo, Chile. The idea has spread rapidly.[13]

Another variation on fog harvesting involves a pattern mimicked from a desert beetle that obtains water by its own "bobbled upper surface with a . . . hexagonal pattern of tiny peaks and troughs [which] appear to push tiny droplets [of fog] together to form larger droplets, which then roll off the beetle's back and into its mouth." The approach has been patented, and companies are developing such fog collectors for building rooftops and other places.[14]

Dam Breaching

Although dam breaching may not seem like a form of obtaining *more* water, dam breaching would greatly improve the quality of water and restore many of the important services that rivers carry out around the world. In the United States, twenty dams were removed in the 1970s, ninety one in the 1980s, and one hundred seventy one in the 1990s. In the Pacific Northwest, dams will be breached on the Elhwa River in the Olympic National Park, and discussions continue on breaching the dams on the Snake River, which flows into the Columbia. Sandra Postel notes that when Edwards Dam on the Kennebec River in Maine was removed, two million alewife fish returned within a year, and other species, including Atlantic salmon and sturgeon, were spotted above the former dam's location.[15]

Certainly one of the most promising developments does not involve obtaining "more" water as much as obtaining clean water for the millions who lack access to potable water. The device is a nine-inch "Lifestraw," a plastic tube through which a person literally sucks water from questionable sources. The tube has seven increasingly fine mesh filters that block contaminants. Any bacteria that remain are killed along with some parasites and viruses through iodine beads. The iodine taste is neutralized by active carbon that also kills more parasites. Remarkably, the device, manufactured by the Danish textile company Vestergaard Frandsen costs only $3 and lasts approximately one year. Although it does not filter metals such as arsenic, nor some viruses or the parasite giardia, the Lifestraw offers hope to millions around the globe. At present only some 100,000 have been handed out, mainly through aid agencies, but Vestergaard Frandsen is preparing for mass production.[16] Another promising method of obtaining more pure water has been developed by Ashok Gadgil, a Mumbai native, now a scientist at the Lawrence Berkeley National Laboratory in California. In 1966 Gadgil patented an inexpensive method for disinfecting water by using ultraviolet light. The company WaterHealth International has also helped more than one million people obtain drinkable water.[17]

Using Less Water: Agriculture

Rainwater Harvesting

Before the British arrived in India, villages supported the workers and managers of the irrigation system that harvested rain. Then in the colonial period, British overlords dismissed the support systems as "religious and charitable allowances," and rainwater harvesting fell into disuse. The British moved to large-scale water projects, particularly in the twentieth century.[18] What follows are the stories of a revival of these ancient technologies for the twenty-first century.

In the area surrounding Rajasthan, India, a *modern Gandhi*, as Bendra Singh is called, has started a rainwater-harvesting movement opposing privatization while working at the local level. Beginning in 1984, Singh organized farmers and others to collect and save water through rainwater harvesting, collecting the precious resource in small reservoirs. Supported by a growing women's water movement, the Rajasthan movement has been very successful, and currently over 500,000 villages carry out rainwater harvesting. "Small local action can change global thinking in a second,"[19] says Singh.

One approach to rainwater harvesting in India is to catch the rain in ponds; villagers do not use the water directly from the ponds but allow the

water to seep into the underground water resources to replenish wells. Sometimes the ponds are arranged to catch monsoon rains slowly, each pond filling and overflowing into a lower pond while the water continues to refill the
aquifer below. Local farmers also utilize *tanka*, small mud-walled reservoirs
from which they divert the waters through channels for irrigation or let the
water sink into the soil, replenishing the water table. Today, there are some
140,000 such "tanks" across India. Check dams are a similar method of con-
structing barriers in streams and gullies to hold water long enough to perco-
late underground. Other practices involve percolation tanks, contour building on terraces, and additional dug wells. The dramatic results mean more
water in village wells, higher-yielding crops, and year-round farming of
grains. In many instances incomes have increased double and even fourfold.
Thus water issues are directly related to poverty relief. Rainwater harvesting
is becoming an important tool in meeting water needs as well as helping to
meet the crises of rural poverty by generating employment in rural areas and
so mitigating the flow of migration from rural to urban areas.[20] In this way
the pressure on urban needs and resources is diminished.

The keys to these promising efforts lie in small-scale village collaboration
and community-based operations, using principles of subsidiarity and solidarity. Separately the farmers could not effect results since the water would
too quickly dissipate, but collectively the results are very successful. Tushaar
Shah, founder of the International Water Management Institute in Gujarat,
Rajasthan, sees the rainwater-harvesting movement as "mobilizing social energy on a scale and with an intensity that may be one of the most effective
responses to an environmental challenge anywhere in the world"—a dramatic part of a new, yet old, communal water ethic.[21]

While India provides the most dramatic example of rainwater harvesting, China under Chairman Mao and the Cultural Revolution revived
similar ancient practices. Harvesting in rural China is done through cel-
lars for domestic use and cisterns in the fields for agriculture. Although
the number of people utilizing rainwater harvesting is small compared
with China's burgeoning population, the current government actively promotes rainwater harvesting. In one dry province, Gansu, near the middle
section of the Yellow River, over two million people get their water
through rainwater harvesting.[22]

Almost every ancient civilization and many modern ones practiced or
practice some form of rainwater harvesting. Whether catching water in large
vats, such as I saw throughout Belize, diverting flash floods into ponds and
channels, putting check dams across streams, erecting earth dams in the Jor-
danian desert, or capturing floodwaters in *wadis* (gullies) in Yemen, Somalia,

and other African nations,[23] millions of acres in dry parts of the world were once used for water harvesting. The revived technique is spreading to parts of the world as diverse as Japan, Nepal, Bangladesh, Israel, Kenya, Pakistan, Sri Lanka, Germany, and Singapore. Some two billion people across Asia already are having their water shortages alleviated by rainwater harvesting. The same is true for the desperate situations in many parts of Africa.[24] Huge potential exists.

Rainwater harvesting applies many of the principles outlined in the previous chapter, namely, active citizen participation, a recognition of the dignity of all persons, and subsidiarity in communities large or small. The practice of rainwater harvesting is one promising alternative to the continuing depletion and contamination of rivers, streams, and other groundwater resources. It challenges state policies that emphasize large-scale state- or corporate-sponsored projects centralized in remote centers with little accountability to citizens.

Qanats

Another fascinating ancient technique revived today involves *qanats* found throughout the Middle East, Central Asia, and North Africa. When rains fall in these dry areas, and rain falls irregularly, it accumulates in the rough mountains and seeps underground. The ancient Persians, ancestors to the Iranians, first discovered that by digging horizontal tunnels into the mountains they could divert water from underground springs to use in their cities and villages. Iran today has some 50,000 *qanats* dug more than three thousand years ago, some extending for miles. *Qanats* discharged water in Iran, at least until the 1960s, at a volume of more than twelve Nile rivers. The technology spread to Iraq, Jordan, Afghanistan, as far west as Libya and Algeria where they are still in use, and as far east as China. Modern technological methods could make utilizing *qanats* and building and maintaining new ones very cost-effective. Once again, one of the keys to the success of *qanats* is their collective nature. No matter where they emerge, everyone surrounding the *qanat* is entitled to a share.[25]

Other traditional practices include *dambo*-farming, involving intensive cultivation of small garden plots in seasonally water-logged areas. Such plots provide approximately half of a farmer's income in some parts of central southern Africa, and are essential in helping farmers through the drought years. In these places heavy machinery would damage the soil of the wetlands. Other similar small-scale practices take place successfully and sustainably in over half of all irrigated areas of the Philippines and three-quarters of the areas in Nepal.[26] The key to success in these areas involves local consultation, in many cases local control, and accountability of users and managers in some form of democratic process.

Drip Irrigation

Driving across the vast farmlands of Eastern Washington in mid-summer, you will certainly be struck by the long pipes on large wheels spraying water onto the fields. In the midday heat, it is certain that a large portion of the water is lost to evaporation. Drip irrigation, on the other hand, uses water much more efficiently, and the water directly benefits the crop. Israel's success in agricultural production in an arid land is due almost entirely to drop-by-drop irrigation techniques. Desert Bedouins are using drip irrigation on oasis crops.[27]

The efficiency of drip irrigation and other micro-irrigation techniques is especially promising for poorer farmers around the world. By delivering water directly to the plant's root system these methods can reduce water volume anywhere from 39 to 70 percent while doubling and even tripling water productivity over conventional methods. Currently some 200,000 farmers worldwide are using low-cost drip-irrigation systems, and the technology is catching on worldwide, particularly in India.[28] In addition, techniques such as low-pressure spraying for feed grain crops use 30 percent less water than conventional high-pressure spraying and 60 percent less than conventional irrigation. Other possibilities for less water use include changing from water-intensive crops.[29]

Robert Kandel in discussing drip irrigation asks why these techniques are not used elsewhere in any extensive manner. His answer is that in countries like the United States or his native France where huge amounts of water are wasted, water is too cheap. Why should a farmer invest in new technologies such as drip irrigation or even switch to less thirsty crops when extra water is available cheaply?[30]

In Colorado, farmers pay only 3 percent of the cost of water, and 70 percent of the farmers' profits in the Central Valley of California are funded by taxpayers.[31] So why not increase prices of water and drop or curtail subsidies? De Villiers quotes a study which argues that the urban poor would not be the ones to suffer; subsidies benefit the wealthy since the poor are usually not connected to the water supply and utilize other sources such as private water tanks, at higher prices. The same is true of farmers; the richest have greater access. The Central Valley of California is cited here as one of the greatest examples of welfare for the wealthy. What is needed is sound and equitable water pricing based on what water is worth, not what people can pay. At least for irrigation ". . . If we stopped subsidizing water to plant water-thirsty crops alien to deserts or to irrigate pasture to raise cattle for beef, . . . if we stopped doing the wasteful things for which the American West is famous, we would have water to spare."[32] It will take a great deal of effort and public pressure to change old ways.

Using Less Water: Industry

Industry has shown great improvements in water use. According to a 1998 Geological Survey, U.S. industrial consumption of water has declined by almost 35 percent since 1950.[33] Factories in the industrialized world generally return more than 90 percent of the water they withdraw from rivers,[34] although we have seen that polluted and warmer waters are sometimes the result.

One pioneering company in the United States is well known for its revolutionary approach to the environment, including water use and discharge. In the 1990s one of the largest carpet makers in the country, Interface, changed its entire manner of accounting for its products and included in its costs the ecological impact of its dyes, plastics, water usage, oil usage, and every aspect of production. The results have been dramatic. Energy use is down 41 percent, and greenhouse gas emissions are 56 percent lower—factors that help reduce global warming. Also, water usage is down an astounding 73 percent. President Ray Anderson views his company as a "restorative company" and a model for others.[35]

Wastewater

Several hopeful projects are based on the premise that wastewater is still water and can be used for multiple purposes, from extinguishing fires, to washing automobiles, cooling industrial buildings, and even irrigating crops and watering lawns. Fully 98 percent of wastewater in Denmark is reused, 52 percent in France, 73 percent in the United States, and 39 percent in Japan. Robert Kandel, senior scientist at the National Scientific Research Agency of France, writes that the most easily harnessed energy source in developed countries is wastewaster.[36]

In Pakistan, a quarter of the country's vegetables are grown with sewage. Sewage can be used for nonfood crops or those cooked before eating. Ten percent of the world's main crops are irrigated by sewage. Certainly there are risks. Some form of treatment is necessary to remove dangerous chemicals, and Israel, Jordan, Tunisia, and Mexico already provide such treatment. In England, new treatment plants with high-tech technologies along the Thames deliver recycled sewage effluent to millions of Londoners daily.[37]

Israel routinely reuses 70 percent of its sewer water for irrigation after treatment in wastewater lagoons. Similarly, cities in the western and southwestern United States recycle part of their wastewater. While there are dangers of harmful chemicals in wastewater or sewer sludge, careful management and testing should assure quality. Yet some of these technologies are more expensive than current, more wasteful, practices.[38] Such a conundrum brings calls for higher water rates as incentives to bring about water reductions.

Water from bathing, dishwashing, and other "light" water uses could be inexpensively filtered. Use of such systems in urban housing could have a considerable impact on water use. Phillip Ball writes that it is our own psychological relationship with water that needs rethinking.[39]

Using Less Water: Consumption

In the United States lawns are the largest "crop," and some efforts to mitigate lawn spread and even use are beginning across the country. Some twenty-five years ago the local utility in Denver, Colorado, which sits on a high plain and is in constant need of water, began a program called "Xeriscaping," which employs several basic principles utilizing low-water plants, careful planning and design, efficient irrigation, conservation, mulching, and turf that suits the area.[40]

The program has spread to forty states and five foreign countries. The results can be dramatic: a Las Vegas study over several years by the Water Authority revealed that "where Xeriscaping replaced turf, water use dropped an average of 80 percent—*even though residents received no formal instruction in water conservation.*"[41] Companion programs in Las Vegas, Albuquerque, El Paso, and other cities offer a rebate if residents replace their lawns with more low-water landscaping; in Las Vegas alone over five years, 16,000 residents and 2,200 commercial establishments using the program saved eight billion gallons of water. Las Vegas's Water Waste Investigators sweep the city citing broken sprinklers, overwatering, etc. Albuquerque has similar restrictions, and Phoenix is currently considering such rules.[42]

Around the globe other water use savings will come from the reduction of pipe leakage. Jordan, for example, has a target of reducing leakage from the domestic water supply from 30 percent currently to 18 percent by 2015. In the United States, new water-efficient toilets, washers, urinals, faucets, and showerheads, first appearing in 1997, are estimated to save enough water per year to supply four to six areas the size of New York City.[43]

The other critical issue besides water savings is access to clean water. When we met Jim and Brooke Rufo-Hill in chapter 4, Jim had installed a water filtration system in their home in the Dominican Republic, Biosand Water Filter. The system uses a slow sand filtration method to filter out bacteria and other impurities. Over their two years in the country, Jim helped install some seventy of the 300-lb. concrete filters in the homes of his community and the surrounding area. The costs were subsidized through Rotary International's water program.[44] Other programs range from large, private organizations such as World Vision, Catholic Relief Services' "Water for Life" Program, and the International Red Cross for emergency relief, to private firms such as Enterprise Works, volunteer programs such as Engineers without Borders, and government programs such as the U.S. Agency for Internation Development's work in Haiti.[45]

Earth's Waters

The Sound and the Seas

In late October 2006, as the fall colors spread around the Puget Sound, a small gathering of Native Americans and invited guests assembled at the Nisqually National Wildlife Refuge, just southwest of the Washington state capitol in Olympia. That day the first of Puget Sound's salt waters began to flood a former farming area, once heavily diked to keep the salt waters out. The area is being restored to its original form as marshland, an integral part of the Sound's food chain. Since the tribe began tearing down the dikes in 1996, the changes have been swift; the salt water flows in, and animals begin to establish colonies. Birds and small fish show up almost immediately, and then slowly but surely native marsh grasses and other plants double every year. The waters come alive with food for fish and serve as a refuge for the young Chinook salmon.[46] It is a pattern essential for the restoration of the whole Sound.

At the same time, Washington State's governor, Christine Gregoire, recently declared that "Puget Sound is sick and we must take action now." She has established the Puget Sound Partnership for further restoration. The partnership represents a diverse group established to formulate recommendations for returning the Sound to health by 2020. A formidable task, but an admirable goal.[47]

Rivers

New approaches to river management encompass the entire river basin as an ecological system on a regional, national, and international scale. In 2001 the United States and Canada augmented the Great Lakes Charter between the two countries to include flow restoration measures to accompany any future changes in the Great Lakes basin. The addition regards the basin as a freshwater ecosystem. A new water directive of the European Parliament and the Council for European Union charges the countries involved with ensuring no further deterioration and working toward good health of river ecosystems.[48] One of the oldest water basin approaches is that used by India and Pakistan, who signed the Indus Waters Treaty in 1960, managing these waters jointly in spite of conflicts over Kashmir.[49]

In 2002 due to heavy rainfall, Europe's rivers turned into flooding torrents. Rivers had been straightened; dykes had cut off rivers from floodplains, and the main channels of rivers had systematically been shortened to get the waters to the sea quickly. With these approaches engineers have destroyed the complex hydrology of rivers and "often created danger where they promised safety and intensified the floods they intended to prevent."[50] In England the solution has been to break river banks and re-flood four square miles of Thames floodplain while creating floodplains downstream. Austria, Germany, and The Netherlands are following similar plans.[51]

These approaches are linking efforts to diminish the "floods" in cities long designed with culverts and drains to carry away rainwater quickly to rivers and to the sea. All too often the drains overflow in heavy downpours, and cars and people find themselves slogging through the rising waters. Cities like Berlin are working to design "porous" areas, part of a new "low-impact technology." Instead of ridding the city of its waters, the city will collect the water, a form of urban rainwater harvesting. The new commercial center in Berlin, Potsdamer Platz, is designed so that buildings capture rainwater from rooftops to flush toilets and water roof gardens. The water that falls to the ground fills an artificial lake or percolates underground through porous paving. This high-tech urban center can store a sixth of its annual rainfall and reuse most of the rest.[52] The city also boosts housing developments with similar technology—a porous city.

Global Warming

We have seen the impacts of global warming on the Arctic and Antarctic glaciers, on ocean warming, and on rising water levels. One of the human-made causes is the increase in carbon dioxide emissions from fossil fuels. The failure of the United States to sign the Kyoto Protocol mandating reduction in emissions has provoked responsible action at other levels around the country. In the western United States, small cities and large are undertaking reforms without waiting for national or even state governments. Several mayors have signed onto the Cities for Climate Protection, an international organization formed in 1993 to cut back on greenhouse emissions and reduce global warming. Some seven hundred cities worldwide, with 166 in the United States, have agreed to dramatically reduce emissions. Cities in the West and along the Pacific Coast have taken the lead in these efforts.

Portland, Oregon, was the first U.S. city to develop a strategy to reduce its carbon dioxide emissions and by 2005 had cut back to 1990 levels. On the day on which the Kyoto Protocol became law for the 141 nations that adopted it, Mayor Greg Nichols of Seattle pledged that his city too would meet those goals. He then announced the "U.S. Mayors Climate Protection Agreement" and challenged other mayors to sign on. Thanks to his leadership, by April 2007, 435 mayors had signed the agreement and pledged to meet or go beyond the Kyoto Protocol targets.[53] Although the U.S. official delegation to the UN Climate Change Conference in Montreal in December 2005 continued to oppose mandatory targets, municipal leaders from the United States, including Nichols and others, pledged long-term reduction targets of 30 percent below 1990 levels by 2020 and 80 percent by 2050. In 2003, the governors of California, Oregon, and Washington pledged to work together on climate protection.[54]

Population

The third leg of a sustainable water policy involves the question of population control. There is a direct correlation between population growth and water consumption. The good news is that the slowing of population growth now developing will mean fewer countries, such as India, in critical water shortages. The bad news is that while slowing population growth means fewer people than projected living in water-stressed areas, by 2050 "the percentage of the world's population living in water-stressed countries will increase by anywhere from three- to fivefold."[55] Yet the increasing use of new and ancient approaches to water access, collection, and distribution provides some basis for hope in mitigating the worst of the water-stress conditions, first by changing the projections until a later date but for the long term by educating populations, communities, and active citizens to engage in alternatives even as new technologies continue to develop.

Simple technologies also reduce the impact that growing populations will have on water. Some examples are "roof-top water tanks, lined and covered wells, eco-sanitation [toilets which preserve nutrients in human excreta, recycling them as fertilizer], small bore-hole pipes and sewers," "handpumps, rooftop reservoirs, gravity-fed standpipes at regular and short distances, dry sanitation," capped springs, and composting human waste.[56] New household appliances from toilets to washers are now on the market. In rural areas dry and on-site toilets for local people keep human waste in a dug pit or a brick box, allowing it to settle while the pathogens die.[57]

Stealing Water from Others

Finally there is the possibility of "stealing" water, or outright "water wars." Yet water wars are not inevitable. Rather, national and international agreements can relieve and resolve water conflicts in order to meet the needs of the countries and peoples involved. As far back as 1909, Canada and the United States forged a mechanism and process, the International Joint Commission, for resolving water disputes that carries even to this day.[58] More recently, after meeting for some twelve years under the Nile Basin Initiative, ten countries sharing the Nile River agreed in 2004 to establish a binding legal structure to facilitate cooperation.[59] Namibia, Botswana, and Angola have likewise established a commission to study water rights.

In addition to a long-term agreement between India and Bangladesh over the Ganges, perhaps the most striking example of peaceful agreements instead of water wars is the 1960 agreement between India and Pakistan, two countries often at war for geographical and political reasons.[60] However, more recently, tensions between the two nations have increased, and the possibility of a second water war still exists over the Indus's sacred waters.[61]

Even the dynamics of the first water war between Israel, its neighbors, and the Palestinians may yet yield some agreements. Many Israeli hydrologists argue that Israel must decrease its demand for water. "It is patently ridiculous for Israel to use two-thirds of its water to irrigate crops that generate less than 2 percent of the country's GDP. . . . If it wants to maintain agriculture, it can develop desalination further for drinking water and aim to use that water a second time by recycling treated sewage onto farmland," thereby providing Palestinians with greater amounts of water.[62]

Whether the conditions are ever truly present for an actual military war over water (and one researcher has found only one such possibility, in conflict over the Nile),[63] other issues still emerge around water shortages. Water shortages "lead to food shortages, increased poverty, and the spread of disease. . . . They increase the migrations of peoples. . . . Standards of living deteriorate, and social unrest and violence increase."[64] Thus "war" breaks out because of these indirect results of water conflicts. Still, de Villiers is hopeful. In spite of growing pollution, growing scarcity, and growing population strains on water, "Water wars might be caused by human folly, but they might still be prevented by human inventiveness. . . . [W]e are not without weapons in these wars we are waging against our own worst nature."[65]

New Water Management Policies: Cochabamba Revisited

In the 2006 UN World Water Development Report, the authors argue that the traditional solution to pressure on water sources was to increase supply while also developing new sources and getting more from old sources. However, the report notes that this approach is not in itself sustainable. The report argues instead for "demand management," namely, "using water more efficiently, and fairly, improving the balance between present supplies and demand, and reducing excessive use."[66] Demand management, then, brings us back to Cochabamba. As we saw in a previous chapter, the goal of the Coordinadora in Cochabamba was to develop a "socially owned and self-managed enterprise," as a collective way to define the "common good." Toward that goal since SEMAPA was revived as a public utility in 2001, several important steps have been taken. By working with the one hundred or more community-run water committees around Cochabamba, SEMAPA has forged important working links to the people. To break the "technical-bureaucratic rationality" of planning, managers and technicians of the water systems join with neighborhood sanitation committees to develop plans based on community needs, and local assembly-style, communal forms of politics are the norm.[67]

Certainly problems remain. The present rate structure needs to be re-evaluated using guidelines that reflect "social justice, economic equilibrium, and the rational use of water." There is also recognition of the need to adopt a broader environmental approach. The report also advocates ways to reuse and recycle water and continue with collection of rainwater.[68] Cochabamba represents an alternative pattern to issues of large multinational privatization schemes as well as large, often inefficient state-run approaches.

Oscar Olivera had argued against *two* forms of privatization, the international water corporation on the one hand, and the bureaucratic, inefficient, corrupt state system. In developing models that can provide workable and sustainable alternatives to embody the principles developed in earlier chapters, the editors of *Reclaiming Public Water* draw upon twenty-one case studies to reveal a wide variety of possibilities. For example, Santa Cruz de la Sierra in Argentina uses a system of cooperatives to serve some 1.3 million people in which the users are shareholders. In Malaysia, a public–public partnership (PPP of a different kind) has produced the lowest water rates in the country and some of the lowest in the world. Cities like Grenoble, France; Recife, Brazil; and Monterray, Mexico, have successfully remunicipalized their water utilities. In Ghana, the national government has cooperated with local and international NGOs to produce a model of community-controlled utilities. Porto Alegre, Brazil, one of the most successful alternative models, utilizes a public water and sanitation facility.[69]

A key to many of these alternatives and their abilities to serve the poor portions of their populations, in rural areas as well as large cities, lies in a system of *social tariffs*, i.e., a system in which the rich and the poor pay different prices for water and sanitation and consumption levels are priced appropriately. Sliding rates are applied for personal consumption; commercial and industrial use; and public uses in hospitals, public schools, and government offices. The systems work on strong *cross-subsidies*. A *social tariff* in Porto Alegre, for example, means that low-income people who have a right to use ten cubic meters per month only pay for four; those who consume only for basic needs are subsidized by others whose rates rise exponentially. The result is that Porto Alegre is able to invest in good maintenance and expansion of services.

Sandra Postel also cites sound water management as the key to the global water crisis and suggests several features of management principles in a new water ethos. First, humans must adapt more fully into nature's cycles and rhythms, such as restoring free-flowing rivers and adjusting to droughts, rather than attempting to control flows. Second, we can reduce pressures on freshwater systems by reducing population and consumption. In addition we must increase water "productivity" by utilizing the approaches outlined above: employing drip irrigation, planting water-tolerant crops and replacing water-thirsty ones, shifting from animal to vegetable protein in diets, and challenging the privatization of water in the name of the common good. Finally, in water decisions managers must act as water stewards, not owners, and fully utilize the "precautionary principle," i.e., "err on the side of allocating too much water to ecosystems rather than too little." This "ethic of stewardship" ultimately is "about respecting the beauty and mystery of a natural world we did not create and cannot fully understand."[70]

Conclusion

The many components we just examined are essential and in many cases elementary tools in managing the global water crisis. The problem is not that there is too little water; except for water in aquifers, now in danger of depletion, water is a renewable, but finite, resource. The major issues involve the basic principles behind water management policies and practices. A new ethos for water must replace twentieth-century large-scale, centralized, statist, and nondemocratic ideologies and policies. We have seen a new ethos bursting forth in many places, too strong to be neglected, too efficient to be dismissed. The stories of Cochabamba illustrate the emerging paradigm.

In part this new ethos will involve relearning "some of the old lessons of sharing," protecting against damaging floods by "tear[ing] down dams and dykes, recharge[ing] the underground reservoirs, and remaking the rivers. We will certainly have to pour less concrete—a twentieth-century solution to a twenty-first century problem." We will have to store water sustainably, renew lakes and rivers, restore wetlands, and share waters.[71]

Behind these many promising approaches, new and old, to sustainable, equitable, democratic water management lie the same basic directions that Ricardo Petrella calls for in the World Water Contract. First, there needs to be a "legally binding world water contract which integrates the political, economic, and social right of individual and collective access to water into the Universal Declaration of Human Rights."[72] This effort needs to enshrine such a right into other international declarations as well, making explicit what at times was only implicit. Such declarations are key to legitimizing international regulations and in guiding any form of privatization.

However, the next step is equally important, namely, changing existing water laws across the world or initiating new water laws that reflect the social nature and purpose of water. These guidelines would then inform any kind of *pricing* systems for water established by local communities "as a trust from the world community" in accordance with principles of subsidiarity and with a socially equitable pricing scheme, "graduated in accordance with principles of solidarity and sustainability." Such an approach, then, sees access to water as a basic right but also pushes the moral duty and obligation dimensions of water to the forefront—an obligation to use water with care and, recalling water's religious significance, with reverence.[73]

In all these discussions, the private sector will still play a key role, but one that must be developed in cooperation with public agencies, and it must be transparent and accountable. Given that by one estimate there is a $1.2 trillion investment needed in wastewater treatment and another $100 billion for drinking water over the next twelve years,[74] countries from China to Algeria and Saudi Arabia are letting out water contracts to meet the needs of growing populations, polluted waters, and the disruptions caused by global warming. Public agencies alone and the hopeful developments outlined in this chapter are still insufficient to meet the needs. Nonetheless, whatever room there is for private investment in the world water supply and management, the principles and traditions examined above must form the heart of any future agreements. The reality of water as a public good and a public trust must prevail.

This exploration of water's origins and central place in nourishing the Earth and all that is on it now comes to an end. My hope is that the reader will take away first a strong sense of the problems the entire globe faces over water purity, access, and management and an awakening to the part each of us and all of us play in those problems. But second, I hope that the reader gains a greater awareness of the sacred dimension of water and its meaning in the depths of our spiritual and psychic lives as well as our bodily lives. Perhaps such an awareness will bring greater mindfulness of our obligations to use water with respect in our rituals and daily practices. Finally I hope the reader finds motivation and passion to join with so many others to ensure that our policies and practices will be efficient and sufficient, sustainable, democratic, localized, and just for all concerned. I end these water ruminations with a summary thought from Maggie Black, whose words help chart the path ahead:

> Future water peace will depend less on international diplomacy between water-competing nations . . . than on whether water's status as a commons over which all humanity has rights can be upheld. That in turns depends on whether states and water administrators can be made to assume their proper custodial role toward the resource on which all living systems depend.
>
> Perhaps water will manage to redeem the sacred status it has enjoyed since life appeared on Earth and magically divest itself of the commodity-driven character which is, after all, only a recent incarnation.[75]

Notes

1. Report quoted in Peter Bosshard, "A Drop-Sized Way to Bring Clean Water to a Thirsty World," *Christian Science Monitor*, 10 November 2006.

2. Quoted in Robyn Dixon, "Targeting 'Water Apartheid,'" [*Los Angeles Times* as reported in] *Seattle Times*, 6 November 2006, sec. A.

3. United Nations, *Water: A Shared Responsibility. The United Nations World Water Development Report 2* (New York: Berghahn, 2006), 7–8, 16, 19, 28.

4. Fred Pearce, *When the Rivers Run Dry: Water—The Defining Crisis of the Twenty-First Century* (Boston: Beacon, 2006), 307–308.

5. Pearce, *When the Rivers Run Dry*, 309.

6. Quoted in Maggie Black, *The No-Nonsense Guide to Water* (Oxford: New Internationalist, 2004), 83, 86.

7. Ricardo Petrella, *The Water Manifesto: Arguments for a World Water Contract*, trans. Patrick Camiller (London: Zed Books, 2001), 12–20.

8. Marc de Villiers, *Water: The Fate of Our Most Precious Resource* (New York: Houghton Mifflin, 2000), 275–82.

9. de Villiers, *Water*, 286–291.

10. Pearce, *When the Rivers Run Dry*, 253–255.

11. de Villiers, *Water*, 295–297.

12. Pearce, *When the Rivers Run Dry*, 245–227.

13. Pearce, *When the Rivers Run Dry*, 251–252.

14. Pearce, *When the Rivers Run Dry*, 253.

15. Sandra Postel and Brian Richter, *Rivers for Life: Managing Water for People and Nature* (Washington, D.C.: Island Press, 2003), 40.

16. Donald G. McNeil, "A $3 Water Purifier that Could Save Lives," *New York Times*, 10 October 2006, www.nytimes.com/2006/10/10/science (18 October 2006); Jennie Yabroff, "Water for the World," *Newsweek* (18 June 2007): 20.

17. Barrett Sheridan, "The Flames of Hope," *Newsweek*, 16 July 2007, 80.

18. Christopher Key Chapple, "Hinduism and Deep Ecology," in *Deep Ecology and World Religions*, eds. David L. Barnhill and Roger S. Gottlieb (Albany: State University of New York Press, 2001), 67.

19. Quoted in *Thirst*, a documentary produced and directed by Alan Snitow and Deborah Kaufman (Oley, Penn.: Bullfrog Films. Snitow-Kaufman Productions, 2004).

20. Anil Agarwal et al., eds., *Making Water Everybody's Business* (New Delhi: Centre for Science and Environment, 2001), xii–xiii, xxvii.

21. Pearce, *When the Rivers Run Dry*, 266.

22. Pearce, *When the Rivers Run Dry*, 259–261.

23. See Pearce, *When the Rivers Run Dry*, 267–269 for a fuller description of different techniques by varieties of cultures.

24. Quoted in Pearce, *When the Rivers Run Dry*, 270–271.

25. Pearce, *When the Rivers Run Dry*, 273–278.

26. Black, *No-Nonsense Guide*, 64–65.

27. de Villiers, *Water*, 298–299.

28. Sandra Postel, *Liquid Assets: The Critical Need to Safeguard the Freshwater Ecosystems* (Washington, D.C.: Worldwatch, 2005), 40.

29. de Villiers, *Water*, 298.

30. Robert Kandel, *Water from Heaven: The Story of Water from the Big Bang to the Rise of Civilization and Beyond* (New York: Columbia University Press, 2003), 257.

31. de Villiers, *Water*, 303.

32. de Villiers, *Water*, 305.

33. de Villiers, *Water*, 298.

34. Kandel, *Water from Heaven*, 257.

35. Amy Cortese, "The Carpet Cleaner," *Mother Jones*, November–December 2006, 56–57.

36. Kandel, *Water From Heaven*, 211, 255; Phillip Ball, *Life's Matrix: A Biography of Water* (New York: Farrar, Straus & Giroux, 1999), 356.

37. Pearce, *When the Rivers Run Dry*, 233–234.

38. de Villiers, *Water*, 300.

39. Ball, *Life's Matrix*, 356–357.

40. Michelle Nijhuis, "The Lure of the Lawn: Can Westerners Get Over Their Romance with Turf?" *High Country News*, 21 August 2006, 13.

41. Italics mine.

42. Nijhuis, "Lure of the Lawn," 13–14; for more information contact Denver Water at http://www.denverwater.org; see http://www.ripyourstrip.com for advice on converting grass strips to low water users.

43. Postel, *Liquid Assets*, 37.

44. Jim and Brooke Rufo-Hill, personal correspondence, 27 December 2006. For more information on the process, visit http://www.addyourfight.org/project.

45. For information on these programs visit http://www.worldvision.org; http://www.crs.org; http://www.vita.org; http://www.usaid.org; and http://www.ecosmart.net/homewater.

46. Susan Gordon, "Salt Water Returns to Nisqually Field," *Tacoma (Wash.) News Tribune*, 1 November 2006, sec. A.

47. Cherie Black, "New Alert on Eating Local Salmon," *Seattle Post-Intelligencer*, 27 October 2006, at http://seattlepi.nwsource.com/local/290187_fishwarn27.html.

48. Postel and Richter, *Rivers for Life*, 196.

49. Kandel, *Water from Heaven*, 229.

50. Pearce, *When the Rivers Run Dry*, 285.

51. Quoted in Pearce, *When the Rivers Run Dry*, 289–290.

52. Pearce, *When the Rivers Run Dry*, 291.

53. Anne Underwood, "Mayors Take the Lead," *Newsweek*, 16 April 2007, 68.

54. Michelle Nijhuis, "Save Our Snow," *High and Dry: A High Country News Special Report* (Spring 2006): 42, 45–46.

55. Report from Population Action International, as quoted in de Villiers, *Water*, 307–308.

56. Black, *No-Nonsense Guide*, 36, 41, 82–84.

57. Black, *No-Nonsense Guide*, 41.

58. de Villiers, *Water*, 255.

59. Black, *No-Nonsense Guide*, 126.

60. de Villiers, *Water*, 10.

61. Pearce, *When the Rivers Run Dry*, 177.

62. Pearce, *When the Rivers Run Dry*, 172.

63. de Villiers, *Water*, 310.

64. de Villiers, *Water*, 311.

65. de Villiers, *Water*, 313.

66. United Nations, *Water: A Shared Responsibility*, 14.

67. Raquel Gutierrez-Aguilar, "The Coordinadora One Year After the Water War," in ¡*Cochabamba! Water War in Bolivia*, ed. Oscar Olivera with Tom Lewis (Cambridge, Mass.: South End Press, 2004), 56–64.

68. Report from the International Network, "SEMAPA: Globalizing Solidarity," in ¡*Cochabamba! Water War in Bolivia*, ed. Oscar Olivera with Tom Lewis (Cambridge, Mass.: South End Press, 2004), 97–101.

69. Belén Balanyá et al., eds., *Reclaiming Public Water* (Amsterdam: Transnational Institute and Corporate Europe Observatory, 2005); see especially the editorial team's summary "Empowering Public Water—Ways Forward," 247–275.

70. Postel and Richter, *Rivers for Life*, 202–204.

71. Pearce, *When the Rivers Run Dry*, 309, 311.

72. Petrella, *Water Manifesto*, 94.

73. Petrella, *Water Manifesto*, 96. See Petrella's discussion of the priority targets and recommendations that follow from the principles and objectives of the World Water Contracts, such as the establishment of a World Water Fund through which countries exchange water credits, a World Water Tribunal to resolve water disputes, and a World Centre for Economic and Social Water Rights, similar to UNESCO. Petrella calls upon the world's religious leaders to utilize their resources on water issues, pp. 102–106.

74. Leslie Crawford, "Water Crisis Looms Worldwide," *Los Angeles Times*, 16 April 2007, at www.latimes.com/business/la-ft-water.

75. Black, *No-Nonsense Guide*, 140–141.

~

Selected Bibliography

Abderrahman, Walid A. "Water Demand Management and Islamic Water Management Principles: A Case Study." *Water Resources Development* 16, no. 4 (2000): 465–473.

Abrams, Julie. "Buddhism." At www.thewaterpage.com/religion (accessed 12 June 2006).

Agarwal, Anil. "Can Hindu Beliefs and Values Help India Meet Its Ecological Crisis?" In Chapple and Tucker, eds., *Hinduism and Ecology*, 165–179.

Agenda Edition, no. 1, Haveestehuder Weg. Hamberg: Hoffman und Compe Verlag GilmH., 2004, circulated in a public presentation by Loretta Jancoski, director, Center for Water and Ethics, Seattle University, 23 April 2005.

Allegria, Martin, Department of the Environment, and Ismael Fabro, chief executive officer, Ministry of Natural Resources and Environment. Personal interview, 24 March 2006.

Alley, Kelly D. "Separate Domains: Hinduism, Politics, and Environmental Pollution." In Chapple and Tucker, eds., *Hinduism and Ecology*, 355–387.

Alt, David. *Glacial Lake Missoula and Its Humongous Floods*. Missoula, Mont.: Mountain Press, 2001.

Alter, Stephen. *Sacred Waters: A Pilgrimage up the Ganges River to the Source of Hindu Culture*. New York: Harcourt, 2001.

Altman, Nathaniel. *Sacred Water: The Spiritual Source of Life*. Mahwah, N.J.: Hidden Spring, 2000.

Anderson, E. N. "Flowering Apricot: Environmental Practice, Folk Religion, and Daoism." In Girardot, Miller, and Xiaogan, eds., *Daoism and Ecology: Ways within a Cosmic Landscape*, 157–183.

Anteby, Lisa. "'There's Blood in the House': Negotiating Female Rituals of Purity among Ethiopian Jews in Israel." In *Women and Water: Menstruation in Jewish Life and Law,* edited by Rahel R. Wasserfall, 166–186. Hanover, Mass.: Brandeis University Press, 1999.

Ariyaratne, A. T., and Joanna Macy. "The Island of Temple and Tank." In Batchelor and Brown, *Buddhism and Ecology,* 78–86.

Asmal, Kader. "Chair's Preface." In World Commission on Dams, *Dams and Development,* i–vi.

Austin, Charles. "Symbolic Sins Cast on Water for Rosh Ha-Shanah." *New York Times,* 9 September 1983, late edition, sec. B.

Avrillier, Raymond. "A Return to the Source: Re-Municipalisation of Water Services in Grenoble, France." In Balanyá et al., *Reclaiming Public Water,* 63–71.

Bachelard, Gaston. *Water and Dreams.* Dallas: Pegasus Foundation, 1983. Originally published as *L'Eau et les Reves.* Paris: Librairie Jose Corti, 1942.

BACONGO flier opposed to the Vaca dam. Obtained from Sharon Matola, director, Belize Zoo. Personal interview, 27 March 2006.

Bakker, Karen. "Archipelagos and Networks: Urbanization and Water Privatization in the South." *Geographical Journal,* 169.4 (2003): 328–341.

Balanyá, Belén, Brid Brennan, Olivier Hoedeman, Satoko Kishimoto, and Philipp Terhorst, eds. *Reclaiming Public Water.* Amsterdam: Transnational Institute and Corporation, European Observatory, 2005.

Ball, Phillip. *Life's Matrix: A Biography of Water.* New York: Farrar, Straus & Giroux, 1999.

Barlow, Maude. Speech at the WTO demonstrations, Benaroya Hall, Seattle, 25 November 1999.

Barlow, Maude, and Tony Clarke. *Blue Gold: The Fight to Stop the Corporate Theft of the World's Water.* New York: New Press, 2002.

Barnhill, David L., and Roger S. Gottlieb, eds. *Deep Ecology and World Religions.* Albany: New York State University Press, 2001.

Barua, Dipak Kumar. "Ecological Ethics and Conservation of Forests and Wildlife." In Pathak, *Buddhism and Ecology,* 18–24.

Batchelor, Martine, and Kerry Brown, eds. *Buddhism and Ecology.* London: Cassell, 1992.

"Bathing in Hospitality." *Daily Om,* 4 November 2005. At http://www.dailyom.com.

Bergman, B. J. "The Hidden Life of Computers." *Sierra,* July–August 1999, 32.

Berry, Thomas. *Dream of the Earth.* Mystic, Conn.: Twenty-Third Pub., 1989.

Berthrong, John. "Motifs for a New Confucian Ecological Vision." In Tucker and Berthrong, *Confucianism and Ecology,* 237–263.

Best, Allen. "Glaciers Offer a Glimpse of the Distant Past." *High and Dry: Dispatches on Global Warming from the American West,* Summer 2006, 16.

Black, Cherie. "New Alert on Eating Local Salmon." *Seattle Post-Intelligencer,* 27 Oct. 2006, p. 1.

Black, Maggie. *The No-Nonsense Guide to Water*. Oxford: New Internationalist, 2004.

Blackstock, Michael. "Water: A First Nations' Spiritual and Ecological Perspective." *Perspectives* 1, no. 1 (2001): 1–14.

Blanchard, Tsvi. "Can Judaism Make Environmental Policy?" In Tirosh-Samuelson, *Judaism and Ecology*, 423–448.

Blatter, Joachim, and Helen Ingram, eds. *Reflections on Water: New Approaches to Transboundary Conflicts and Cooperation*. Cambridge, Mass.: MIT Press, 2001.

Blatter, Joachim, Helen Ingram, and Pamela M. Doughman. "Emerging Approaches to Comprehend Changing Global Contexts." In Blatter and Ingram, *Reflections on Water*, 3–30.

Borenstein, Seth. "Report on Climate to Include 'Smoking Gun' on Global Warming." *Seattle Post-Intelligencer,* 23 January 2007, sec. A.

Bosshard, Peter. "A Drop-Sized Way to Bring Clean Water to a Thirsty World." *Christian Science Monitor*, 10 November 2006.

Bowen, Robert. *Surface Water*. New York: Wiley, 1982.

Brown, Kerry. Edited talks with Ajahn Pongsak. "In the Water There Were Fish and the Fields Were Full of Rice." In Batchelor and Brown, *Buddhism and Ecology*, 87–99.

Bryson, Bill. *A Short History of Nearly Everything*. New York: Broadway Books, 2003.

Buddah Dharma Education Association Inc. "Rituals in Buddhism: Buddhist Funeral Rites." At www.buddahnet.net (accessed 2 May 2006).

Burckhardt, Titus. "The Symbolism of Water." In *Seeing God Everywhere: Essays on Nature and the Sacred*, edited by Barry McDonald, 205–212. Bloomington, Ind.: World Wisdom, 2003.

Byron, S.J., William J. "Ten Building Blocks of Catholic Social Teaching." *America* 179, no. 13 (31 October 1998): 9–13.

Callicott, J. Baird. "Conceptual Resources for Environmental Ethics in Asian Traditions of Thought: A Propaedeutic." *Philosophy East and West* 37, no. 2 (April 1987): 115–130.

Catholic Bishops of the Region. *The Columbia River Watershed: Caring for Creation and the Common Good*. Seattle: Columbia River Project, 2001.

Chapple, Christopher Key. "Hinduism and Deep Ecology." In *Deep Ecology and World Religions*, edited by David L. Barnhill and Roger S. Gottlieb, 59–76. Albany: New York State University Press, 2001.

Chapple, Christopher Key, and Mary Evelyn Tucker, eds. *Hinduism and Ecology: The Intersection of Earth, Sky, and Water*. Cambridge, Mass.: Harvard University Press, 2001.

Chishti, Saadia Khawar Khan. "*Fitra*: An Islamic Model for Humans and the Environment." In Foltz, Denny, and Baharuddin, *Islam and Ecology*, 67–82.

Chryssavgis, John. "World of the Icon and Creation: An Orthodox Perspective on Ecology and Pneumatology." In Hessel and Ruether, *Christianity and Ecology*, 83–96.

Clarke, Tony, and David A. McDonald. "Water Privateers." *Alternatives Journal* 29.2 (Spring 2003), 10–11, 13–15.

Coles, Anne. "Geology and Gender: Water Supplies, Ethnicity and Livelihoods in Central Sudan." In *Gender, Water, and Development*, edited by Anne Coles and Tina Wallace, 75–94. New York: Berg Books, 2005.

Cortese, Amy. "The Carpet Cleaner." *Mother Jones*, November–December 2006, 56–57.

Daido Loori, John. "The Precepts and the Environment." In Tucker and Williams, *Buddhism and Ecology*, 177–184.

Deegan, Chris. "The Narmada: Circumambulation of a Sacred Landscape." In Chapple and Tucker, *Hinduism and Ecology*, 389–399.

Dien, Mawil Izzi. "Islam and the Environment." In Foltz, Denny, and Baharuddin, *Islam and Ecology*, 107–120.

"Discovering the Dead Sea Scrolls." Inscription, Seattle Center House exhibit, 31 October 2006.

Dixon, Robyn. "Targeting 'Water Apartheid.'" [*Los Angeles Times* as reported in] *Seattle Times*. 6 November 2006, sec. A.

Dockrat, Hashim Ismail. "Islam, Muslim Society, and Environmental Concerns." In Foltz, Denny, and Baharuddin, *Islam and Ecology*, 341–375.

Donahue, John M., and Barbara R. Johnston, eds. *Water, Culture, and Power*. Washington, D.C.: Island Press, 1998.

Doughton, Sandi. "Climate Scientists Surer Than Ever: Man's to Blame." *Seattle Times*, 2 February 2007, sec. A.

Eisenberg, Evan. "The Ecology of Eden." In Tirosh-Samuelson, *Judaism and Ecology*, 27–59.

Electronics Industry Good Neighbor Campaign. *Sacred Waters: The Life-Blood of Mother Earth*. Tucson, Ariz.: Southwest Network for Environmental and Economic Justice, and Campaign for Responsible Technology, 1997.

Eliade, Mircea. *Images and Symbols*. New York: Sheed and Ward, 1969.

———. *Patterns in Comparative Religion*. New York: Sheed and Ward, 1958.

Eliperin, Juliet. "Growing Acidity of Oceans May Kill Corals." *Washington Post*, 5 July 2006, sec. A.

Endo, Yasuo, *Suigenren* founder, Masa Ujiie, Atsuko Masano, reporter. Personal interview, Tokyo, 14 October 2005.

Environment, Health, and Safety Online. "Drinking Water Information." At http://ehso.com/ehsohome/DrWater/drinkingwater.php#Overview (accessed 22 January 2007).

Environmental Law Alliance Worldwide, in support of BACANGO. At www.elaw.org/resources (accessed 18 December 2006).

Ereira, Alan. *The Elder Brothers*. New York: Vintage, 1993.

Ettinger, Kreg. "A River That Was Once So Strong and Deep." In Donahue and Johnston, *Water, Culture, and Power*, 47–71.

Fehr, Raner, Odile Mekel, Martin Lancombe, and Ulrike Wolf. "Towards Health Impact Assessment of Drinking-Water Privatization." *Bulletin of the World Health Organization* 81, #6 (June 2003): 387–472.

Field, Stephen L. "In Search of Dragons: The Folk Ecology of Fengshui." In Girardot, Miller, and Xiaogan, *Daoism and Ecology*, 185–200.

Fisher, William H. "Sacred Rivers, Sacred Dams: Competing Visions of Social Justice and Sustainable Development along the Narmada." In Chapple and Tucker, *Hinduism and Ecology*, 401–421.

Foltz, Richard C. "Islamic Environmentalism: A Matter of Interpretation." In Foltz, Denny, and Baharuddin, *Islam and Ecology*, 249–279.

Foltz, Richard C., Frederick M. Denny, and Azizan Baharuddin, eds. *Islam and Ecology: A Bestowed Trust*. Cambridge, Mass.: Harvard University Press, 2003.

Friedman, Irving. "A River Went out of Eden." *Parabola* 20, no. 1 (Spring 1995): 66–67.

Gardner, Gary. *Invoking the Spirit: Religion and Spirituality in the Quest for a Sustainable World*. Washington, D.C.: Worldwatch Institute, 2002.

Gardner, W. H., ed. *Gerard Manley Hopkins: A Selection of His Poems and Prose*, no. 63. Harmondsworth, England: Penguin Books Ltd., 1964.

Geertz, Clifford. "Religion as a Cultural System." In *The Religious Situation*, edited by Donald R. Cutler, 639–688. Boston: Beacon, 1969.

Gillman, Neil. "Creation in the Bible and in the Liturgy." In Tirosh-Samuelson, *Judaism and Ecology*, 133–154.

Girardot, N. J., James Miller, and Liu Xiaogan, eds. *Daoism and Ecology: Ways within a Cosmic Landscape*. Cambridge, Mass.: Harvard University Press, 2001.

Glenhorn, Michael. "Taoism and Christianity." At http://www.probe.org/content/view/892/65 (accessed 3 May 2006).

"Global Water Crisis: A Test of Solidarity." *National Catholic Reporter*, 30 May 2003.

Goldstein, Elyse. "Taking Back the Water." Letter to editor. *Canadian Forum* (December 1998): 6–7.

Gordon, Susan. "Salt Water Returns to Nisqually Field." *Tacoma (Wash.) News Tribune*, 1 November 2006, sec. A.

Got?, Seiko, and Julia Ching. "Confucianism and Garden Design: A Comparison of Koishikawa K?rakuen and Wörlitzer Park." In Tucker and Berthrong, *Confucianism and Ecology*, 275–292.

Granberg-Michaelson, Wesley. "Creation in Ecumenical Theology." In *Ecotheology: Voices from South and North*, edited by David G. Hallman, 96–106. Maryknoll, N.Y.: Orbis, 1994.

Green, Arthur. "A Kabbalah for the Environmental Age." In Tirosh-Samuelson, *Judaism and Ecology*, 3–15.

Gutierrez-Aguilar, Raquel. "The Coordinadora One Year after the War." In Olivera with Lewis, *¡Cochabamba!* 53–64.

Haberman, David L. "River of Love in an Age of Pollution." In Chapple and Tucker, *Hinduism and Ecology*, 339–354.

Habito, Ruben L. F. "Mountains and Rivers and the Great Earth: Zen and Ecology." In Tucker and Williams, *Buddhism and Ecology*, 165–175.

Hahn, Thomas. "An Introductory Study on Daoist Notions of Wilderness." In Girardot, Miller, and Xiaogan, *Daoism and Ecology*, 201–218.

Hall, David. "Introduction." In Balanyá et al., eds., *Reclaiming Public Water*. 15–28.

Hanh, Thich Nhat. "Look Deep and Smile: Thoughts and Writings of Thich Nhat Hanh." In Batchelor and Brown, *Buddhism and Ecology*, 100–109.

Haq, S. Nomanul. "Islam and Ecology: Toward Retrieval and Reconstruction." In Foltz, Denny, and Baharuddin, *Islam and Ecology*, 121–154.

Harney, Corbin. *The Way It Is: One Water, One Air, One Mother Earth*. Nevada City, Calif.: Blue Dolphin, 1995.

Haught, John. *The Promise of Nature*. New York: Paulist Press, 1993.

Hecht, Mark Erik. "A Pure Perspective on Water." *Human Right Tribune* 9, no. 3 (30 April 2003): 2.

Hessel, Dieter, and Rosemary Radford Ruether. *Christianity and Ecology*. Cambridge, Mass.: Harvard University Press, 2000.

Hoeg, Peter. *Ms. Smilla's Feeling for Snow*. London: Varvill, 1993.

Holley, David. "A Rising Tide: The Aral's Return." *Seattle Times*, 26 May 2006.

Houlberg, Marilyn. "Sirens and Snakes: Water Spirits in the Art of the Haitian Vodou." *African Arts* 29, no. 2 (Spring 1996): 30–35.

Izzi Dien, Mawil Y. "Islamic Ethics and the Environment." In Khalid and O'Brien, *Islam and Ecology*, 25–35.

Jacobs, Mark X. "Jewish Environmentalism: Past Accomplishments and Future Challenges." In Tirosh-Samuelson, *Judaism and Ecology*, 449–480.

Jeffrey, Paul. "Wells Run Dry: Coke Faces Thirsty Opponents in India." *National Catholic Reporter*, 24 March 2006.

Jenkins, Matt. "The Wet Net." *High Country News*, 2 October 2006.

Jiyu, Zhang, and Li Yuanguo. "The Concept of 'Mutual Stealing among the Three Numinous Powers' in the *Scripture on Unconscious Unification* (Yinfu jing)." In Girardot, Miller, and Xiaogan, *Daoism and Ecology*, 113–124.

John Paul II. "Water Is Sacred: Protect It." *National Catholic Reporter*, 19 February 1993.

Johnson, John, Jr. "New Evidence of Liquid Water Makes Enceladus a 'Better Bet.'" *Seattle Times*, 10 March 2006.

Kammer, Charles, III. *Ethics and Liberation*. Maryknoll, N.Y.: Orbis, 1988.

Kanai, Yutaka, and Setsu Furukawa. Wild Bird Society, Conservation Division, Tokyo. Personal interview, 17 October 2005.

Kandel, Robert. *Water from Heaven: The Story of Water from the Big Bang to the Rise of Civilization and Beyond*. New York: Columbia University Press, 2003.

Kassam, Tazim R. "The Aga Khan Development Network: An Ethic of Sustainable Development and Social Conscience." In Foltz, Denny, and Baharuddin, *Islam and Ecology*, 478–496.

Katz, Eric. "Judaism and the Ecological Crisis." In Tucker and Grim, *Worldviews and Ecology*, 55–70.

Kaza, Stephanie. "American Buddhist Response to the Land: Ecological Practice at Two West Coast Retreat Centers." In Tucker and Williams, *Buddhism and Ecology: The Interconnection of Dharma and Deeds*, 219–248.

Kearns, Laurel. "Saving the Creation: Christian Environmentalism in the United States." *Sociology of Religion* 57 (1996): 55–70.

Kessler, E. J. "Taking the Waters." *Forward*, no. 31 (13 September 1996): 22.

Khalid, Fazlun M. "The Application of Islamic Environmental Ethics to Promote Marine Conservation in Zanzibar: a Case Study." January 2003. At http:// ifees.org.uk/ index.php?option=com_content\&task=view&id=40&Itemid=55> (accessed 5 May 2007).

Khalid, Fazlun M., and Joanne O'Brien, eds. *Islam and Ecology*. London: Cassell, 1992.

Kimber, Richard G. "Australian Aboriginals' Perceptions of Their Desert Home-lands: Part One." *Arid Lands Newsletter* 50 (November/December 2001). http://ag .arizona.edu/ALS/ALN/aln50/kimberpart1 (14 April 2006).

Kinsley, David. *Ecology and Religion: Ecological Spirituality in Cross-Cultural Perspec-tive*. Englewood Cliffs, N.J.: Prentice Hall, 1995.

Kraft, Kenneth. "The Greening of Buddhist Practice," *Cross Currents* 44, no. 2 (Sum-mer 1994): 163–179.

LaGate, Penny. "Ethiopia." *6:00 News*, CBS. 14 August 2005.

Lebacqz, Karen. *Six Theories of Justice: Perspectives from Philosophical and Theological Ethics*. Minneapolis: Augsburg, 1986.

Leopold, Aldo. *A Sand County Almanac*. New York: Ballantine, 1970.

Lewis, Tom. "Direction SEMAPA: An Interview with Luis Sanchez-Gomez." In Olivera with Lewis, ¡*Cochabamba!* 87–94.

Lindsey, Rebecca. "Earth Observatory." Publication of NASA's Earth Science Enter-prise. 1 March 2006, 1–4.

Llewellyn, Othman Abd-ar-Rahman. "The Basis for a Discipline of Islamic Environ-mental Law." In Foltz, Denny, and Baharuddin, *Islam and Ecology*, 185–247.

Loy, David. "The Religion of the Market." In *Visions of a New Earth*, edited by Harold Coward and Daniel C. Maguire, 15–28. Albany: State University of New York Press, 2000.

Ma, R. "Water-related figurative language in the rhetoric of Mencius." In *Rhetoric in Intercultural Contexts (International and Intercultural Communication Annual 22)*, ed-ited by A. Gonzalez and D. V. Tanno, 119–129. Thousand Oaks, Calif.: Sage, 2000.

MacKinnon, Mary Heather, and Moni McIntyre, eds. *Readings in Ecology and Femi-nist Theology*. Kansas City, Mo.: Sheed and Ward, 1995.

Macy, Joanna. "The Ecological Self: Postmodern Ground for Right Action." In MacKinnon and McIntyre, *Readings in Ecology and Feminist Theology*, 259–268.

Maguire, Daniel. *On Moral Grounds*. New York: Crossroad, 1991.

Maltz, Helio. "Porto Alegre's Water: Public and for All." In Balanyá et al., *Reclaim-ing Public Water*, 29–36.

Martin, Jonathan. "Victoria Revisits Issue of Treating its Sewage." *Seattle Times*, 14 July 2006, sec. B.

Masri, Al-Hafiz. "Islam and Ecology." In Khalid and O'Brien, *Islam and Ecology*, 1–24.

Matola, Sharon, Director, Belize Zoo, one of the BACONGO nine. Personal interview, Belize City, 28 March 2006.

McClure, Robert, and Lisa Stiffler, "Marine Life Is Disappearing from Puget Sound, and Fast," *Seattle Post-Intelligencer*, 9 October 2006.

———. "Scientists Agree: Humans Causing Global Warming." *Seattle Post-Intelligencer*, 2 February 2007, sec. A.

McDonagh, Sean. *Dying for Water*. Dublin: Veritas, 2003.

McNiven, Ian J. "Saltwater People: Spiritscapes, Maritime Rituals and the Archeology of Australian Indigenous Landscapes." *World Archaeology* 35, no. 3 (December 2003): 329–349.

Narayanan, Vasudha. "Water, Wood, and Wisdom: Ecological Perspectives from the Hindu Traditions." *Daedalus* 130, no. 4 (Fall 2001): 179–206.

Nasr, Seyyed Hossein. "Islam, the Contemporary Islamic World, and the Environmental Crisis." In Foltz, Denny, and Azizan, *Islam and Ecology*, 85–105.

National Council of Churches. "God's Earth Is Sacred: An Open Letter to Church and Society in the United States." At www.ncccusa.org/news/14.02.05theological-statement (accessed 10 April 2006).

———. "Safe Drinking Water for Those Who Are Thirsty: Wells in Bangladesh." At www.nccecojustice.org (accessed 23 April 2007).

———. "Water: The Key to Sustaining Life—An Open Statement to Governing Bodies and Concerned Citizens." At www.nccecojustice.org/waterltr.htm (accessed 2 May 2007).

National Park Service. Ice Age Floods Study Team. "Ice Age Floods, Study of Alternatives. Section D: Background." At http://www.nps.gov/iceagefloods/d.htm (accessed 10 May 2006).

Negus, Yunus. "Science within Islam: Learning How to Care for Our World." In Khalid and O'Brien, *Islam and Ecology*, 37–49.

News from the National Council of Churches. 14 March 2007. At www.nccusa.org/news (accessed 26 April 2007).

Nijhuis, Michelle. "The Lure of the Lawn: Can Westerners Get Over Their Romance with Turf?" *High Country News*, 28 August 2006, 8ff.

———. "Save Our Snow." *High and Dry: A High Country News Special Report* (Spring 2006).

———. "What Happened to Winter?" *High and Dry: Dispatches on Global Warming from the American West*. Boulder, Colo.: High Country News, Summer 2006.

NPR News, KUOW Seattle, 9 a.m. news report. 6 September 2006.

O'Brien, David, and Thomas Shannon, eds. *Catholic Social Thought: The Documentary Heritage*. Maryknoll, N.Y.: Orbis, 1998.

Odin, Steve. "The Japanese Concept of Nature in Relation to the Environmental Ethics and Conservation Aesthetics of Aldo Leopold." In Tucker and Williams, *Buddhism and Ecology*, 89–109.

Olivera, Oscar. "Petroleum and Natural Gas: Recovering Our Collective Patrimony." In Olivera with Lewis, ¡Cochabamba! 153–159.

Olivera, Oscar, with Tom Lewis, eds. ¡Cochabamba! Water War in Bolivia. Cambridge, Mass.: South End Press, 2004.

Ozdemir, Ibrahim. "Toward an Understanding of Environmental Ethics from a Qur'anic Perspective." In Foltz, Denny, and Baharuddin, Islam and Ecology, 3–37.

Pathak, S. K., ed. Buddhism and Ecology. New Delhi: Om Publications, 2004.

Pearce, Fred. When the Rivers Run Dry: Water—The Defining Crisis of the Twenty-First Century. Boston: Beacon, 2006.

Perelmuter, Hayim. "'Do Not Destroy:' Ecology in the Fabric of Judaism." In Ecological Challenge, edited by Richard Fragomeni and John Palowsk, 129–138. Collegeville, Minn.: Liturgical Press, 1994.

Peterson, Anna. Being Human: Ethics, Environment, and Our Place in the World. Berkeley: University of California Press, 2001.

Petrella, Ricardo. The Water Manifesto: Arguments for a World Water Contract. Trans. Patrick Camiller. London: Zed Books, 2001.

Pielou, E. C. Fresh Water. Chicago: University of Chicago Press, 1998.

Postel, Sandra. Liquid Assets: The Critical Need to Safeguard the Freshwater Ecosystems. Washington, D.C.: Worldwatch, 2005.

Postel, Sandra, and Brian Richter. Rivers for Life: Managing Water for People and Nature. Washington, D.C.: Island Press, 2003.

"Principle No. 4." The Dublin Statement on Water and Sustainable Development. International Conference on Water and the Environment, organized by the United Nations. Dublin, Ireland, January 1992.

Quinn, Jane Bryant. "Investing Goes Back to Basics." Newsweek, 19 December 2005, 57.

The Qur'an. Trans. M. H. Shakir. Elmhurst, N.Y.: Tahrike Tarsile Qur'an, 1997.

Rao, K. L. Seshagiri. "The Five Great Elements (Pañcamah?bh?ta): An Ecological Perspective." In Chapple and Tucker, Hinduism and Ecology, 29–38.

Rasmussen, Larry. Earth Community, Earth Ethics. Maryknoll, N.Y.: Orbis, 1996.

Rauber, Paul. "Secrets of the Supermarket." Sierra 91, no. 6 (November–December 2006): 50–75.

———. "Signs of a Changing Planet." Sierra 91, no. 4 (July–August 2006): 17.

Reisner, Mark. Cadillac Desert: The American West and Its Disappearing Water. New York: Viking, 1986.

Robinson, B.A. "Taoism (a.k.a. Daoism)." Ontario Consultants on Religious Tolerance. 1995–2006. At http://www.religioustolerance.org/taoism.htm (accessed 3 May 2006).

Rossing, Barbara. "River of Life in God's New Jerusalem: An Eschatological Vision for Earth's Future." In Hessel and Ruether, Christianity and Ecology, 205–224.

Rouyer, Alwyn R. "Zionism and Water: Influences on Israel's Future Water Policy during the Pre-State Period." Arab Studies Quarterly 18, no. 4 (Fall 1996): 25–47.

Roy, Arundhati. "The Greater Common Good." In Arundhati Roy, The Cost of Living. New York: Modern Library, 1999.

Rufo-Hill, James, and Brooke Rufo-Hill. Personal interview, Seattle, 13 May 2006.

Ruiz-Marrero, Carmelo. "Free Trade and Water Privatization: The Wet Side of the FTAA." Americas Program, Interhemispheric Resource Center (December 2, 2004).

Sahagun, Louis. "Holy Waters, Slot Machines and a Gamble in Taos, New Mexico: A Ruling May Close Tribal Casinos." *Los Angeles Times*, 11 January 1996, sec. A.

Sandor, Marjorie. "Waiting for a Miracle: A Jew Goes Fishing." *Georgia Review* 53, no. 2 (Summer 1999): 231–233.

Sankarnarayan, K. "Buddhist Ecology and Scriptures of Mahayana." In Pathak, *Buddhism and Ecology*, 19–27.

Santiago, Charles. "Public-Public Partnership: An Alternative Strategy in Water Management in Malaysia." In Balanyá et al., *Reclaiming Public Water*, 55–61.

Shafer, Ingrid H. "Confucianism." Revised 6 January 2002. At www.usao.edu/~usao-ids3313/ids/html/confucianism (accessed 25 July 2006).

Shiva, Vandana. *Water Wars: Privatization, Pollution, and Profit*. Cambridge, Mass.: South End Press, 2002.

———. "World Bank, WTO, and Corporate Control over Water," *International Socialist Review*, August–September 2001, 41.

Shultz, Jim. "Bolivia: The Water Wars Widen." *NACLA Report on the Americas* 36.3 (2003): 1–3.

Shuppy, Annie. "Prime Numbers: H_2OU." *The Chronicle of Higher Education*. 3 Nov. 2006. A7.

Silko, Leslie Marmon. *Sacred Water: Narratives and Pictures*. Tucson, Ariz.: Flood Plain Press, 1993.

de Silva, Lily. "The Hills Wherein My Soul Delights." In Batchelor and Brown, *Buddhism and Ecology*, 18–30.

de Silva, Padmasiri. *Buddhism, Ethics and Society: The Conflicts and Dilemmas of Our Times*. Clayton, Australia: Monash University Press, 2002.

Slater, Dashka. "Big-Box Talk." *Sierra Magazine* 91, no. 6 (November–December 2006): 19–21.

Smith, Mick. *An Ethics of Place: Radical Ecology, Postmodernity, and Social Theory*. Albany: State University of New York Press, 2001.

Specter, Michael. "The Last Drop: Confronting the Possibility of a Global Catastrophe." *New Yorker* 82, no. 34 (23 October 2006): 60–71.

Starke, Linda, ed. *Vital Signs, 2006-2007: The Trends That Are Shaping Our Future*. New York: Norton, 2005.

Stein, Jonathan. "Enemies of the Ocean." *Mother Jones* 31, no. 2 (March–April 2006): 50.

Stiffler, Lisa, and Robert McClure. "Reality Already Is Soaking In." *Seattle Post-Intelligencer*, 11 October 2006, sec. A.

———. "Saving Puget Sound Could Cost $12 Billion." *Seattle Post-Intelligencer*, 13 October 2006, sec. A.

Struck, Doug. "Scientists Say It's Just a Matter of When." [*Washington Post*, as reported in] *Seattle Times*, 10 November 2006, sec. A.

Suzuki, David. *The Sacred Balance*. Vancouver, B.C.: Greystone, 1997.

Swearer, Donald K. "The Hermeneutics of Buddhist Ecology in Contemporary Thailand: Buddhadīsa and Dhammapitaka." In Tucker and Williams, *Buddhism and Ecology*, 21–44.

Swearer, Donald K., Sommai Premchit, and Phaithoon Dokbuakaew. *Sacred Mountains of Northern Thailand and Their Legends*. Chiang Mai: Silkworm Books, 2004.

"Taoism/Daoism," *Meditations and Reflections in Zen, Buddhism, Taoism, Mystical Religions, and Early Christianity*. At www.yakrider.com (accessed 3 May 2006).

Taylor, Rodney L. "Companionship with the World: Roots and Branches of a Confucian Ecology." In Tucker and Berthrong, *Confucianism and Ecology*, 37–58.

Thirst. Produced and directed by Alan Snitow and Deborah Kaufman. Oley, Pa.: Bullfrog Films. Snitow-Kaufman Productions, 2004.

Timm, Roger E. "The Ecological Fallout of Islamic Creation Theology." In Tucker and Grim, *Worldviews and Ecology*, 93–95.

Tirosh-Samuelson, Hava, ed. *Judaism and Ecology: Created World and Revealed Word*. Cambridge, Mass.: Harvard University Press, 2002.

Tounounga, Camille Talkeu. "The Liquid of the Gods." *Unesco Courier*, no. 5 (May 1993): 38–39.

Tucker, Mary Evelyn. "The Philosophy of Ch'i as an Ecological Cosmology." In Tucker and Berthrong, *Confucianism and Ecology*, 187–207.

Tucker, Mary Evelyn, and John Berthrong, eds. *Confucianism and Ecology: the Interrelation of Heaven, Earth, and Human*. Cambridge, Mass.: Harvard University Press, 1998.

Tucker, Mary Evelyn, and John Grim. "Series Foreword." In Tucker and Berthrong, *Confucianism and Ecology*, xv–xxxi.

Tucker, Mary Evelyn, and John Grim, eds. *Worldviews and Ecology*. Maryknoll, N.Y.: Orbis, 1994.

Tucker, Mary Evelyn, and Duncan Ryūken Williams, eds. *Buddhism and Ecology: The Interconnection of Dharma and Deeds*. Cambridge, Mass.: Harvard University Press, 1997.

United Nations. *Water for People, Water for Life: The United Nations World Water Development Report*. Geneva: UNESCO, 2003.

United Nations. *Water: A Shared Responsibility. The United Nations World Water Development Report 2*. New York: Berghahn, 2006.

Unno, Taitetsu. *River of Fire, River of Water*. New York: Doubleday, 1998.

Unsworth, Tim. "Holy Waters Run Deep," *U.S. Catholic*, February 1996, 50.

Velez, Hildebrando. "Public Services in Colombia: A Matter of Democracy." In Balanyá et al., *Reclaiming Public Water*, 103–109.

de Villiers, Marc. *Water: The Fate of Our Most Precious Resource*. New York: Houghton Mifflin, 2000.

"Water, People, Land and Conflict." Center for Defense Information. Video #1143, narrated by Rear Admiral Eugene Carroll, US Navy (retired), deputy director, July 1998.

"What's on Tap? Grading Drinking Water in U.S. Cities: Tap Water Quality and Safety." National Resource Defense Council. 10 June 2003. At www.nrde.org/water/drinking (accessed 20 November 2006).

White, Lynn, Jr. "The Historical Roots of Our Ecologic Crisis." In MacKinnon and McIntyre, *Readings in Ecology and Feminist Theory.*

Whitty, Julia. "The Fate of the Ocean." *Mother Jones* 31, no. 2 (March-April 2006): 32–48.

———. "The Thirteenth Tipping Point," *Mother Jones* 31, no. 6 (November-December 2006): 44–101.

Wicker, Kathleen O'Brien. "Miami Water in African Religion and Spirituality." In *African Spirituality: Forms, Meanings, and Expressions,* edited by Jacob K. Olupona, 198–223. New York: Crossroad, 2000.

Witt, Howard. "Arctic Town Isn't So Hot on Warming." [*Chicago Tribune,* as reported in] *Seattle Times,* 6 Oct. 2006, sec. A.

Woodworth, Cameron. "A Clean Drink of Water: Choices and Responsibilities." *Sound Consumer,* August 2006.

World Commission on Dams. *Dams and Development: Report of the World Commission on Dams.* London, Earthscan, 2000.

World Council of Churches. *Statement on Water for Life.* At www.oikoumene.org/index.lpho?id=1955 (accessed 3 May 2007).

World Health Organization. WHO and UNICEF Joint Monitoring Programme. *Global Water Supply and Sanitation Assessment 2000 Report.* Geneva: UNICEF, 2000.

Worm, Boris, et al. "Impacts of Biodiversity Loss on Ocean Ecosystem Services." *Science* 314, no. 5800 (3 November 2006): 787–790.

Worster, Donald. *Rivers of Empire.* New York: Oxford University Press, 1985.

Yavari, Luis Fernando. "Management of Basic Drinking Water and Sanitation Services by a Cooperative in Bolivia." In Balanyá et al., *Reclaiming Public Water,* 37–44.

Young, Robert. *Determining the Value of Water: Concepts and Methods.* Washington, D.C.: Resources for the Future, 2005.

~

Web Resources

General

blueplanetproject.net

Fourth World Water Forum: http://www.worldwaterforum4.org.mx/home/
home.asp

Islam and Ecology: http://environment.harvard.edu/religion/religion/islam/
bibliography.html

People's World Water Forum Group: http://www.wateryear2003.org/en/
ev.php

thirstthemovie.org

www.adb.org/water/default.asp

www.citizen.org/cmep/water

www.experiencingfestival.com/a/Holy_Water/id

www.iwha.net

www.measuredhs.com

www.nccecojustice.org

www.piur.com

www.savingwater.org

www.un.org/waterforlifrdecade/statements.html

www.unhabitat.org

www.unher.org

www.un-urbanwater.net

www.unwac.org

International NGOs

The Access Initiative: www.accessinitiative.org
Action against Hunger (AAH): www.actionagainsthunger.org/
The African Water Page: www.thewaterpage.com
Beijer Institute website on environmental economics: www.beijer.kva.se/
Centre on Housing Rights and Evictions (COHRE): www.cohre.org/water/
CGIAR (Consultative Group on International Agriculture Research)–Challenge
Comprehensive Assessment of Water Management in Agriculture (CA): www.iwmi.cgiar.org/Assessment/Index.asp
FAO–Global Perspective Studies: www.fao.org/es/ESD/gstudies.htm
FAO–State of Food Insecurity (SOFI): www.fao.org/sof/sofi/index_en.htm
FAO–State of World Fisheries and Aquaculture (SOFIA): www.fao.org/sof/sofia/index_en.htm
Global Water Partnership: www.gwpforum.org
International Federation of Red Cross and Red Crescent Societies (IFRC): www.cred.be/
International Water Management Institute (IWMI): www.iwmi.cgiar.org and
Program on Water and Food: www.waterforfood.org/
Transparency International: www.transparency.org/
Utstein Anti-Corruption Resource Centre: www.u4.no/
The World Bank Institute: www.worldbank.org/wbi/governance/
World Resources Institute: www.wri.org
www.iwmidsp.org/iwmi/info/main.asp

International Organizations

Asian Development Bank: www.adb.org
European Commission on the Environment on water policy: www.europa.eu.int/comm./environment/water/index.html
FEWS (Famine Early Warning Systems Network): www.fews.net
Health, Nutrition, and Population Programme: www.adb.org/Health
ICID (International Commission on Irrigation and Drainage): www.icid.org/
IFAD (International Fund for Agricultural Development)—Rural Poverty: www.ifad.org/poverty/
IUCN's Water and Nature Initiative on valuing water: www.iucn.org/themes/wani/value/index.html
OECD website on water financing: www.oecd.org/document/7/0,2340,en_2649_201185_33719751_1_1_1_1,00.html

Stockholm Convention: www.pops.int/

UNEP-GEMS Water (Global Environment Monitoring System): www.gems water.org

Unilever: www.unilever.com/environmentalsociety/

Water for All Programme: www.adb.org/Water

Water Supply and Sanitation Collaborative Council: www.wsscc.org

Wetlands International, 2005, Annual History of Ramsar Site Designations: www.wetlands.org

World Bank Water and Sanitation Blue Gold Series: www.wsp.org/08_Blue Gold.asp

World Bank Water Supply and Sanitation Programme: www.worldbank .org/watsan

World Bank's Public-Private Infrastructure Advisory Facility (PPIAF) re- garding large scale PPPs: www.ppiaf.org/

World Health Organization: www.who.int

World Lakes Organisation: www.worldlakes.org/

World Resources Institute: www.wri.org/

World Water Council on virtual water: www.worldwatercouncil .org/index.php?id=866

World Water Resources and Their Use—a joint SHI/UNESCO project: www.unesco.org/water

WWF Freshwater programme: www.panda.org/about_wwf/what_we_do/ freshwater/index.cfm

www.ecosystemvaluation.org

www.wetlands.org/RDB/global/Designations.html

UNDP Governance Centre, Sources for Democratic Governance Indicators: www.undp.org/water

UNDP on public-private partnerships (medium sized): www.pppue.undp .org/index.cfm

UNDP Water Governance Facility at Siwi: www.watergovernance.org

UNECE Convention on the Protection and Use of Transboundary Water- courses and International Lakes (Water Convention): www.unece .org/env/water/

UNEP Division of Technology, Industry and Economics: www.uneptie.org/

UNESCO-IHE website on virtual water: www.waterfootpring.org/

UNICEF Water, Environment, and Sanitation: www.unicef.org/wes

UNIDO: www.unido.org/

United Nations: igrac.nitg.tno.nl/homepage.html

Index

acequia ditches, 15

acidification, of oceans, 105

Adamah, Shomrei, 164

Africa, 2, 7, 13, 14, 70, 71, 103, 105, 117, 120, 121, 132, 133–34, 166, 180, 183–84

Aga Kahn Development Network, 170

Agarwal, Anil, 20, 159

agriculture, 2, 64, 81–82, 84, 90, 102–4, 108, 137, 140, 155, 169, 179, 181–83, 191; and water, 15, 82, 84, 102, 103, 108, 169, 182–83, 191

ahimsa, 21

Ajakarani River, 23, 144

algae, 82, 84, 103

Allah, 52, 53, 54, 55, 150, 168, 169

Alley, Kelly, 20

Altman, Nathaniel, 53

Amazon, the rainforest, 106

Amazon, the river, 70, 86

Amnesty International, 132

Antarctic, the (South Pole), 68, 69, 72–73, 82, 106, 189

anti-dam movement, 95 *See also* dams

Aquafina water, 101

aqueducts, Roman, 80, 85–86

aquifers, 66, 69, 72, 84, 100, 102–4, 133, 181, 193; in Central California, 100; and *mining* of, 102, 104; Ogallala, 69, 100, 141; and West Bank, Israel, 107

Arctic, the (North Pole), 68, 72–73, 82, 106, 189

Aristotle, 66, 152n27

arsenic, 83, 91n18, 166

Asmal, Kader, 98

Australian aboriginals, 13–14

Bachelard, Gaston, 55–57

BACONGO (Belize Alliance of Conservation NGOs), 95, 110n13–14. *See also* countries, Belize

Ball, Phillip, 64, 106, 157, 187

Banzer, Hugo, 122

baptism, 46–50, 168

Barlow, Chris, 108

Barlow, Maude, 81, 127

Bechtel, 117, 121–22

Belize 94–96, 120, 183

Ben Pazi, Judah, 41

Bernstein, Ellen, 164
Berry, Thomas, 158
Bhagavadgita, 17. *See also* Hinduism
Bhagavita Purana, 17. *See also* Hinduism
Bhikkhu, Buddhadasa, 22
Big Bang, 65
Bini people (Nigeria), 14
Black, Maggie, 68, 156–57, 179, 195
Blatter, Joachim, 4–5, 157
bottled water, 101–2, 146; and brands, Aquafina (Pepsi), Dasani (Coca-Cola), Fiji, 101; Perrier, 101
Bouygues-SAUR, 117
Brazil, 7, 13, 83; and nursing, 97, 100, 121, 167, 192
British Columbia, 71, 74, 105, 118, 119; pollution in Victoria, 183. *See also* Canada
Buddhism, origins, rituals and practices, 21–25; bodhi tree, 21; bodhisattva, 22, 31, 160; Buddha, 21, 23, 160; dharma, 20; ethics, 142–44; *gatha* versus, 161; "green, " 161; Kalachakra ceremony, 23; karma, 21, 23; lotus flower, 23; Mahayana Buddhism, 25, 143; mandala, 23; water ethos, 160–62, 168, 171; Zen Buddhism, 24–25

cadmium, 83, 102
Callicott, J. Baird, 153n44, 159
Canada, 13, 72, 85, 97, 119, 167, 188, 191; and agreement with U.S., 188, 191
carbon dioxide, 88, 97, 189. *See also* gasses; greenhouse gasses
Care International, 170
Carthusians, and toilets, 80
Cascade mountains, 2, 74, 105
Cascal Company, 120
Cassini spacecraft, 67
Catholic Social Teaching, 139, 141–42, 151n27, 167

Celts, 45, 46
Center for Naval Analyses, 109
Centre for Science and Environment, 101. *See also* India
channelization, of rivers, 86
chemicals, 84, 87–88, 102, 104, 180, 186
Chishti, Saadia Khawar Khan, 173
cholera, 81, 119, 120
Christianity, 3, 12, 39, 44–46, 50, 156, 163, 165–68, 171; baptism, 46, 48, 168; creation in, 44–45; and desacralization, 44; and Easter, 47; and Eden (Garden of), 41, 43; and Eucharist, 47; and holy water, 47, 49–50; and manager (of creation), 39
Chrysostom, John, 46
Chryssavgis, John, 48
Cistercian monks, 46
cities, Bruges, 80; London, 80; New York City, 82; Paris, 86; Rome, 47, 49, 81, 86; Tokyo, 86; Victoria, B.C., 82; Washington, D.C., 83
climate change. *See* global warming
cloud seeding, 181
clouds, 2, 14, 41, 57, 66–68, 71, 73–74, 78n45. *See also* water, forms of
Coalition on the Environment and Jewish Life, 164–165
Coca-Cola Company (Coke), bottled water brand, 101; contamination in India, 101–2
Cochabamba, Bolivia, 7, 120, 121–23, 145, 146, 148–49, 173, 192–93
Coalition for the Defense of Water and Life. *See* La Coordinadora
common good, 109, 127, 132, 141–42, 148–49, 166, 167, 179, 191–94
conation, 136
condensation, process of, 68
contamination, defined, 82, 83; and bacteria, 86; gasoline, 82; from

groundwater, 104; oil, 82; solvents, 82, 83
Coordinadora, 121–22, 148, 191; and norms, 148
coral reefs, 88, 170
coulees, 63
countries, Afghanistan, 81, 184; Argentina, 100, 121, 133, 192; Assyria, 80; Australia, 106; Babylonia, 40, 81; Bangladesh, 70, 83, 106, 108, 167, 183, 191; Belize, 94–96, 120, 183; Bolivia, 7, 71, 120, 121–23, 129n52, 147, 173; Brazil, 7, 13, 83, 97, 100, 121, 167, 192; Cambodia, 108, 120; Canada, 13, 72, 85, 97, 119, 167, 188, 191; China, 7, 29–32, 85, 86, 88, 94–95, 97–98, 100, 105, 108, 114, 180, 183, 184, 194; Colombia, 11, 13, 121, 149, (Kogi and 11, 13); Czech Republic, 86; Dominican Republic, 79, 187; Egypt, 40, 41, 42, 69, 81, 94, 96–97, 108; Ethiopia, 81, 108; Ghana, 13, 53, 120, 121, 192; Greenland, 69, 73, 106; Haiti, 14, 181, 187; Honduras, 138; India, 7, 21–27, 118, 122, 131, 141, 142, 143, 151, 191; Iran, 114; Iraq, 114, 150; Israel, 150–51; Japan, 25, 31, 86, 88, 94, 95, 100, 103, 127, 135, 136, 139, 166, 183, 186; Jordan, 107, 180, 183, 184, 186, 187; Laos, 108; Malaysia 121, 156, 192; Mexico, 94, 95, 100, 134, 158, 166, 186, 192; Morocco, 100; Nepal, 108, 181, 183, 184; the Netherlands, 70; Nigeria, 14; Pakistan, 2, 100, 119, 173, 183, 186, 188, 191; Peru, 2, 71; the Philippines, 119, 184; Russia, 81, 88, 136; Rwanda, 118; Saudi Arabia, 100, 170, 179, 194; Scandinavia, 85; South Africa, 120–21, 133, 134, 180; Spain, 94, 180; Sudan, 108; Sweden, 85; Syria, 107; Switzerland, 105; Tanzania, 2, 128; Thailand, 81, 108, 160; Tibet, 23, 106; Turkey, 107, 180; former Union of Soviet Socialist Republics, 85, 87; United Kingdom, 106, 120, 125; United States, 13, 15, 74, 83–85, 88, 94, 99, 100, 101, 103, 104, 108, 109, 117–18, 121, 132, 135, 143, 147, 158, 163, 172, 180, 185, 187–90, 191; Uruguay, 120, 137; Vietnam, 82, 108
Cree people, and mercury contamination, 97. See also Native Americans and First Nation Peoples

Dagara people (Burkina Faso and Ghana), 13
dambo farming, 184
dams, 93–99; Aswan High Dam, 94–97; Banqiao, China, 99; breaching, 101, 182; Chalillo, Belize, 95; costs, 95–98; as development tools, 94; for flood control, 94; Glen Canyon, 94; Grand Coulee, 93–94; Hoover, 93, 94; and human rights, 98; for hydroelectric power, 94; for irrigation, 94; capacities of large, 94; major builders, 94–95; resettlement, 94–96, 97, 98, 132, 133, 135, 137; Shasta, 94; and sustainability, 98; Three Gorges, 95; uses, 94; Vaca, Belize, 95
Daza, Victor Hugo, 122
deforestation, 30, 103
Democracy Center, 122
desalination, 180, 191; negative effects, 180; reverse osmosis, 180
desertification, 100, 103
de Villiers, Marq, 80, 180, 185, 191
dengue fever 81
development, 135; sustainable, 134
dew collecting, 181

dharma, 20
diarrheal disease, 2, 81
diseases, 81–82, 86, 87
divestment, 123
Dochrat, Hashim Ismail, 169
Dogon people (Mali), 13
Dome of the Rock, 52
Doon Valley, 125
drilling, 125; percussion drills, 80; techniques, 80
drip irrigation, 184–85
Dry Falls, 63–64. *See also* Pacific Northwest
dysentery, 81

Earth, creation of 5, 13, 15–17, 19, 21, 28, 29, 39, 40, 41, 44, 51, 52, 55, 137, 142, 156, 160, 163–68; basalt formations, 69; craters, 71; deltas, 58, 70, 140; lava, 69; magma, 65, 66, 69; plants and vegetation, 30, 55, 58, 63, 69, 71, 73, 84, 85, 87, 96, 97, 103, 106, 124, 144, 164, 188; rift valleys, 71
Earth Summit (2002), 124
eco-feminism, 144–47
Eden (Garden of), 41, 43. *See also* Christianity
effluent, 83, 88, 120, 170, 186
Egypt, vi, 40–42, 80, 94, 96, 97, 108; deliverance from, 40, 41, 42; Egyptian sandstones, 69. *See also* countries, Egypt
Eisenberg, Evan, 41
El Niño, 106
electricity, 64, 94, 95, 97, 98
elements, 16, 17, 23, 30, 32, 40, 41, 43, 45, 51, 65, 66. *See also* water, as element
Eliade, Mircea, 12, 13, 50
Empedocles, 66
Engelman, Robert, 107
Enron-Azruix, 117

Environmental Protection Agency, 84, 101
environmentalism, 165
equity, 98, 99, 116, 126, 141, 179
Ereira, Alan, 11
Ethics, definition of, 3, 5, 6, 9; 137; 137–39; Buddhist and, 142–44; Catholic Social Teaching and, 141–42; environmental and eco-feminist and, 144–47; utilitarian and, 139–41
Ethos, 136–39; summary of principles, 150
Europe, 7, 45, 48, 80, 85, 86, 88, 89, 100, 104, 116, 132, 135, 172, 189
European Community, 101; water purity and, 102
Evangelical Lutheran Church in America, 166
evaporation, process of, 68, 70, 84, 100, 105, 108, 185
extraterrestrial life, 67

Farallon Islands, 88
Fiji, 101
flooding, 86, 88, 95, 99, 103, 105, 106, 141, 189; flood control, 86, 94
fog harvesting, 181
Fon people (Benin), 14
Food and Drug Administration, 101
fossil-fuel, 85, 97
Friedman, Irving, 40, 53, 59, 203

Ganges River (also Ganga), 16–20, 34, 70, 159, 160, 191
Gasses 73, 122, 156, 186; carbon dioxide, 88, 97, 189; methane, 82, 97, 106, 136; nitrogen, 65, 85, 103; sulphur, 85. *See also* greenhouse gasses
Geertz, Clifford, 12, 58
General Agreement on Trade in Services (GATS), 118

Genesis, 41, 59, 164
geysers, 67
ghats, 21
glaciers, glacial snows, 11, 63, 71, 105, 115, 189
global warming, 2, 69, 72, 79, 81, 82, 88, 90, 93, 105, 106, 109; 186, 189, 194; dilution 69
gods, Aspu (Sumerian), 40; Ea (Mesopotamian), 40; Gilgamesh, 40; Hapi (Egyptian), 40; Indra (Hindu), 23; Krishna (Hindu), 18; Nun (Babylonian), 40; Shiva (Hindu), 16, 17, 19, 34, 146
Goldman, Elyse, 43, golf courses, 82, 103, 135
Grand Canyon, 108
Grand Coulee Dam, 93, 94. See also dams; Pacific Northwest
gravity, 65, 66, 69, 80, 190
Great Depression, 63, 70, 93
Great Lakes Charter, 188
greenhouse gasses, 82, 88, 97, 105, 180, 186, 189; carbon dioxide and methane, 82, 88, 97, 106, 189
Groundwater, 71, 74, 80, 84, 100, 101, 117, 121, 133, 137, 140, 155, 186
guinea worm, 81, 120
Gulf Coast, 70

"Hadean" period, 66
Habito, Rubin, 24
Hahn, Thich Nhat, 21, 22, 160
hepatitis, 81
Hessel, Dieter, 44
Hinduism, 4, 8, 12, 16, 19, 20, 32, 56, 159, 160, 171; Bhagavadgita, 17; Bhagavita Purana, 18; ghats, 21; Indra (god), 17; Krishna (god), 18; Maha Kumbh Mela festival, 19; Regveda (also Rig Veda), 18; Shiva (goddess), 16, 17, 19, 23, 26, 34, 146. See also India

Hmong people, 81
HMS Challenger, 68
Hoeg, Peter 73
Hopi people, 158; and Peabody Coal, 158
Hopkins, Gerard Manley, 155
human rights, 9, 98, 132, 136, 163, 193
Hurricane Katrina, 70, 121; Hurricane Mitch, 98
hydrologic cycle, 41, 68, 75, 105; "conveyor belt," 68–69; hydroelectric power. See dams

Ice, 11, 41, 63, 64, 66, 67, 68, 69, 71, 72, 73, 74, 81, 106, 180; ice age, 71, 72; ice cliffs, 71; ice dams, 71; "ice-front" lakes, 71; moraines, 71; reflecting sun, 72, 74, 106; underground, 66, 68, 73
immersion, 12, 13, 42, 43, 46, 47, 48, 53, 56
Imperial Valley, 108
India 7, 16–20, 56, 83, 86, 94, 96, 100–2, 108, 121, 124, 125, 159, 160, 170, 173, 182–84, 188, 190; Centre for Science and Environment, 101–2; conservation, 126; pollution, 20, 83, 86, 102, 159; religion, 16–20, 159–60, 171; Brahman, 17; Ganges River (also Ganga), 16–20, 70, 159, 160, 190; ghats, 16
indigenous peoples, 4, 15, 95, 155, 167; and relocation, 87, 97
indigenous traditions 8, 13–16, 158–59, 164, 171
Indus Waters Treaty, 188
industry, 81, 83, 89, 95, 96, 101, 104, 117, 121, 133, 137, 140, 155, 186
infant mortality, increases in, 87, 99
Ingram, Helen, 4, 159
initiation 12, 13–15, 23, 24, 42, 43, 46, 49, 53; for indigenous peoples, 13–15

Institute for Human and Environmental Development (Islam), 109
Interface carpeting, 186
Intergovernmental Panel on Climate Change, 105
International Agreements on Water, 189–91
International Convention on the Rights of the Child, 132
International Covenant on Economic, Social and Cultural Rights, 133
International Drinking Water and Sanitation Decade, 133
International Joint Commission (Canada and United States), 191
International Monetary Fund, 117, 118
International Year of Freshwater, 134
Ireland 45, 168
irrigation, 3, 28, 42, 54, 80, 86–87, 94–96, 99, 100, 102, 103, 107, 108, 161, 167, 170, 179, 181–82, 184–87, 193; water for, 54, 80, 86–87, 99, 100, 102, 103, 107, 108, 167, 170
Islam, 4, 8, 12, 33, 39, 40, 50–55, 136, 163, 167, 168–71, 173
Islamic Foundation for Ecology and Environmental Sciences, 170
Israel, 40–41, 101, 180, 183, 184, 186, 191; and Judaism, 40–41; and war, 107, 191; and water 180, 185, 186, 191. See also Judaism

Jacobs, Mark, 164
Jerusalem, 46, 47, 50, 165
Jesus, 46–47, 50, 165
John Paul II, Pope, 141–42
John XXIII, Pope, 133, 141
Judaism, 4, 8, 12, 33, 39–43, 136, 163–65, 167; book of Deuteronomy, 43; caretaker (of creation), 39; Exodus story, 41–42; Hasidic Judaism, 39; meal and washing, 42; mikveh, 42–43; Moses, 41–42; Rosh

ha-Shanah, 43; Sabbath, 42, 163–64; Torah, 40; Yahweh, 41. See also washing; water
Jupiter, 67; moons Callisto, Europa, Ganymede, 67

Kammer, Charles, 4
Kandel, Robert, 185, 186
Karaja people (Brazil), 13
Katz, Eric, 41
Kinsley, David, 21
Kogi people, 11, 13, 70
Krishna (god), 18
Kyoto Protocol, 190

La Coordinadora, 121–22
lakes, 2, 11, 13, 14, 27, 63, 66, 67, 69, 70–71, 73, 81–83, 85, 89, 94, 96, 103, 115, 188, 189; Caspian Sea, 70–71; Crater, 71; Great Lakes, 71, 188; "Kettlehole" lakes, 71; Malawi, 71; Mead, 94; Nasser, 94; Roosevelt, 63, 94; Tanganyika, 71; Titicaca, 71
Lead, 83; as toxic, 83
Leopold, Aldo, 146
London, 80, 124, 186; water pumps 80
lotus flower, 12, 23
Love Canal, 104
Loy, David, 3

Macy, Joanna, 143
Maguire, Daniel, 6, 138
malaria, 81
mangroves, 88, 160
Mars, 67
Masayesva, Vernon, 158
Mbibi, John, 15
McDonagh, Sean, 168
meditation, mindfulness, 17, 21, 24, 57, 143–44, 161, 171, 173, 195
Mekong River Commission, 108
mercury, 83, 84, 96, 97; aluminum, 83; cadmium, 83, 102; cobalt, 83;

contamination by, 84, 96; copper, 83, 89; lead, 83; manganese, 83; mercury, 83, 84, 96, 97; as pollutant, 83, 97; pollution metals, 66, 83, 84, 104; tin, 83; as toxic, 83, 104; in waters, 84; zinc, 83. *See also* contamination; metals; pollution

methane, 82, 97, 106. *See also* gasses

mikveh 42–43, 53; for purification, 42, 43, 53; for fertility, 42. *See also* Judaism

Millennium Declaration, 135, 137

Millennium Development Goals, 124, 179

mining, 83, 100, 125, 158, 167; tailings, 83

Mishra, V. B., 160

Mohammed, 54. *See also* Islam

monsoon, in Asia, 106, 182

moon, Earth's, 65, 67

mountains, 2, 11, 13, 25, 26–28, 30, 41, 68, 74, 80, 81, 85, 105, 144, 161, 162, 164, 170, 184; Adirondacks, 85; Cascade range, 2, 74, 105; Catskills, 85; Mt. Adams, 71; Mt. Hood, 71; Mt. Rainier, 71; Rocky Mountain range, 74. *See also* volcanoes

Muslim, 51–55, 168–69

Narmada River, 16–19, 96

Nash, James, 136

Nash, Mick, 137

Nasr, Seyyed Hossein, 51–52

National Aeronautics and Space Administration (NASA), 67, 106

National Council of Churches, 165

National Public Radio, 84

National Resources Defense Council, 101

National Snow and Ice Data Center, 106

Native Americans and First Nation Peoples, 187; Cree, 13, 82, 97; Hopi, 13, 158; Lakota, 13; and mercury contamination, 96–97; Omaha, 13; Pueblo, 15; Salish, 13; Taos, 13; Western Shoshone, 13

Navajo peoples, 158

New York City, 83, 187

Nichols, Greg, 191

Nirvana, 21–22

Nisqually National Wildlife Refuge, 188

nitrates, 82, 88. *See also* contamination; pollution

North American Free Trade Agreement (NAFTA), 118

Narayanan, Vasudha, 19, 20

nuclear power, 88, 95

obligations, 137, 149

oceans, 2, 55, 66–68, 72, 88, 103, 105, 156; as acidic, 88, 105; Arctic, 67, 73, 81, 106, 189; Atlantic, 67, 14, 68, 106, 181; Indian, 68, 170; Pacific, 13, 57, 68–89; Southern (Antarctic) Ocean, 73, 67, 81, 106, 189; surface currents, 68

oil, 13, 83, 84, 186. *See also* contamination; pollution

Olivera, Oscar, 122, 148, 192

Oslo Accords, 107

oxygen, 65, 67, 72, 82; depletion, 82

ozone hole, 106

Pacific Northwest, 13, 57, 69, 73, 167, 181; Rialto Beach, 70

Palestinians, 107, 191; and water war, 107, 191; and wells, 107

Patriarch Bartholomew, Orthodox Church, 165, 167

Paul (Biblical), 47

Payen, Gerard, 127

Peabody Coal, 158

Pearce, Fred, 100, 107, 137, 156, 178, 179, 180

Pepsi, 101–2; bottled water brand, 101–2; contamination in India, 101–2. *See also* water, bottled
permafrost, 66, 67, 72, 106
Perrier water, 101. *See also* water, bottled
pesticides, 84, 101; PCBs, 83, 85, 88. *See also* contamination; pollution
Peterson, Anna, 3, 143, 150
Petrella, Ricardo, 149
pharmaceuticals, 84. *See also* contamination; pollution
phosphates, 82, 88
Pielou, E. C., 71, 82, 83, 85, 86, 97
Pitak, Prhaku, 160
pollution, 2, 3, 20, 24, 43, 54, 56, 58, 79, 81, 93, 102, 109, 119–20, 135, 155, 159, 167, 69–171, 191; agriculture and, 2, 81, 84, 89, 103, 179; DDT, 87; defined, 82; dioxin, 83; fertilizers and, 84, 103; golf courses and, 82, 103, 135; herbicides, 84; from industrial plants, 81, 89, 104, 170, 179; oceans and, 88
Pongsak, Ajahn, 22
Population Action Institute, 107
population, 2, 76, 81, 83, 85, 89, 90, 93, 95, 96, 99, 100, 103, 106, 107, 109, 115, 116, 118, 155, 171, 180, 183, 190–91; increases in, 2, 76, 81, 85, 89, 90, 93, 99, 103, 107, 109, 155, 180, 183, 190–91
Postel, Sandra, 181, 192–93
Prince William Sound, 84
principles, accountability, 146, 150, 184; community of interests, 147; equality, 93, 126, 142, 146, 148; fair and reasonable use, 147–48; of new water ethos, 150; participation, 12, 48, 93, 99, 16, 120, 123–24, 126, 142, 146, 150, 178, 184; preferential option, 142, 148, 150, 166; prior appropriation, 108, 130; riparian

rights, 131–32; solidarity, 6, 131, 142, 149, 150, 166, 172, 178, 179, 194; stewardship, 142, 163–65, 193; subsidiarity, 142, 146, 148, 150, 179, 183, 184, 194; sufficiency, 147; sustainability, 6–8, 55, 76, 93, 99, 116, 120, 145–47, 149–50, 150, 157, 159, 170, 173, 179, 180, 194
"prior appropriation," doctrine of, 108, 132
Private Sector Participation (PSP), 124
privatization, 8, 116–20, 132, 140, 147–48, 182, 192–93
Privy Council, of Great Britain, 95
prophets, 41, 43, 54, 169, 172; Isaiah, 40–41; Jeremiah, 41
prohibitions, 24, 43, 51, 53, 54, 55, 119, 144, 168, 171; al-Wudu, Faraid, 53; in Buddhism, 24, 144; Hesiod, 55; in Islam, 51, 53–55, 168, 171; muhtasib, 53
Public-Private Partnerships (PPPs), 124, 127, 147
Public-Public Partnerships (PPPs), 192
Puget Sound, 2, 89, 188

qanats, 80, 184
Qur'an, 50–51, 52, 53, 54, 170. *See also* Islam

rain, 2, 14, 15, 17, 21, 23, 30, 42, 45, 57, 66–67, 69–74, 83, 84, 85, 101–3, 105, 106, 158, 160, 181–84, 188, 189; formation of, 66–67; acid rain, 85
rainmakers, 14–15
rainwater harvesting, 102, 182–83, 189; in China, 183; in India, 182–83; Singh, Bendra, 182
Red Sea, 40
Rees, Judith, 123, 126
Regveda (also *Rig Veda*), 17, 18. *See also* Hinduism

religion, 3–5; definition of, 4, 12, 16; of the market, 3
relocation, 123
reservoir, 69, 87, 93–97; problems in, 97
resettlement, due to dams, 94, 95, 96, 97
resistance, 115–16, 120–22, 145
Revelation, Book of, 49
Rig Veda. See *Regveda*
rights, 131–33, 235–37, 2 149; defined, 136; to life, 131; of nature, 136; to participation, 142, 146; of persons, 141; private property rights, 132; riparian rights, 131; to water, 132, 149
ritual. *See* water
rivers, Amazon, 70, 86; Clyde, 45; Colorado, 39, 70, 94, 108, 148; Columbia, 63, 64, 69, 93, 167, 181; Congo, 70, 86; Cuyahoga (Cleveland, US), 104; ephemeral rivers, rivulets, tributaries, 70; Euphrates, 40, 80, 107; Ganga (also Ganges), 16–20, 70, 159, 160, 190; Hudson, 83; Jordan, 41, 46, 70, 107; Macal (Belize), 95; Marne, 45; Mekong, 108; Narmada, 16, 17–18, 19, 96; Niger, 70; Nile, 40, 41, 70, 80, 94, 96, 184, 190–91; Potomac, 84; Rhine, 45, 70; sediments in, 69, 71, 82–85, 94, 97; Seine, 45, 80; Tigris, 40, 80, 107; Thames, 80, 186, 189; Topajoz, Brazil, 82; Yamuna River, 16, 18, 19; Yangtze Kiang, 87, 95; Yellow, 86, 87, 183
Roman Catholic Church, 15, 47, 53, 122, 165, 167, 188 ; and Catholic Social Teaching, 139–42; Pontifical Council for Justice and Peace on Water, 166; and water, 165
Rome, 47, 49, 80, 86
Rossing, Barbara, 49
Roy, Arundhati, 96, 125

Ruether, Rosemany Radford, 44
Rufo-Hill, Jim and Brooke, ix, 79, 187
Russia, 81, 88, 135
RWE-Thames Water, 117, 121

Sagar, King (Hinduism), 17
Sahara Desert, the, 13, 106, 117
Sahel, North Africa, 103
salinization, 79, 96, 100, 103, 109; and salt dust, 87
salmon, 63, 89, 181, 188
Sandor, Marjorie, 39–40
sanitation, 3, 79–81, 86, 99, 102–15, 117, 120, 124–25, 132, 133–35, 137, 149, 150, 177–78, 190, 192; and disease, 86; in house, 80
Sarvodaya Sharmadana (Sri Lanka), 160–61
Saturn, 67; moon Enceladus, 67
Schellnhurer, John, 106
schistosomiasis, 94
seas, 87–88; Aral, 87; Baltic, 86, 126; Caspian, 70; Mediterranean, 47, 49, 76, 94, 180; North, 86; Sea of Galilee, 47
sediment, buildup, 69–70, 71, 82–85, 94, 97. *See also* rivers
SEMAPA, 122, 148, 191–92
sewage, 82, 83, 86, 88, 100, 104, 115, 120, 123, 159, 177, 186, 191
Sherman, Martin, 107
ships, cruise, 88
Shiva (Hindu goddess), 17, 19; Vandana, 16, 124–25, 146–47, 157
Siddhartha, 21. *See also* Buddhism
Sinai Desert, 42
Singh, Bendra, and rainwater harvesting, 182
Six-Day War, 107
Smith, Mick, 6, 138
solar system, 67
states in United States, Alaska, 13, 72, 84, 106, 115, 180; Arizona, 108, 158;

California, 7, 88, 94, 95, 100, 104, 108, 119, 121, 161, 173, 180, 185, 190; Colorado, 84, 185, 186; Florida, 69, 84, 180; Idaho, 63, 69, 94; Montana, 63; Nebraska, 69, 100; New Mexico, 100; New York, 85; Ohio, 84; Oregon, 63, 69, 71, 74, 94, 105, 190; Texas, 69, 84, 100, 180; Washington, 63, 64, 69–71, 74, 89, 94, 105, 185, 187–88, 190
Stockton Water Company, 121
Strait of Georgia, 69
Strait of Juan de Fuca, 83, 89
Suez (ONDEN/Suez Lyonnaise des Eaux), 117, 120, 124, 127
Suigenren (Water Resource Development Issue and Communication Network), 95
Sun Belt Water, 119
sun, the, 55, 57, 64, 67, 72, 74, 106, 109; as symbol, 12, 26
sunyata, 22
Superfund, 104
sustainability, 6–8, 55, 76, 93, 116, 120, 145–47, 149–50, 157, 159, 170, 173, 179–80, 194–95; and dams, 99
Suzuki, David, 156
sweat lodge, 15. *See also* Native Americans and First Nation peoples
symbolism. *See* water

Tenari Water (*Aguas de Tenari*), 121–22
Tertullian, 45, 50
Thales, 66
Thunderhawk, Madonna, 13
Tibet, plateau in, 106
tipping points, twelve, 93, 106
toilets, 2, 189–90; flow-through, 80; low-flow, 161
Torah, 40. *See also* Judaism
Train, Russell, 5, 156, 171

tsunamis, 88
turf grass, lawn, 103, 107, 135, 140, 187
Tyndall Centre for Climate Change Research (UK), 106
typhoid, 81
Typhoon, 88, 98

United Nations, 8, 103, 133, 135, 144; Climate Change Conference (2005), 190; Collaborative Council on Water Supply and Sanitation, 132; Conference on the Environment and Development, 133; Convention on the Law of Non-Navigational uses of International Water Courses, 147; Declaration of Human Rights, 132; Development Report 2006, 2; International Convention on the Rights of the Child, 132; Millennium Goals, 124, 134, 137, 179; World Water Development Report (2003), 82, 99; World Water Development Report 2 (2006), 6, 99, 126, 134–35, 178
United States, 13, 15, 74, 83–85, 88, 94, 99, 100, 101, 103, 104, 108, 109, 117–18, 121, 132, 135, 143, 147, 158, 163, 172, 180, 185, 187–90
United States, Mayors Climate Protection Agreement, 190
United Utilities, 117
Urban, 49, 108, 115, 126, 118, 120, 155, 178, 182, 185–86, 189; and the poor, 185; and urbanization, 99, 103, 108, 109, 116; and the wealthy, 155, 178

Varnasi, 16, 18
vicegerent, 39, 51, 168
Vivendi/General des Eaux, 117
vodou (voodoo), 14. *See also* countries, Haiti

volcanoes, 66, 67, 101; outgassing, 66; and volcanic activity, 101. *See also* mountains

voodoo. *See* vodou

Wal-Mart, 84

washing, 15, 126; in Islam, 53–54; in Judaism, 42

wastes, body, 20, 85, 99; chemical, 83; human, accumulation of, 99; radioactive, 88

wastewater, 146; and reuse, 170, 186–87

water and commerce, 64; economic value of, 131, 135, 178

water and desertification, 100, 103, 165, 167; flooding, 86, 88, 95, 99, 103, 105, 106, 141, 188; management of, ix, 3, 5–6, 8, 28, 58, 83, 93, 116–18, 120, 121–26, 134–42, 145–50, 170–72, 178–79, 183, 186, 191–93

water and purification, purity, in Buddhism, 24; in Christianity, 50; in Hinduism, 16, 19–20; for indigenous peoples, 13, 15; in Islam, 53; in Judaism, 42–43

water and ritual, in Buddhism, 23, 24; in Christianity, 47, 48; in Hinduism, 18–19; for indigenous peoples, 14; in Islam, 53–54; in Judaism, 42–43

water and symbol, 55–56; as maternal, mother, 18, 40, 43, 52, 159; as milk, 16, 18, 56, 58

water as biography, 63–76; characteristics of, 67–86; water's "memory," 72; in the human body, 74, 75

water as element, 16, 17, 22, 25, 32, 41, 43, 45, 51, 65, 66, 67, 126

water as sacred, water as creation, birthplace, in Buddhism, 22, 23; in Christianity (Genesis), 40, 41; in Hinduism, 16; for indigenous peoples, 13, 14; in Islam, 52; in Judaism, 40, 41

water basins, 69–70; as clouds, 73–74; density, 69; fog, 73; hail, 69; ice, 71–74; ponds, 72; and self-cleansing of, 68; snow, 71, 74; super cooled, 72

water ethos, 5–6, 9, 49, 79, 127, 135, 137–40, 149, 156–57, 160, 162, 163 167, 171, 173, 178, 192; general principles, 172, 178

water "straw," 181

water filtration, 79, 187

water storms, hurricane, typhoons, tsunamis, 88, 98

water wars, 79, 90, 93, 107–9, 191

water, fresh, 58, 85, 99, 100, 104, 134, 188, 193

water, rights of, 137; rules, 131

Watkins, Andrew, 105

wells, as sacred; Cartes, 45; Chalice Well, 45; Lourdes, 45; and Palestinians, 107; St. Beuno's Well, 45; St. Mandron's Well, 45; St. Winifred's Well, 45; Zamzam, 52

West Bank, 107–8

wetlands, 71, 140, 160, 165–66, 184, 193; bogs, fens, marshes, peatlands, potholes, sloughs, swamps, 71

White, Lynn, 44

Wild Bird Society of Japan, 86

Women, 18, 42–43, 54, 74, 87, 101, 124–26, 144–45, 161, 166, 178, 182; and management, 124–26

Wordsworth, William, 57

World Bank, and International Center for the Settle of Investment Disputes (ISCID), 96, 116, 117–18, 121, 124, 126, 133, 146, 178

World Commission on Dams, 86–133

World Commission on Water, 122

World Council of Churches (1966 statement), 44, 156, 165, 166

World Dam Commission, 133

World Health Organization, 81, 83, 84, 99, 119

World Monetary Fund, 116
World Summit on Sustainable
    Development, 134, 178
World Toilet Summit, 134
World Trade Organization, 118
World Water Commission, 133
World Water Contract, 149, 172, 194
World Water Day, 133, 166
World Water Forum, 117, 125, 127,
    133, 134, 158, 166
World Wide Fund for Nature, 51, 156,
    170

World Wildlife Fund, 6
worldview, definition of, 4

Xeriscaping, 186–87

Yamuna River, 16, 18–19
Yoruba people (Nigeria), 14
Young, Robert, 139–40

Zanzibar, archipelago and fishing,
    170
Zulu people, 15

About the Author

Gary Chamberlain is professor of Christian ethics in the Theology and Religious Studies Department at Seattle University. He regularly teaches courses in peace and social justice, ecology and religion, human sexuality, and faith and morality. Dr. Chamberlain has published previously in *America*, *Journal for Peace and Justice Studies*, *National Catholic Reporter*, *New Catholic World*, *Christianity and Crisis*, *Theology Today*, *Worship*, *Journal of Religious Education*, *Chicago Studies*, *Journal of Peace and Justice Studies*, *Belizean Studies*, *The Iliff Review*, *Review of Business*, *Seattle Journal of Social Justice*, *The Critic*, *Encounter*, *Japan Christian Quarterly*, *The Journal of Value Inquiry*, and several other journals and magazines. His book, *Fostering Faith*, was published by Paulist Press, February 1989, and he co-edited, with Fr. Patrick Howell, S.J., *Empowering Authority*, published by Sheed & Ward in 1990. He has presented the results of his scholarship for several years locally and at regional, national, and international conferences.

His research on issues such as family planning, reproductive health, abortion, along with ecology and water, all from a religious/ethical perspective has taken him to Belize annually for eleven years and Japan four times.

He resides in Seattle, Washington, with his wife Sharon and has twin sons, Michael and Benjamin, who also live in Seattle.